Nutshell Series
Hornbook Series
and
Black Letter Series
of
WEST PUBLISHING COMPANY
P.O. Box 64526
St. Paul, Minnesota 55164–0526

Accounting

FARIS' ACCOUNTING AND LAW IN A NUTSHELL, 377 pages, 1984. Softcover. (Text)

Administrative Law

GELLHORN AND LEVIN'S ADMINISTRATIVE LAW AND PROCESS IN A NUTSHELL, Third Edition, 479 pages, 1990. Softcover. (Text)

Admiralty

MARAIST'S ADMIRALTY IN A NUTSHELL, Second Edition, 379 pages, 1988. Softcover. (Text)

SCHOENBAUM'S HORNBOOK ON ADMIRALTY AND MARITIME LAW, Student Edition, 692 pages, 1987 with 1989 pocket part. (Text)

Agency—Partnership

REUSCHLEIN AND GREGORY'S HORNBOOK ON THE LAW OF AGENCY AND PARTNERSHIP, Second Edition, 683 pages, 1990. (Text)

STEFFEN'S AGENCY-PARTNERSHIP IN A NUTSHELL, 364 pages, 1977. Softcover. (Text)

American Indian Law

CANBY'S AMERICAN INDIAN LAW IN A NUTSHELL, Second Edition, 336 pages, 1988. Softcover. (Text)

Antitrust—see also Regulated Industries, Trade Regulation

GELLHORN'S ANTITRUST LAW AND ECONOMICS IN A NUTSHELL, Third Edition, 472 pages,

---

Commercial Law—Continued

STONE'S UNIFORM COMMERCIAL CODE IN A NUTSHELL, Third Edition, 580 pages, 1989. Softcover. (Text)

WEBER AND SPEIDEL'S COMMERCIAL PAPER IN A NUTSHELL, Third Edition, 404 pages, 1982. Softcover. (Text)

WHITE AND SUMMERS' HORNBOOK ON THE UNIFORM COMMERCIAL CODE, Third Edition, Student Edition, 1386 pages, 1988. (Text)

Community Property

MENNELL AND BOYKOFF'S COMMUNITY PROPERTY IN A NUTSHELL, Second Edition, 432 pages, 1988. Softcover. (Text)

Comparative Law

GLENDON, GORDON AND OSAKWE'S COMPARATIVE LEGAL TRADITIONS IN A NUTSHELL. 402 pages, 1982. Softcover. (Text)

Conflict of Laws

HAY'S BLACK LETTER ON CONFLICT OF LAWS, 330 pages, 1989. Softcover. (Review)

SCOLES AND HAY'S HORNBOOK ON CONFLICT OF LAWS, Student Edition, approximately 1025 pages, 1992. (Text)

SIEGEL'S CONFLICTS IN A NUTSHELL, 470 pages, 1982. Softcover. (Text)

Constitutional Law—Civil Rights

BARRON AND DIENES' BLACK LETTER ON CONSTITUTIONAL LAW, Third Edition, 440 pages, 1991. Softcover. (Review)

BARRON AND DIENES' CONSTITUTIONAL LAW IN A NUTSHELL, Second Edition, 483 pages, 1991. Softcover. (Text)

ENGDAHL'S CONSTITUTIONAL FEDERALISM IN A NUTSHELL, Second Edition, 411 pages, 1987. Softcover. (Text)

MARKS AND COOPER'S STATE CONSTITUTIONAL LAW IN A NUTSHELL, 329 pages, 1988. Softcover. (Text)

NOWAK AND ROTUNDA'S HORNBOOK ON CONSTITUTIONAL LAW, Fourth Edition, 1357 pages, 1991. (Text)

VIEIRA'S CONSTITUTIONAL CIVIL RIGHTS IN A NUTSHELL, Second Edition, 322 pages, 1990. Softcover. (Text)

WILLIAMS' CONSTITUTIONAL ANALYSIS IN A NUTSHELL, 388 pages, 1979. Softcover. (Text)

Consumer Law—see also Commercial Law

EPSTEIN AND NICKLES' CONSUMER LAW IN A NUTSHELL, Second Edition, 418 pages, 1981. Softcover. (Text)

Contracts

CALAMARI AND PERILLO'S BLACK LETTER ON CONTRACTS, Second Edition, 462 pages, 1990. Softcover. (Review)

CALAMARI AND PERILLO'S HORNBOOK ON CONTRACTS, Third Edition, 1049 pages, 1987. (Text)

CORBIN'S TEXT ON CONTRACTS, One Volume Student Edition, 1224 pages, 1952. (Text)

FRIEDMAN'S CONTRACT REMEDIES IN A NUTSHELL, 323 pages, 1981. Softcover. (Text)

KEYES' GOVERNMENT CONTRACTS IN A NUTSHELL, Second Edition, 557 pages, 1990. Softcover. (Text)

SCHABER AND ROHWER'S CONTRACTS IN A NUTSHELL, Third Edition, 457 pages, 1990. Softcover. (Text)

Copyright—see Patent and Copyright Law

Corporations

HAMILTON'S BLACK LETTER ON CORPORATIONS, Second Edition, 513 pages, 1986. Softcover. (Review)

HAMILTON'S THE LAW OF CORPORATIONS IN A NUTSHELL, Third Edition, 518 pages, 1991. Softcover. (Text)

HENN AND ALEXANDER'S HORNBOOK ON LAWS OF CORPORATIONS, Third Edition, Student Edition, 1371 pages, 1983, with 1986 pocket part. (Text)

Corrections

KRANTZ' THE LAW OF CORRECTIONS AND PRISONERS' RIGHTS IN A NUTSHELL, Third Edition, 407 pages, 1988. Softcover. (Text)

Creditors' Rights

EPSTEIN'S DEBTOR-CREDITOR LAW IN A NUTSHELL, Fourth Edition, 401 pages, 1991. Softcover. (Text)

NICKLES AND EPSTEIN'S BLACK LETTER ON CREDITORS' RIGHTS AND BANKRUPTCY, 576 pages, 1989. (Review)

Criminal Law and Criminal Procedure—see also Corrections, Juvenile Justice

ISRAEL AND LaFAVE'S CRIMINAL PROCEDURE—CONSTITUTIONAL LIMITATIONS IN A NUTSHELL, Fourth Edition, 461 pages, 1988. Softcover. (Text)

LaFAVE AND ISRAEL'S HORN-

Criminal Law and Criminal Procedure—Continued

BOOK ON CRIMINAL PROCEDURE, Second Edition, approximately 1350 pages, 1992. (Text)

LaFAVE AND SCOTT'S HORNBOOK ON CRIMINAL LAW, Second Edition, 918 pages, 1986. (Text)

LOEWY'S CRIMINAL LAW IN A NUTSHELL, Second Edition, 321 pages, 1987. Softcover. (Text)

LOW'S BLACK LETTER ON CRIMINAL LAW, Revised First Edition, 443 pages, 1990. Softcover. (Review)

Domestic Relations

CLARK'S HORNBOOK ON DOMESTIC RELATIONS, Second Edition, Student Edition, 1050 pages, 1988. (Text)

KRAUSE'S BLACK LETTER ON FAMILY LAW, 314 pages, 1988. Softcover. (Review)

KRAUSE'S FAMILY LAW IN A NUTSHELL, Second Edition, 444 pages, 1986. Softcover. (Text)

MALLOY'S LAW AND ECONOMICS: A COMPARATIVE APPROACH TO THEORY AND PRACTICE, 166 pages, 1990. Softcover. (Text)

Education Law

ALEXANDER AND ALEXANDER'S THE LAW OF SCHOOLS, STUDENTS AND TEACHERS IN A NUTSHELL, 409 pages, 1984. Softcover. (Text)

Employment Discrimination—see also Gender Discrimination

PLAYER'S FEDERAL LAW OF EMPLOYMENT DISCRIMINATION IN A NUTSHELL, Third Edition, approximately 270 pages, 1992. Softcover. (Text)

PLAYER'S HORNBOOK ON EMPLOYMENT DISCRIMINATION LAW, Student Edition, 708 pages, 1988. (Text)

Energy and Natural Resources Law—see also Oil and Gas

LAITOS AND TOMAIN'S ENERGY AND NATURAL RESOURCES LAW IN A NUTSHELL, Approximately 525 pages, 1992. Softcover. (Text)

Environmental Law—see also Energy and Natural Resources Law; Sea, Law of

FINDLEY AND FARBER'S ENVIRONMENTAL LAW IN A NUTSHELL, Third Edition, approximately 375 pages, February, 1992 Pub. Softcover. (Text)

RODGERS' HORNBOOK ON ENVIRONMENTAL LAW, 956 pages,

Immigration Law—Continued pages, 1989, Softcover. (Text)

Indian Law—see American Indian Law

Insurance Law

DOBBYN'S INSURANCE LAW IN A NUTSHELL, Second Edition, 316 pages, 1989. Softcover. (Text)

KEETON AND WIDISS' INSURANCE LAW, Student Edition, 1359 pages, 1988. (Text)

International Law—see also Sea, Law of

BUERGENTHAL'S INTERNATIONAL HUMAN RIGHTS IN A NUTSHELL, 283 pages, 1988. Softcover. (Text)

BUERGENTHAL AND MAIER'S PUBLIC INTERNATIONAL LAW IN A NUTSHELL, Second Edition, 275 pages, 1990. Softcover. (Text)

FOLSOM'S EUROPEAN COMMUNITY LAW IN A NUTSHELL, Approximately 425 pages, 1992. Softcover. (Text)

FOLSOM, GORDON AND SPANOGLE'S INTERNATIONAL BUSINESS TRANSACTIONS IN A NUTSHELL, Third Edition, 509 pages, 1988. Softcover. (Text)

Interviewing and Counseling

SHAFFER AND ELKINS' LEGAL INTERVIEWING AND COUNSELING IN A NUTSHELL, Second Edition, 487 pages, 1987. Softcover. (Text)

Introduction to Law—see Legal Method and Legal System

Introduction to Law Study

HEGLAND'S INTRODUCTION TO THE STUDY AND PRACTICE OF LAW IN A NUTSHELL, 418 pages, 1983. Softcover. (Text)

KINYON'S INTRODUCTION TO LAW STUDY AND LAW EXAMINATIONS IN A NUTSHELL, 389 pages, 1971. Softcover. (Text)

Judicial Process—see Legal Method and Legal System

Juvenile Justice

FOX'S JUVENILE COURTS IN A NUTSHELL, Third Edition, 291 pages, 1984. Softcover. (Text)

Labor and Employment Law— see also Employment Discrimination, Workers' Compensation

LESLIE'S LABOR LAW IN A NUTSHELL, Third Edition, approximately 400 pages, 1992. Softcover. (Text)

Professional Responsibility— Continued

IN A NUTSHELL, Second Edition, 514 pages, 1991. Softcover. (Text)

ROTUNDA'S BLACK LETTER ON PROFESSIONAL RESPONSIBILITY, Third Edition, approximately 400 pages, 1992. Softcover. (Review)

WOLFRAM'S HORNBOOK ON MODERN LEGAL ETHICS, Student Edition, 1120 pages, 1986. (Text)

Property—see also Real Estate Transactions, Land Use, Trusts and Estates

BERNHARDT'S BLACK LETTER ON PROPERTY, Second Edition, 388 pages, 1991. Softcover. (Review)

BERNHARDT'S REAL PROPERTY IN A NUTSHELL, Second Edition, 448 pages, 1981. Softcover. (Text)

BOYER, HOVENKAMP AND KURTZ' THE LAW OF PROPERTY, AN INTRODUCTORY SURVEY, Fourth Edition, 696 pages, 1991. (Text)

BURKE'S PERSONAL PROPERTY IN A NUTSHELL, 322 pages, 1983. Softcover. (Text)

CUNNINGHAM, STOEBUCK AND WHITMAN'S HORNBOOK ON THE LAW OF PROPERTY, Student Edition, 916 pages, 1984, with 1987 pocket part. (Text)

HILL'S LANDLORD AND TENANT LAW IN A NUTSHELL, Second Edition, 311 pages, 1986. Softcover. (Text)

Real Estate Transactions

BRUCE'S REAL ESTATE FINANCE IN A NUTSHELL, Third Edition, 287 pages, 1991. Softcover. (Text)

NELSON AND WHITMAN'S BLACK LETTER ON LAND TRANSACTIONS AND FINANCE, Second Edition, 466 pages, 1988. Softcover. (Review)

NELSON AND WHITMAN'S HORNBOOK ON REAL ESTATE FINANCE LAW, Second Edition, 941 pages, 1985 with 1989 pocket part. (Text)

Regulated Industries—see also Mass Communication Law, Banking Law

GELLHORN AND PIERCE'S REGULATED INDUSTRIES IN A NUTSHELL, Second Edition, 389 pages, 1987. Softcover. (Text)

Remedies

DOBBS' HORNBOOK ON REMEDIES, 1067 pages, 1973. (Text)

DOBBYN'S INJUNCTIONS IN A NUTSHELL, 264 pages, 1974.

Remedies—Continued

Softcover. (Text)

FRIEDMAN'S CONTRACT REME-DIES IN A NUTSHELL, 323 pages, 1981. Softcover. (Text)

O'CONNELL'S REMEDIES IN A NUTSHELL, Second Edition, 320 pages, 1985. Softcover. (Text)

Sea, Law of

SOHN AND GUSTAFSON'S THE LAW OF THE SEA IN A NUT-SHELL, 264 pages, 1984. Soft-cover. (Text)

Securities Regulation

HAZEN'S HORNBOOK ON THE LAW OF SECURITIES REGULA-TION, Second Edition, Student Edition, 1082 pages, 1990. (Text)

RATNER'S SECURITIES REGULA-TION IN A NUTSHELL, Third Edi-tion, 316 pages, 1988. Soft-cover. (Text)

Sports Law

SCHUBERT, SMITH AND TRENTADUE'S SPORTS LAW, 395 pages, 1986. (Text)

Tax Practice and Procedure

MORGAN'S TAX PROCEDURE AND TAX FRAUD IN A NUTSHELL, 400 pages, 1990. Softcover. (Text)

Taxation—Corporate

SCHWARZ AND LATHROPE'S BLACK LETTER ON CORPORATE AND PARTNERSHIP TAXATION, 537 pages, 1991. Softcover. (Review)

WEIDENBRUCH AND BURKE'S FEDERAL INCOME TAXATION OF CORPORATIONS AND STOCKHOLD-ERS IN A NUTSHELL, Third Edi-tion, 309 pages, 1989. Soft-cover. (Text)

Taxation—Estate & Gift—see also Estate Planning, Trusts and Estates

MCNULTY'S FEDERAL ESTATE AND GIFT TAXATION IN A NUT-SHELL, Fourth Edition, 496 pages, 1989. Softcover. (Text)

PEAT AND WILLBANKS' FEDERAL ESTATE AND GIFT TAXATION: AN ANALYSIS AND CRITIQUE, 265 pages, 1991. Softcover. (Text)

Taxation—Individual

DODGE'S THE LOGIC OF TAX, 343 pages, 1989. Softcover. (Text)

HUDSON AND LIND'S BLACK LET-TER ON FEDERAL INCOME TAXA-TION, Third Edition, 406 pages, 1990. Softcover. (Review)

MCNULTY'S FEDERAL INCOME TAXATION OF INDIVIDUALS IN A

Advisory Board

[XIV]

WORKERS' COMPENSATION AND EMPLOYEE PROTECTION LAWS

IN A NUTSHELL

Second Edition

JACK B. HOOD
Adjunct Professor of Law
Mercer University Law School

BENJAMIN A. HARDY, Jr.
Former Associate Professor of Law
Cumberland School of Law
Samford University

HAROLD S. LEWIS, Jr.
Professor of Law
Fordham University
School of Law

ST. PAUL, MINN.
WEST PUBLISHING CO.
1990

COPYRIGHT © 1984 WEST PUBLISHING CO.
COPYRIGHT © 1990 By WEST PUBLISHING CO.
                    610 Opperman Drive
                    P.O. Box 64526
                    St. Paul, MN 55164–0526

Library of Congress Cataloging in Publication Data

Hood, Jack B.
    Workers' compensation and employee protection laws in a nutshell /
by Jack B. Hood, Benjamin A. Hardy, Jr., and Harold S. Lewis, Jr.—
2nd ed.
        p.   cm.—(Nutshell series)
    ISBN 0–314–71824–9
    1. Workers' compensation—Law and legislation—United States.
2. Employers' liability—United States. 3. Labor laws and
legislation—United States. I. Hardy, Benjamin A. II. Lewis,
Harold S., 1947–   . III. Title. IV. Series.
KF3615.Z9H64   1990
344.73'021—dc20
[347.30421]
                                                    90–30706
                                                       CIP

ISBN 0–314–71824–9

        (H.H.&L.) Workers' Comp. 2d Ed. NS
        1st Reprint—1992

TO
Pat, Sara, and Laura
Linda and Andy
Cecelia, Carmen, and Marcia

*

PREFACE

Our purpose in writing this Nutshell is to provide an overview of the laws affecting employees in the workplace. It is our hope that the sections on workers' compensation and employment discrimination will provide both students and lawyers with insight into most of the common questions in the field. Only a summary has been attempted in the sections dealing with other employee protection legislation, as the subject areas were simply too large for detailed explanation.

An excellent and comprehensive treatment of workers' compensation is to be found in Professor Arthur Larson's multi-volume treatise on the subject, and we have given useful citations to that work at relevant points. The West Nutshells by Professor Player on the federal law of employment discrimination, by Professor Leslie on labor law, and by Professor Maraist on admiralty are also useful references.

We would like to acknowledge and thank Dean Philip Shelton of the Mercer University Law School, along with Deanna Parrish, Mercer Law School student and research assistant. We also acknowledge and thank Deans John D. Feerick and Georgene M. Vairo of Fordham University Law

School. A special thanks to Professor Steve Thel of the Fordham Law School for an insightful first read. Warm thanks are extended to Anita Pascocello, Carol DeVito and Marilyn Alexander for expert word processing assistance and administrative support. Finally, we would like to express our appreciation to the law libraries of Mercer, Fordham and the University of Georgia.

JACK B. HOOD
BENJAMIN A. HARDY, JR.
HAROLD S. LEWIS, JR.

November, 1989
Macon, Georgia

OUTLINE

PART 1: HISTORICAL BACKGROUND OF COMPENSATION LEGISLATION

XV

TABLE OF CASES

References are to Pages

A

B

C

D

E

F

G

H

K

L

M

N

O

P

R

S

T

U

W

Z

WORKERS' COMPENSATION AND EMPLOYEE PROTECTION LAWS

IN A NUTSHELL

Second Edition

*

PART 1

HISTORICAL BACKGROUND OF COMPENSATION LEGISLATION

CHAPTER 1

EMPLOYMENT RELATED ACTIONS AND LEGISLATION

A. EMPLOYEE'S COMMON–LAW REMEDIES

The common-law imposed a number of duties on employers for the protection of their employees, and an action existed for the breach of these duties, however, as a practical matter the common-law failed to provide adequate remedies for such injuries and deaths. The common-law duties imposed upon the master were as follows:

(1) to provide a safe place to work;

(2) to provide safe appliances, tools and equipment;

(3) to give warnings of dangers of which the employee might reasonably be expected to remain in ignorance;

(4) to provide a sufficient number of fit, trained, or suitable fellow servants to perform assigned tasks; and

1

(5) to promulgate and enforce rules relating to employee conduct which would make the work safe.

Employee remedies based upon a breach of the foregoing duties were restricted by the "unholy trinity" of common-law defenses: (1) fellow-servant doctrine; (2) contributory negligence; and (3) assumption of risk. See Prosser and Keeton on Torts § 80 (5th ed. 1984).

1.   FELLOW–SERVANT DOCTRINE

Unless there was an express contract the rule at common law was that a master was not liable to a servant for injuries due to the negligence of a fellow servant. Priestly v. Fowler (1837); see Murray v. South Carolina Railroad Co. (1841). The doctrine provided that the negligence of a co-employee was not to be imputed to the master; of course, the injured employee, for what it was worth could still sue a co-employee. The fellow-servant rule was not founded in abstract or natural justice, and the rule was an exception to the rule of agency and the general rule that a master was responsible for injuries caused to third persons by the negligence of servants who were acting within the scope of their employment. In support of the fellow-servant doctrine it was said that the negligence of a fellow-servant was one of the risks incident to employment, and the risk was assumed by the servant as an implied term of the employment contract. Public policy in support of the doctrine was to the effect that the rule would make servants careful and watchful with regard to each other, thus promoting greater care in the performance of their duties.

The harshness of the fellow-servant doctrine was lessened by the recognition of certain exceptions. For example, servants who did not have a common master and who were not engaged in the same enterprise, were not barred from recovery by the fellow servant rules. Furthermore, if they were employed in different departments of the same enterprise, the employees were not generally to be treated as fellow-servants. The most important exception involved the negligence of a "vice-principal" because the fellow-servant bar did not apply to the vice-principal. One approach required that the vice-principal be a supervisory employee, representing the employer in his duty toward the employee. The vice-principal exception has been held to apply to any servant, as opposed to just superior servants. The key inquiry aimed at an employer's liability was whether a servant (alleged vice-principal) owed an obligation to the injured employee to meet the common-law duties of the employer. In order for the master to be liable, these duties were viewed as being non-delegable. The vice-principal exception was subject to an important qualification. It was not applicable to those incidental dangers which arose out of the operational details of a fellow-servant's work. No duty was owed by the master with regard to these risks.

2. CONTRIBUTORY NEGLIGENCE

An employee or servant was required to exercise reasonable care for his own safety, and his failure to use the precautions that ordinary prudence required, barred any recovery under the contributory negligence defense. Exceptions existed on the basis of the last clear chance doctrine and in situations in which the master's conduct was willful or wanton. As a result of the doctrine's harshness, statutes sometimes abrogated the defense and statutorily imposed requirements for worker safety, placing certain servants in a special, protected category. In some jurisdictions comparative negligence statutes aided employees.

3. ASSUMPTION OF RISK

The assumption of risk defense was grounded in the notion that the servant or employee had voluntarily agreed to assume the dangers normally and ordinarily incident to the work. Risks were covered which a mature worker was presumed to know, regardless of whether one had actual knowledge. The employee further assumed such extraordinary and abnormal risks of which he had knowledge and appreciation. Assumption of risk was customarily based upon contract theory, as opposed to contributory negligence which was based upon tort theory. Contributory negligence involved the notion of fault and a breach of duty to one's self, whereas assumption of risk could exist in the absence of fault because of its contractual nature. Employees or servants did not assume those risks growing out of the negligence of the master, or a vice principal. Generally risks arising out of the non-delegable duties doctrine were not viewed as the ordinary sort of risks which one could assume; these were treated as extraordinary risks which one did not assume. It should be kept in mind that recovery could still be barred by one's contributory negligence.

In summary, the foregoing "unholy trinity" may be explained in large part on the basis of the highly individualistic attitude of the common-law courts and society's desire to encourage industrial expansion and development by lessening the financial costs upon industry for industrial injuries and deaths. See generally Dodd, Administration of Workmen's Compensation, § 7 (1936); Prosser and Keeton on Torts § 80 (5th ed. 1984).

B. EMPLOYERS' LIABILITY ACTS

Employers' liability acts came into being in response to rising industrial injury and death rates in the 19th Century, and in response to dissatisfaction with the common-law remedies available to employees. For example, in 1855, the State of Georgia enacted a statute making railroads liable to employees and others for negligence in situations previously barred by the fellow-servant defense. By 1908, almost every American jurisdiction had passed similar legislation. Congress, in

1908, placed interstate railroad employees under an employers' liability act system and later extended this same coverage to seamen. The state and federal acts generally barred the use of the fellow-servant rule, substituted comparative negligence for pure contributory negligence, and later barred the use of the assumption of risk defense. These employers' liability laws were, however, soon found to be unsatisfactory for several reasons: workers or their survivors had to bring law suits for damages; the employers' defenses, while considerably weakened, still made it difficult for workers to prosecute their cases; the outcome of the cases were always uncertain; actions were costly to bring and were lengthy; cases produced ill-will between the employers and employees and posed a constant threat to job security.

C. EUROPEAN COMPENSATION LEGISLATION

The historical origins of modern workers' compensation legislation may be found first in Germany and then in England. Philosophers and politicians, especially socialists, were of great influence in the development of European compensation legislation which later influenced the development of similar compensation legislation in the United States.

1.　GERMANY

The German influence began in 1838 with the enactment of an employers' liability act that was applicable to railroads. In 1873 Germany extended coverage to workers in factories, mines and quarries. In 1884, Germany enacted a compulsory system of accident insurance which is regarded as the first true workers' compensation act, and it covered all employees engaged in manufacturing, mining and transportation. Similar workers' compensation laws were enacted in Austria in 1887, Norway in 1894, Finland in 1895, and Great Britain in 1897.

2.　GREAT BRITAIN

The Workmen's Compensation Act of 1897 provided the prototype, and was the forerunner of the majority of compensation acts passed in the early 1900's in the United States. The Act contained important limitations: only hazardous employments were covered; there were no insurance provisions; and the employer bore the complete burden of compensation benefit costs. The statute also gave rise to the key phrase, "arising out of and in the course of employment," which is generally found today in compensation statutes in the United States. The British legislation differed from the German. Germany attempted to provide broader coverage in the area of social insurance and to provide a more complete compensation system.

The British Act gave a workman only moderate recovery, with the cost being borne by the employer as an expense of doing business.

D. STATE COMPENSATION ACTS

There was a gradual recognition after the turn of the century that the common-law remedies of employees injured or killed on the job, were filled with inequities. The states were slow, however, to adopt workers' compensation laws, and initial attempts to do so faced legal and political opposition. Early compensation legislation was very limited and legislators exercised great caution in replacing the common-law recovery system. While it is beyond the scope of this work to address the various attempts of the states to enact compensation legislation, a sampling is necessary for historical appreciation of workers' compensation legislation in the United States.

1. MARYLAND

In 1902, Maryland passed the first workers' compensation act in the United States. It applied to death cases only, and provided coverage to a limited number of workers. This act was declared unconstitutional in Franklin v. United Railways and Electric Co. (1904), because it was held to deprive the parties of the right to jury trial and said to be violative of the separation of powers doctrine (an insurance commissioner, under the executive branch, was performing judicial functions). In 1910, Maryland enacted a voluntary workers' compensation statute, but apathy on behalf of employers and employees rendered the legislation ineffective.

2. MONTANA

In 1909, Montana enacted a compulsory workers' compensation statute, which was designed for employees in the coal industry. The employer and employee were both required to contribute to a state fund, and a covered employee or his beneficiaries could elect to sue at law or receive compensation from the fund; however, workers could not receive the benefits of both. This legislation was declared unconstitutional in Cunningham v. Northwestern Improvement Co. (1911), because it was held that employers were denied equal protection of the laws, in that there was the potential for double liability (employers had to contribute to the state compensation fund and additionally were open to suit if an employee or beneficiary so elected).

3. MASSACHUSETTS

Massachusetts, in 1908, passed a voluntary workers' compensation statute. The voluntary nature of the act was designed to avoid some of the theoretical constitutional problems concerning compensation acts. As a result of the voluntary nature of the act, both employers and employees had no incentive to commit themselves to the scheme.

Thus, the Massachusetts act proved to be ineffective.

4. NEW YORK

In 1909, in New York, a commission on Employers' Liability was created (popularly known as the "Wainwright Commission"). It was to inquire into the liabilities of employers to employees for industrial accidents, and to compare and study: efficiencies, costs, justice, merits and defects in the laws of the other industrial states and countries. The Commission reported that the current common-law system with its employers' liability act exceptions provided insufficient compensation; was wasteful in terms of resources; caused unsatisfactory delays and was essentially antagonistic in nature. The Commission proposed two statutes in light of constitutional problems. One proposal was aimed at employers and employees when especially dangerous employments were involved. The other statute was designed as an elective statute to cover employments outside of the especially dangerous work categories. In 1910, both compulsory and voluntary acts were passed. Predictably, the voluntary statute suffered from employer indifference, and the compulsory statute was declared unconstitutional in Ives v. South Buffalo Railway (1911). Employers were viewed as having been denied due process under both the state and federal constitutions in that employers' property, i.e., money, was taken without consent and without fault.

In 1913, New York amended its constitution to permit the enactment of a compulsory workers' compensation statute and in 1914 the New York legislature passed a compulsory workers' compensation law that applied only to hazardous employments. In Jensen v. Southern Pacific Railroad (1915), the New York Court of Appeals upheld the statute as a valid exercise of police power. As might be expected, thereafter mandatory coverage was extended and broadened in New York.

5.   FLORIDA

By 1920, most states had adopted some form of workers' compensation legislation. The last state to adopt a compensation act was Mississippi in 1949. In 1935 the State of Florida enacted its first workers' compensation act which was elective in theory. The development of the law in this area in Florida is typical of its development in the United States. For example, from 1935 forward, practically every session of the Florida legislature amended the compensation act. It must be pointed out, however, that the Florida legislature in 1978, because of its concern over excessive awards and a backlog of claims, initiated a study of the problems. In 1979 the legislature enacted a Workers' Compensation Reform Act which "re-established the centrality of the wage-loss principle," and represented a departure from the development in many other jurisdictions. The current theory in Florida is that awards should not be based on the medical nature of the injury alone but should focus on the economic impact of the injury. Florida's wage-loss approach is designed to avoid compensating a worker for an injury per se, or basing an award on conjecture as to the future course of a specific injury; instead, its goal is to provide compensation for an employee's economic losses as they arise. See Abinger & Granoff, Legislative Overview: The Florida Workers' Compensation Act, 1979, 4 Nova L.J. 91 (1980). This approach has been used by Florida in an advertising effort to attract new industry. Florida may not have the most progressive and acceptable of workers' compensation programs, however its innovations will no doubt influence other jurisdictions. The Florida experience exemplifies the continuing political battles fought in legislatures between employees in the work force and employers and insurance carriers.

E. FEDERAL LEGISLATION

There are a variety of federal acts designed to provide compensation or recovery for certain employees injured or killed on the job. Additionally, there has been federal legislation aimed at regulation of safety practices, labor standards, discrimination, social security benefits, etc. and which may affect employees' rights in the workplace. Provided below is a brief history and introduction of the more important federal acts providing compensation or recovery; other employee protection laws will be addressed in Part III.

1. FEDERAL EMPLOYEES' COMPENSATION ACT

In 1908, Congress enacted a workers' compensation act for a limited group of federal employees, and, in 1916, it expanded the coverage to all civil employees of the United States government without regard to the hazards of their employment. An extensive revision of the FECA was undertaken in 1949, and today, the FECA, 5 U.S.C.A. § 8101 et seq., is considered to be one of the most liberal workers' compensation acts in existence, and provides coverage for federal employees and their dependents for death or disability resulting from personal injury "sustained while in the performance of duty." Congressional appropriations finance all administrative and benefit costs, thus making the government a self-insurer. The Secretary of Labor supervises administrative claims procedures through the Office of Workers' Compensation Programs. The Employees' Compensation Appeals Board reviews appeals from final decisions. When an employee is covered by the FECA, all other rights against the government are barred. Third party actions may be commenced when appropriate, and there may be an election of civil service retirement benefits (assuming eligibility), as opposed to compensation benefits. The Supreme Court, in Westfall v. Erwin (1988), indicated that co-employee liability was possible in FECA situations; however, Congress legislatively overruled *Westfall* by enacting the Federal Employees

Liability Reform and Tort Compensation Act of 1988 (28 U.S.C.A. § 2679). The FECA's exclusive liability provision does not directly preclude third-party indemnity actions against the United States. Lockheed Aircraft Corp. v. United States (1983).

Members of the armed forces of the United States are not covered by the FECA, however, analogous legislation does provide them with disability compensation and death benefits. 10 U.S.C.A. Ch. 61 & 75; 38 U.S.C.A. § 301 et seq. Coverage is allowed in cases of service-connected disability or death. The military scheme requires a "line of duty" determination to be made in each case, and either the particular branch of service and/or the Veterans Administration provides the machinery for the claims process and supervision. It should be noted that the Feres doctrine precludes servicemen's recoveries under the Federal Tort Claims Act against the United States for injury, death, or loss "incident to service." Feres v. United States (1950). Furthermore, service personnel cannot generally maintain damage actions against superior officers for violation of constitutional rights. Chappell v. Wallace (1983).

2. FEDERAL EMPLOYERS' LIABILITY ACT

In 1906, Congress passed the first Federal Employers' Liability Act, but the United States Supreme Court held the Act unconstitutional because it infringed upon state rights in that the Act applied to intrastate as well as interstate commerce. Howard v. Illinois Central Railroad (1908). This first FELA was held constitutional, however, as far as the District of Columbia and the territories of the United States were concerned. El Paso & Northeastern Railway v. Gutierrez (1909). In 1908, Congress enacted a second FELA which applied to common carriers engaged in interstate commerce only. It is this second FELA statute which remains effective to this day and is codified at 45 U.S.C.A. §§ 51–60. The FELA is not a true workers' compensation act for it requires an employee to prove negligence even though the burden of proving that negligence has been greatly liberalized by the courts. The FELA at the time of its passage was considered the most progressive of the various employers' liability acts that existed at the time. Comparative fault replaced contributory negligence and the fellow-servant rule was abolished completely. In 1939, Congress amended the act with an eye toward the elimination of the assumption of risk defense. Subsequent court decisions make it clear that there is no assumption of inherent risks based upon the risk of ordinary railroading; nor can there be assumption of risk for obvious dangers knowingly encountered by the railroad employee, but of course, comparative fault may come into play.

One should note that the Safety Appliance Act and the Boiler Inspection Act impose absolute and mandatory duties upon the defendant carriers, which can provide the basis for liability under the FELA. The traditional common-law tort compensatory approach is taken toward personal injury damages under the FELA, but the Supreme Court has remained receptive to new claims, especially in the emotional distress area. Atchison, Topeka & Santa Fe Ry. Co. v. Buell (1987). In death cases, a pecuniary loss approach is employed for beneficiaries. Most courts have held that punitive damages are not recoverable. Actions may be filed in state or federal courts; if filed in state court the action cannot be removed to federal court.

3. THE JONES ACT

Historically, under the general maritime law, seamen were allowed maintenance and cure which consisted of subsistence, medical care and unearned wages, but they had no effective negligence remedy. At the turn of the Twentieth Century, the Supreme Court began fashioning the doctrine of unseaworthiness, which provided a proper cause of action, but a limited remedy for seamen. See The Osceola (1903). Because of concern for the welfare of seamen, Congress enacted the Seamen's Act of 1915, which abolished the fellow-servant defense, but this legislation was effectively nullified in Chelentis v. Luckenbach Steamship Co. (1918). In 1920, Congress passed the Merchant Marine Act of 1920, commonly known as the Jones Act. It provided seamen with the same negligence remedy that is available to railroad employees under the Federal Employers Liability Act. 46 U.S.C.A. § 688 et seq. Both state and federal courts may entertain these actions and comparative negligence applies. In the 1940's, the Supreme Court transformed the unseaworthiness doctrine into an effective liability basis for recoveries by seamen. The unseaworthiness doctrine essentially imposes liability without fault on the part of a shipowner who fails to provide a safe and seaworthy vessel. Thus, today once a person is classified as a seaman he may join actions for maintenance and cure, Jones Act negligence and unseaworthiness in order to obtain compensation for his personal injuries. Fitzgerald v. United States Lines Co. (1963). Punitive damages may be allowed in connection with maintenance and cure claims. Hines v. J. A. LaPorte, Inc. (1987). Punitives are not permitted under the Jones Act, but may be allowed under general maritime law unseaworthiness. Complaint of Merry Shipping, Inc. (1981).

Sometimes there can be an overlap between seamen's rights to recovery under the aforementioned theories and the various state workers' compensation laws. This area is sometimes called a "twilight zone" of coverage. See Ch. 9, C., infra.

In 1970, the Supreme Court in Moragne v. States Marine Lines, Inc. (1970), created a general maritime law cause of action for deaths occurring on territorial or inland waters. Beyond one marine league from shore the Death on the High Seas Act of 1920, 46 U.S.C.A. §§ 761–767, is generally applicable. These remedies do not preclude or displace Jones Act remedies available to a seaman's survivors. For an illustration of the damages issues that can arise under the Jones Act, Death on the High Seas Act, and general maritime law unseaworthiness in the wrongful death context, see Bergen v. F/V St. Patrick (1987). A proper joinder of the various remedies is required in the cases of seamen's deaths, and an analysis must be made on the basis of: (1) status as a seaman; (2) situs of the injury producing death; and (3) cause of action and theory of recovery. See Hood & Hardy, Seamen's Damages, §§ 4–1, 5–1, 6–1 (1983).

It should be noted that the penalty wage statute, 46 U.S.C.A. §§ 10313(f)–(i), 10501(b)–(d), permits an action for delayed payment of wages. In appropriate circumstances, this action may be joined with other seamen's remedies. Griffin v. Oceanic Contractors, Inc. (1982).

4. LONGSHORE AND HARBOR WORKERS' COMPENSATION ACT

In 1927, Congress enacted a national workers' compensation statute for the benefit of longshoremen and other persons engaged in maritime employment on navigable waters. The Longshoremen's and Harbor Workers' Compensation Act (hereinafter "LHWCA") was prompted by the case of Southern Pacific Co. v. Jensen (1917), which had nullified a New York workers' compensation statute as applied to longshoremen. Coverage under the 1927 legislation was said to exist only if the accident occurred on navigable waters; Nacirema Operating Co. v. Johnson (1969); and the fact that a worker's employment was maritime in nature, was not a coverage issue. Calbeck v. Travelers Insurance Co. (1962). By decisions of the Supreme Court, covered workers were also given an unseaworthiness remedy against a vessel, Seas Shipping Co. v. Sieracki (1946), and the vessel owner was given an indemnity action against the stevedore employer, Ryan Stevedoring Co. v. Pan-Atlantic Steamship Corp. (1956).

In 1972, Congress significantly amended the LHWCA. In summary, the amendments increased benefits, eliminated the unseaworthiness remedy against vessels, abolished the vessel owner's right of indemnity against stevedore employers, and instituted needed administrative changes. Most importantly the 1972 amendments broadened coverage, by using both "situs" and "status" for coverage. The situs test is no longer confined to navigable waters, but it includes dockside workers on adjoining shore areas. See Northeast Marine Terminal Co. v. Caputo (1977). The status test is met if a worker is engaged in "maritime employment." 33 U.S.C.A. § 902(3). See Chesapeake & Ohio Railway Co. v. Schwalb (1989).

In 1984, Congress amended the LHWCA, restricting coverage and changing the name of the act to the Longshore and Harbor Workers' Compensation

Act; 33 U.S.C.A. § 901 et seq. All private maritime employments upon navigable waters or adjoining land areas are generally covered by the LHWCA. Specifically excluded are seamen and government employees. Also excluded are clerical employees, recreation employees, temporary employees not engaged in longshore or harbor work, agricultural employees, employees on certain small commercial vessels, and employees who repair or break recreational vessels under 65 feet in length, so long as there is state workers' compensation coverage for these employees.

As might be expected, jurisdictional battles arise because claimants wish to assert seaman status, and while employers prefer to claim immunity from suit under the LHWCA. Seaman status is usually a jury question, but not in all circumstances. Kerr–McGee Corp. v. Ma–Ju Marine Services, Inc. (1987).

When there is an overlap of coverage due to state workers' compensation law, the LHWCA does not necessarily pre-empt. The Supreme Court's concurrent jurisdiction doctrines (sometimes applied in twilight zone cases) indicate that generally, an employee covered by both has an option. See Sun Ship, Inc. v. Pennsylvania (1980). See Ch. 9, C., infra.

It should be pointed out that the receipt of LHWCA benefits does not preclude the initiation of a third-party action based upon traditional negligence concepts. 33 U.S.C.A. § 905(b); see Scindia

Steam Navigation Co. Limited v. De Los Santos (1981). Furthermore, a longshoreman can pursue a negligence remedy under the LHWCA against a vessel owner who acts as his own stevedore, despite the fact that the longshoreman has received compensation under the LHWCA from the stevedore-vessel owner. Jones & Laughlin Steel Corp. v. Pfeifer (1983). But ship repairers' actions are barred by § 905(b).

The LHWCA has been applied by Congress to employees other than longshoremen and maritime workers. The Defense Base Act applies the LHWCA to injuries on deaths of certain persons engaged in public works contracts outside the continental United States and to certain persons employed at military bases outside the United States. 42 U.S. C.A. § 1651 et seq. The War Hazards Compensation Act (42 U.S.C.A. § 1701 et seq.) provides a compensation remedy for death, injury, or detention of certain persons employed overseas by U.S. government contractors or by the United States government; benefits, disability, etc., are determined by reference to the LHWCA. Administration of these claims is accomplished under the Federal Employees' Compensation Act. Subject to certain criteria, employees of nonappropriated fund instrumentalities of the United States are also entitled to the benefits of the LHWCA. 5 U.S. C.A. §§ 8171, 8172.

In 1928, Congress extended the substantive and procedural provisions of the LHWCA to employees in the District of Columbia (D.C. Code §§ 36–501, 36–502 (1973)). These provisions have now been replaced by the District of Columbia Workers' Compensation Act. D.C. Code 1981, § 1–233; See District of Columbia v. Greater Washington Board of Trade (1982).

Finally, the Outer Continental Shelf Lands Act (43 U.S.C.A. §§ 1331–1343) incorporates the provisions of the LHWCA for the benefit of certain employees engaged in natural resources exploration, development, transportation, etc., outside the states' seaward boundaries on the continental shelves. See Herb's Welding, Inc. v. Gray (1985); Mills v. Director (1989). See generally, Schoenbaum, Admiralty and Maritime Law (1987).

5. FEDERAL BLACK LUNG BENEFITS LEGISLATION

As an incident to the Federal Coal Mine Health and Safety Act of 1969, a basic income maintenance program was established for certain coal miners and their dependents. 30 U.S.C.A. § 801 et seq. The program was designed to provide compensation benefits in certain cases in which coal miners had suffered or died from pneumonoconiosis ("black lung"). In 1972, Congress passed the Black Lung Benefits Act, and thereby authorized a national workers' compensation program to be administered under the U.S. Department of Labor. Since that time several important amendments have occurred. In 1978, Congress passed the Black

Lung Benefits Reform Act of 1977 and the Black Lung Benefits Review Act of 1977. Later, Congress enacted the Black Lung Benefits Revenue Act of 1981, the Black Lung Benefits Amendments of 1981 and the Consolidated Omnibus Budget Reconciliation Act of 1985. Because of the controversial and political nature of this federal workers' compensation legislation, there is no doubt that future amendments and revisions will occur. For a more detailed description of the black lung compensation legislation, see Chapter 15, infra.

PART 2

THE LAW OF WORKERS' COMPENSATION

CHAPTER 2

THEORIES AND POLICIES OF WORKERS' COMPENSATION

A. CONSTITUTIONAL THEORIES

Traditionally there have been several key constitutional objections to workers' compensation legislation. Most of these objections have centered on the following constitutional issues: due process of law, equal protection, impairment of contract obligations, trial by jury, and the privileges and immunities of the citizens of the different states. Initially, many of these constitutional objections were sustained; however, most constitutional problems have fallen by the wayside, particularly with the adoption by most states of specific constitutional amendments that authorize workers' compensation legislation. These constitutional problems are not always of just historical interest. They can be of importance to a modern day analysis of a particular compensation scheme; for example, see State ex rel. Doersam v. Industrial Commission (1988); Reed v. Brunson (1988).

1. FREEDOM OF CONTRACT

The U.S. Constitution prohibits the states from enacting laws that impair contract obligations. U.S. Const. Art. 1, § 10. As a result of this general prohibition and the parallel provisions sometimes found within state constitutions, some workers' compensation acts were held at one time to be violative of these provisions. However, the general view is to the effect that even if a workers' compensation act impairs an existing contract obligation between an employer and employee, the impairment may nevertheless be valid because a proper exercise of the police power has occurred. The health, safety and welfare of the people are of overriding importance.

2. ELECTION

Many of the original workers' compensation acts were said to be "elective" in order to avoid the constitutional difficulties imposed by the impairment of contract clause. An elective compensation act could thus be said to be a part of or to be "read into" every contract of employment, and the act contained provisions for employers or employees to opt in or out. There were usually penalty provisions that encouraged coverage. Later, most elective acts were said to be presumptive, that is, the employer and employee were presumed to be covered unless they had taken specific steps in accordance with the act to avoid coverage. Many acts appear to retain their elective and contractual character because of the manner in which they were written, despite the fact that today most state workers' compensation acts are compulsory.

The majority of states have enacted constitutional amendments that eliminate the constitutional difficulties originally posed in this area. Virtually all states today have compulsory coverage. Any system other than a compulsory one appears to be at odds with the purposes and policies of workers' compensation. It should be recalled that when coverage fails for one reason or another, the employee must then rely upon the common law remedies, or those remedies provided by the employers' liability acts.

3. PRESUMPTIVE COVERAGE

As previously mentioned, many compensation acts were elective, thus affording the employer and employee the right to accept or reject coverage. While most acts today are compulsory in character, the few remaining elective acts can pose coverage problems. For example, an employer could refuse on the basis of costs to carry workers' compensation insurance, and some employees may not be sufficiently knowledgable of their rights to make intelligent elections. Consequently, some of the elective acts contain presumptive coverage provisions. In other words, the acts may provide for an election, but, coverage is presumed unless specific steps are taken by the employee or employer to preclude coverage.

4. COMPULSORY COVERAGE

A majority of states employ a compulsory coverage system of workers' compensation. This has generally been accomplished by state constitutional amendments authorizing workers' compensation statutes; see Schmidt v. Wolf Contracting Co. (1945). These state amendments grant the necessary legislative power for the enactment of workers' compensation laws. These grants include the power to enact all reasonable and proper provisions necessary to effectuate the law and to fulfill the objectives of the constitutional provisions. Needless to say, the legislation cannot exceed whatever limitations exist in the constitutional provision.

5. EXCLUSIVENESS OF REMEDY

Regardless of whether a workers' compensation act is compulsory or elective, it generally affords the exclusive remedy for employees or dependents against employers for personal injuries, diseases, or deaths arising out of and in the course of employment. The exclusivity provision of workers' compensation acts is the keystone of all such legislation. The employee or dependents recover without regard to fault, and the employer is spared the possibility of large tort verdicts. Initial assaults on the exclusive remedy provided by workers' compensation were based on allegations of denial of due process of law. Common law and statutory actions were being abrogated along with common law defenses. There was strong early resistance (just as there is today) to the adoption of no-fault statutory systems of compensation. Needless to say, constitutional controversies surrounded meanings of employment, requirements to secure payment of compensation, and the hazardous employment classifications. Additionally, equal protection arguments were made. For a discussion of constitutional issues see generally Cudahy Packing Co. v. Parramore (1923); Arizona Employers' Liability Cases (1919); Jensen v. Southern Pacific Co. (1915). Most constitutional issues have been laid to rest by state constitutional amendments and by more liberal and realistic judicial decisions.

B. SOCIAL AND ECONOMIC POLICIES

1. EMPLOYEE–EMPLOYER "BARGAIN"

It is sometimes said that the employee and employer have entered into an "industrial bargain." The employee has given up his right to sue his employer for negligence and possibly receive a potentially greater damage award, and the employer has surrendered the common law defenses available in negligence actions. In exchange the employee is entitled to prompt but modest compensation for injuries, (or one's dependents for death) arising out of the employment relationship regardless of fault. The employer avoids costly litigation, and faces fixed and limited liability that can be covered by insurance.

2. INDUSTRIAL BURDEN FOR INJURIES AND DEATH

An important economic and social theory underlying the workers' compensation idea is that the cost of employment related injuries, diseases and deaths ultimately should be borne by the purchasers' and consumers' products and services. In other words, built into the cost of any product is the employer's insurance premium for the cost of workers' compensation or the cost of self-insurance. Thus, the costs of employment related injuries, diseases and deaths are properly distributed throughout society.

3. MEDICAL LOSS AND WAGE LOSS

The benefits payable vary from jurisdiction to jurisdiction. An essential inquiry to be made in each jurisdiction is whether the particular statute is based upon a medical loss theory, a wage loss theory, or both. A medical loss theory dictates, for example, that in the case of one who has lost an arm, compensation is required for the loss of that limb regardless of whether there has been an adverse impact upon earning capacity or lost wages. On the other hand, the wage loss theory is based upon the idea that a person should be compensated for loss of wages or diminished earning capacity and not for any pure medical losses that have occurred. Many jurisdictions mix the two theories and provide compensation based upon wage and medical losses. One may find in a purportedly wage loss jurisdiction the utilization of an injury schedule which provides compensation for pure medical losses enumerated in the schedule. For example, one would be entitled a specific amount of compensation for the loss of an arm regardless of any diminution in earning capacity.

It is worthy of note that the State of Florida in recent years has attempted to employ an almost pure wage loss theory. As a result, Florida has reduced the costs to employers of its workers' compensation system. Regardless of the theory chosen, it should be kept in mind that generally workers' compensation benefits remain modest and have failed to keep abreast of inflation.

4. SOCIAL INSURANCE

It must be emphasized that workers' compensation in the United States is privately funded with an insurance base, whereas, in some countries, as for example, in Great Britain, a comprehensive social insurance system encompassing workers' compensation exists. There have been reform proposals in the United States aimed at establishing a more comprehensive national system, however, the American system remains a private one grounded in insurance. Certainly, a legitimate criticism of the current system can be made because compensation allocations are made regardless of need. It would at first appear that the general public bears the costs of workers' compensation, however, the actual costs are probably borne by limited groups of consumers of particular products and services. As a result of the fact that workers' compensation is a statutory no-fault scheme, many lose sight of the relevance of tort law and its notions of culpability and fault. For example, intoxication on the job and intentional self-injuries can prevent the recovery of compensation despite the no-fault theory of the system. For a further discussion of compensation as social insurance, see 1 A. Larson, The Law of Workmen's Compensation §§ 3.10–3.40 (1972). [hereinafter cited as Larson].

5. ECONOMIC APPRAISAL

In comparison with the tort compensation system, workers' compensation provides a more efficient economic model. For example, in the case of automobile accidents the tort system provides recovery to victims and families of only 44% of the sums provided by the system, with the remainder of the costs consumed by the inefficiency of the system itself, i.e., court costs, lawyers fees, insurance administration, etc. Workers' compensation ordinarily does not require lengthy and costly hearings; attorney's fees are regulated by statute; and while issues of fault do creep into compensation decisions, ordinarily compensation is assured when a work related injury or death is demonstrated, as opposed to the perils of the tort system.

In evaluating the workers' compensation system one must consider, however, the economic status of today's industrial worker. Wages generally have not kept up with inflation and workers' compensation payments do not reflect current costs of living; further the system fails to provide the amounts necessary for effective educational retraining and vocational rehabilitation. Compensation benefits simply do not reflect the degree of economic harm suffered by a worker and his family; all persons are treated in a uniform manner by the particular workers' compensation act. Additionally, there is generally no provision allowing for increases and escalations due to inflation. As a final criticism, workers' compensation benefits vary a great deal from state to state. Because of this disparity a National Workers' Compensation Standards Act has been proposed (see Appendix I).

C. LIBERAL CONSTRUCTION OF COMPENSATION ACTS

It is generally said that there is to be a liberal construction of all workers' compensation acts because such legislation is remedial in nature. In fact, many workers' compensation acts have an express provision requiring liberal construction. The humane and beneficient purposes of workers' compensation legislation are certainly taken to heart by judges and compensation commissions.

For example, see Pacific Employers Insurance Co. v. Industrial Accident Commission (1945). While as a general rule workers' compensation acts are to be liberally construed, liberality of construction should not rise to the level of judicial legislation.

CHAPTER 3

WORKERS' COMPENSATION AND THE LAW OF TORTS

A. COMMON LAW AND STATUTORY ACTIONS

The common law remedies, and the statutory actions provided by the various employers' liability acts, form the underlying layer of law upon which a remedy can be based when the applicable workers' compensation act fails to provide coverage. Thus, common law and statutory actions still remain important. Common law and statutory actions are also extremely important when there is third party involvement and recovery is sought against them. Third parties are not covered by the act and are not allowed to limit their liability in the same manner as an employer.

B. THE STRUGGLE FOR COVERAGE AND NON–COVERAGE

Workers are constantly searching for greater compensation than that provided by the applicable workers' compensation system. Whenever possible, and certainly in situations in which there has been no fault on the part of the worker, attempts will be made to obtain increased recoveries through the utilization of traditional tort theories.

Attorneys have certainly been creative in this area and there have been many attempts to circumvent the limitations on tort recovery imposed by workers' compensation legislation. Needless to say, because of the potential economic harm posed by large tort damages awards, employers want to insure that workers' compensation remains as a viable shield to tort recoveries. The more important areas in which the struggle for coverage and noncoverage exists are: co-employee suits, dual capacity situations, property damages, negligent inspectors; bad faith liability, products liability, negligent physicians, intentional torts, nonphysical torts and retaliatory discharge.

1. CO–EMPLOYEES

The majority of states provide co-employees with immunity from ordinary tort liability in connection with the employer immunity provisions found in the workers' compensation acts. In a few states, however, common law or statutory actions may be brought against all persons other than one's employer, and this would include a right against a co-employee who may have negligently injured or killed a fellow employee. The co-employee immunity which exists in the majority of states can be found both in statutes and in judicial decisions. For an example of a statutory provision creating co-employee immunity, see New York—McKinney's Workers' Compensation Law § 64.29; for an example of a judicial decision in favor of co-employee immunity which was grounded on public policy, see Miller v. Scott (1960). Even when immunity exists, it will not be available to a co-employee in most intentional tort situations.

2. DUAL CAPACITY EMPLOYERS

Despite the fact that the employer is generally immune from tort liability, the dual capacity doctrine may place an employer in a position to be sued in an alternative capacity, thus avoiding the immunity provided by a workers' compensation act. The majority of courts are reluctant to find a dual capacity on the part of an employer. See Wilder v. United States (1989) (noting the doctrine to be disfavored). There have been rare instances of success on the basis of dual capacity theories. See 2A. Larson § 72.80.

3. PROPERTY ACTIONS

It should always be remembered that the exclusive remedy provisions granting immunity to employers do not deny a worker's tort claim for any property damage. See Superb Carpet Mills, Inc. v. Thomason (1987) (property action allowed but no punitive damages permitted); Haddad v. Justice (1975). Liberal and modern views of what constitute property interests raise questions with regard to what types of actions might be maintainable against employers.

4. NEGLIGENT INSPECTORS

Some jurisdictions extend the employer's immunity to insurance carriers and others that may conduct safety inspections. In other jurisdictions, however, an insurance carrier or, for example, a union or union inspector, may be held liable under traditional tort concepts for the negligent performance of such an inspection. Compare Bryant v. Old Republic Insurance Co. (1970) with Unruh v. Truck Insurance Exchange (1972).

5. BAD FAITH

The possibility exists of a successful bad faith action against either the employer or the insurance compensation carrier based upon the manner in which an employee's claim for workers' compensation benefits is administered. See Simkins v. Great West Cas. Co. (1987). A strong argument for bad faith on the part of an insurance company can be made when it fails to process an employee's legitimate claim for workers' compensation in a manner which demonstrates good faith. Thus, the potential exists for a large tort recovery even if a simple or fairly minor injury has occurred.

6. PRODUCTS LIABILITY

Perhaps the area of greatest interest for third party consideration is that of products liability. In practically every workers' compensation case when an employee has been injured by a particular product or instrumentality, attorneys should consider that deeper pocket provided by the product manufacturer. This is especially true today in light of the impact of Section 402A of the Restatement (Second) of Torts, and its strict liability approach.

Furthermore, the possibility exists for a products liability action by a worker against his employer through a dual capacity theory. For example, an employee of a company manufacturing a product may be injured in the normal course of his employment through the use of that particular product. In Mercer v. Uniroyal, Inc. (1976) an employee truck driver was injured as a result of the blow-out of a defective tire on the truck he was driving. The defective tire was manufactured by his employer, and the employer was found to be liable for workers' compensation and also in tort under the doctrine of dual capacity as the manufacturer of a defective product.

7. PHYSICIANS

Ordinarily a physician who commits malpractice on an injured employee who is covered by workers' compensation is liable in tort to the employee just as the physician would be to any other patient in the particular jurisdiction. However, workers' compensation acts providing co-employees with immunity may provide protection to a physician employed by the employer. See, e.g., Hayes v. Marshall Field & Co. (1953). It should be noted that the dual capacity theory could be used to impose tort liability on an employer for the negligence of a physician employee which causes additional harm to a worker. Furthermore, a physician employee could be viewed as an independent contractor and thus subject to tort liability as a third person.

8. INTENTIONAL TORTS OF EMPLOYERS

Generally there is tort liability on the part of an employer for intentional torts committed against a worker. See generally, Smolarek v. Chrysler Corp. (1989) (retaliation and discrimination); Paroline v. Unisys Corp. (1989) (sexual assault); Childers v. Chesapeake & Potomac Tel. Co. (1989) (intentional infliction of emotional distress). Problems are posed by those difficult cases in which an employer has knowledge of a continuing dangerous condition to a worker and then knowingly fails to take appropriate action to eliminate the hazard. It is possible for the employer's conduct to be characterized as an "intentional tort" which is outside the coverage of the act. For example, see Johns–Manville Products Corp. v. Contra Costa Superior Court (1980); Blankenship v. Cincinnati Milacron Chemicals, Inc. (1982); but see, Kofron v. Amoco Chemicals Corp. (1982).

It should be noted that there is a growing trend in some states to provide enhanced workers' compensation awards for intentional torts in the workplace. These provisions punish the employer while providing a more efficient remedy to the employee who would otherwise have to resort to a traditional tort action with its cost, delay and uncertainty.

Further, there is a recent trend to impose criminal responsibility for certain employer conduct that injures or kills employees. See Illinois v. Chicago Magnet Wire Corp. (1989) (aggravated battery charged for exposing employees to hazardous substances in the workplace; no federal preemption by OSHA). These criminal proceedings can be of assistance to claimants pursuing compensation and other civil remedies.

9. NONPHYSICAL TORTS

The exclusive remedy provisions of workers' compensation acts generally do not bar what are sometimes referred to as nonphysical torts. These would include actions for false arrest or imprisonment, libel and slander. Additionally, actions for sex, race and handicap discrimination, etc., would not be excluded. See generally, Reese v. Sears, Roebuck & Co. (1987) (handicap discrimination); Cole v. Fair Oaks Fire Protection District (1987); Boscaglia v. Michigan Bell Tel. Co. (1984); Dorr v. C.B. Johnson, Inc. (1983) (slander).

10. RETALIATORY DISCHARGE

Retaliatory discharge actions are permitted in most states when an employer discharges an employee for filing a workers' compensation claim. See e.g., Griess v. Consolidated Freightways Corp. (1989) (public policy supports retaliatory discharge claim). See also Lingle v. Norge Div. of Magic Chef, Inc. (1988) (retaliatory discharge action arising out of the filing of a workers' compensation claim is not preempted by 301 of the Labor Management Relations Act).

CHAPTER 4

THE EMPLOYEE–EMPLOYER RELATIONSHIP

A. EMPLOYEES AND EMPLOYERS GENERALLY

The common law defined a master as one who employed another to perform services and who controls or has a right of control over the other's conduct in performing such services. The master had to have not only the power to control, choose, and direct the servant with regard to the object to be accomplished but also had to possess the power to control the details of the work. The common law definitions are still of importance in establishing who is an employer and employee, however, definitions provided in workers' compensation legislation are controlling. Typically, an employee for workers' compensation coverage purposes is defined as one who works for, and under the control of, another for hire. A liberal construction should be given to the definitions of employer and employee because of the objectives of workers' compensation and the need to make coverage as expansive as possible. The Restatement (Second) of Agency § 220 relating to master and servant provides the basic definitions of employee and employer. The Restatement places primary emphasis on the employer's right to control the details of the work in order for a sufficient employment relationship to exist. Professor Larson has criticized this test and advocates in its place that an inquiry be directed at the nature of the claimant's work in relation to the employer's regular business. He argues that if the particular work has become a part of the cost of the product or services, then the particular work and thus the employee should be covered by compensation. Professor Larson indicates that the right of control test is a false one and that the independent contractor-employee classification issue can lead to unsatisfactory results. See 1 C. Larson § 43.30. Despite this criticism, the traditional test of the employer/employee relationship continues, and the following factors, inter alia, are to be considered: who has assumed the direction and control of the employee; who possesses the power to hire and fire or recall; who bears responsibility for wages and compensation; in whose work was the employee engaged and for whose benefit was the work primarily being done; who furnished any equipment to be used by the employee; and who bore responsibility for the employee's working conditions.

B. EMPLOYEES

On the basis of statutes and judicial decisions, particular classes of employees are sometimes specifically included in or excluded from worker's compensation coverage. Typical employee classifications are provided hereinafter.

1.　CASUAL EMPLOYEES

Casual employees are sometimes excluded from workers' compensation coverage. Real difficulties exist in determining who is a casual employee because of a failure to distinguish properly between casual and non-casual employments. Determinations may be based upon the following issues: the contract of hire; the nature of the service or work to be rendered; the scope and purpose of the employment; and the duration and regularity of the service. Ordinarily employment may be casual if it is temporary in nature and limited in purpose, or if it is incidental, accidental or irregular. The casual classification is not determined solely by a lack of frequency or length. As might be expected, the law in this area varies greatly from jurisdiction to jurisdiction, but the majority view may well be to exclude an employment from compensation coverage only if the employment is both casual and outside of the course of the employer's business.

2.　AGRICULTURAL EMPLOYEES

The majority of workers' compensation acts specifically exclude agricultural and farm laborers from coverage. Difficulties in this area exist with regard to the appropriate label; for example, one who trained a race horse was not an agricultural employee. See Tuma v. Kosterman (1984). The focus ordinarily is upon the substance of the employee's work as opposed to the employer's class of business. Because of the great number of workers employed in activities incidental to farm enterprises, the line between compensation coverage for ordinary employment and non-coverage for agricultural workers can be a perplexing one. For example, one employed as an agricultural worker, whose duties also include the repair of farm buildings, might not be covered; while one specially employed to repair a farm building would receive the benefits of workers' compensation coverage. See Cannon v. Industrial Accident Commission (1959).

3. DOMESTIC EMPLOYEES

Most compensation acts exempt domestic and household employment from coverage. The test for domestic or household employment is generally whether or not the duties performed are directed at the maintenance of the home. Some jurisdictions treat domestic employees as "casual" employees; others exclude them from coverage because of the "non-business" nature of their employment; and they are excluded in other jurisdictions because of the coverage exception applicable to employers who have less than the statutory requisite number of employees.

4. LOANED EMPLOYEES

The case law addressing the issue of loaned employees is confusing and conflicting. The common law rules are relevant to a determination of who is a lent employee and who occupies the status of the employee's general or special employer. The traditional test of special employment focuses on whether the employee has moved out of the control of the general employer and into the direction and control of the special employer. The inquiry is frequently made in tort cases in an effort to establish the proper employer for purposes of vicarious liability. It must be stressed that the issue in workers' compensation cases is simply the need to find an employer who can provide coverage. While in some states lent employee issues are resolved by statute, other states address the questions through case law which may impose compensation liability on the general or special employer, or both.

5. STATE AND MUNICIPAL EMPLOYEES

State, municipal and public agency employees may be covered by the provisions of state workers' compensation acts, or by some alternative state compensation system. Workers' compensation statutes vary considerably and each state's act must be consulted individually in an effort to learn if a particular public employee is covered. Some of the more common issues are: whether municipal corporations are "employers" under the act; whether one is a state officer or official and thus outside coverage or is an employee. Generally, individuals exercising some portion of a state's sovereign power are considered officials. Police officers and firemen, in particular, have posed problems with regard to workers' compensation coverage. Generally, they are not viewed as "workmen" or "employees," and thus, are not covered; however, many workers' compensation acts have special provisions covering for these occupations.

6. FEDERAL EMPLOYEES

Employees and civil officers of the various branches of the United States Government or any of its wholly owned instrumentalities who are injured or killed in the performance of their duties are provided compensation under the Federal Employee's Compensation Act, 5 U.S.C.A. § 8101 et seq. The FECA is liberally construed, administered by the Secretary of Labor, and provides federal employees with their exclusive remedy against the United States for injuries or deaths sustained in the performance of their duties. Traditional third-party liability is not disturbed. The term "employee" under the Act is defined by statute and various classes of employees are specifically covered and others are specifically excluded. See 5 U.S.C.A. § 8101. The amounts and duration of compensation payable under the Act are among the most liberal in the United States. The amount of compensation payable under the FECA is generally based on the employee's monthly pay. Disputed claims for compensation are handled adminis-

tratively under the Department of Labor.
Hearings may be had and final decisions of the
Secretary of Labor are subject to review by the
Employees' Compensation Appeals Board within
the U.S. Department of Labor.

Active duty members of the military services are
not covered by state compensation acts or the
FECA. They are subject to special federal statutory provisions that cover injury and death sustained
in the line of duty. See Chapter 1, E, supra.

7. PARTICIPATION OF EMPLOYEES IN ENTERPRISE

Originally, workers' compensation acts excluded
executives, partners, corporate officers and the
like, from coverage because they did not fall under
the definition of a workman. Additionally, it was
felt that workers' compensation legislation was not
intended to apply to these groups. Today, the fact
that a claimant is a corporate officer does not
generally preclude coverage. Even if an injury
occurs while one is acting in a managerial capacity, one may still be considered an employee under
an act. It is possible, however, because of stock
ownership and a controlling interest for one, in
effect, to be the business. In these instances there
would be no coverage, unless perhaps one could be
classified as an employee on the basis of the activities one was engaged in at the time of injury (i.e.,
non-executive activities). This result is reached on
the basis of the dual capacity doctrine (not to be

confused here with the dual capacity doctrine concerning an employer's potential tort liability; see Chapter 3, B., 2.), which makes it possible for an executive, who at the time of injury was acting as an employee rather than as an executive, to recover compensation. See Hirsch v. Hirsch Brothers, Inc. (1952).

Partners are treated differently because there is no separate employer entity; partners share equal liability and possess comparable rights in management. In the absence of special legislation, partners are not considered to be employees within compensation coverage even if they have been injured in situations in which they would have been entitled to compensation had they been employees.

8. VOLUNTEERS

One who works for another as a volunteer is not generally entitled to the benefits of workers' compensation because one is not deemed to be an employee. Under most acts only those persons who perform a service for hire are employees and, therefore, volunteers are excluded.

9. ALIENS

The term "employee" in the various workers' compensation acts includes all persons who perform services for hire and includes aliens. It should be pointed out, however, that some acts require that one be a state resident in order to receive workers' compensation benefits. States are not uniform in this regard and in the absence of a provision to the contrary, it is generally said that residency is not a requirement for compensation. It should be noted that certain classes of nonresident alien dependents are often excluded from the receipt of death benefits. See Alvarez Martinez v. Industrial Commission (1986).

10. MINORS

Generally, any person may be an "employee" for the purposes of workers' compensation coverage, and one is not excluded from such coverage simply because of minority. Most states have specific provisions in their compensation acts regarding minors. In some states minors are entitled to double compensation, and in others minors may either opt for compensation or sue for damages. A minor's unlawful employment may itself provide a separate tort basis for liability. See Restatement (Second) of Torts § 286 Comment e (1966).

11. ILLEGAL EMPLOYMENTS

Illegally employed workers can present unique coverage problems. The difficulty usually relates to the question of whether the employment itself is prohibited by statute; for example, prostitution would be a prohibited employment in most jurisdictions, and thus if one is employed to perform acts in violation of a penal statute, coverage would be denied. On the other hand, one who has been illegally employed still enjoys coverage when the employment contract is unlawful because of a provision relating to the legality of such an agreement; for example, laws prohibiting the employment of a minor should not interfere with coverage if a minor is injured in an otherwise lawful employment.

12.　INDEPENDENT CONTRACTORS

If one is classified as an independent contractor, rather than the servant or employee of another, one may lose the right to workers' compensation coverage. The independent contractor issue is one of the most frequently litigated questions in the law of workers' compensation. The Restatement (Second) of Agency, § 220 provides the usual definition and tests utilized in this area. The most common factors considered are: the right of control; the method of payment; the providing of materials, tools, or supplies; control over the work site; and the right to discharge the employee.

Independent contractor decisions are often conflicting and irreconcilable. The difficulty in this area stems from attempts by the courts to resolve independent contractor issues in tort cases in which the question is one of vicarious liability. It is questionable whether an inquiry aimed at the avoidance of vicarious liability should be of any relevance to a determination of workers' compensation coverage, given the social and economic policies underlying worker's compensation legislation. See Laurel Daily Leader, Inc. v. James (1955). See also 1 C. Larson § 43.50. Professor Larson argues that a relative nature of work test should be used because it is supported by workers' compensation theory. This test provides that any worker whose efforts are regularly and continually included in the costs of products or services should receive compensation from the manufacturer of such products, or the provider of such services.

13. PROFESSIONAL EMPLOYEES

While often professionals may be viewed as independent contractors, it is certainly possible for them in certain employment circumstances to be employees for purposes of workers' compensation coverage. For example nurses and interns regularly employed by hospitals are generally employees and included within coverage. Additionally, it is possible for an attorney to have an employer and be an "employee" for workers' compensation coverage. See Egan v. New York State Joint Legislative Committee (1956).

C. EMPLOYERS GENERALLY

Workers' compensation acts must be consulted for the definition of "employer." As in the case of "employees" the statutory definition of "employer" is the controlling one to the extent that common law concepts of master and servant are modified. Typically, "employer" means a master or principal who employs another to perform services for hire; who controls or has the right of control of the other; and who usually pays another's wages directly. Situations may arise in which an employee appears to have two employers. For example, an employer's employee may hire another without informing the hiree of the true employer's identity. Since an employer for workers' compensation coverage is usually provided on agency theories, the employee is permitted to elect a covered "employer" for compensation purposes. See Hesse v. J. J. Oys & Co. (1958).

1.   MINIMUM NUMBER OF EMPLOYEES

A minority of workers' compensation acts contain provisions that mandate coverage only in situations in which an employer has a specified number of regular employees. Typical provisions of this nature would, for example, require coverage in the case of three or more employees. Minimum employee requirements are liberally construed in favor of coverage. See Jackson v. Fly (1952).

Furthermore, the usual requirement of workers "regularly" employed does not necessarily mean constant or continuous employment in order to meet the minimum threshold for coverage.

2.   GENERAL AND SPECIAL EMPLOYERS

General and special employer issues usually arise in loaned employee cases. The term "general employer" refers to a worker's original employer, while the term "special employer" refers to the one to whom a worker is loaned. It is possible for one to be the employee of both at the same time, and thus seek compensation against one or both. Special employment relationships require the consent and knowledge of the employee. The basic test for determining one's employer in the loaned employee situation is: who had the right of control and direction over the worker at the relevant time. The pertinent factors, inter alia, include: the power to fire; who paid the wages; and whose business was being furthered. See also Chapter 4, A.4., Loaned Employees, supra.

3. SUBCONTRACTORS AND STATUTORY EMPLOYERS

A majority of states have provisions in their workers' compensation acts which are designed to prevent a general contractor from shielding himself from compensation liability through the use of subcontractors. These "statutory employer" or "contracting under" provisions are intended to provide protection for employees injured or killed while working for uninsured or judgment proof subcontractors. In order to successfully maintain a compensation claim against a statutory employer, the subcontractor's employee must establish that the work that gave rise to the injury was a part of the regular business of the statutory employer. The statutory employer may also be benefited in that tort liability can be precluded. See Black v. Cabot Petroleum Corp. (1989) (exclusive remedy protection involving upstream and downstream contractors); Kelpfer v. Joyce (1961). It must be pointed out, however, that issues of primary versus secondary liability, the status of the statutory employer as guarantor or insurer under some acts, and the subcontractor's failure to carry insurance, may affect third party tort liability on the part of the statutory employer, even if he has paid workers' compensation benefits. See 2 A. Larson, § 72.31. The possibility exists for a statutory employer to obtain reimbursement from a solvent subcontractor. See, e.g., New York—McKinney's Workers' Compensation Law § 56.

4. CHARITABLE ORGANIZATIONS

Employees of charitable or nonprofit organizations may not be covered by workers' compensation in some states. Some acts expressly exclude charitable employers. Charities and nonprofit organizations may be excluded as employers because they involve employments not carried on "for pecuniary gain." In those jurisdictions that require that one be engaged "in the trade or business of the employer" in order to be covered there are conflicting decisions with regard to the coverage of an employee of a charitable organization. The better view allows coverage. See Smith v. Lincoln Memorial University (1957).

5.   CONCURRENT EMPLOYERS

An employee may have more than one employer for workers' compensation purposes. These employers may be characterized as either concurrent employers or as joint employers. When one is injured or killed in the service of such employers, several approaches have been taken toward compensation. Liability may be joint, or apportioned, or placed upon only one employer. In apportionment situations employers may be required to provide compensation in proportion to the wages they paid the employee. See Newman v. Bennett (1973).

6.   SUCCESSIVE EMPLOYERS

It is not uncommon for an employee to have successive employers, and difficulties can arise in determining which employer is the "employer" for workers' compensation purposes. One method of determining one's responsible employer is to focus simply on the date of injury, and to view the employer at that time as the appropriate one. In those cases in which a disability or injury has resulted from successive employments, the various employers may be required to provide compensation on the basis of their contribution to such disability or injury. Some injuries and certainly death, as in tort cases, can be viewed as single and indivisible, or as incapable of apportionment, with entire liability imposed upon the employers.

In cases of occupational disease and successive employers the following possibilities exist: liability is placed upon the employer in whose service the disease was contracted; liability is borne by the last employer in whose employ the worker was last exposed to the disease's hazards; or liability may be apportioned among several employers. Statutory variations exist with respect to the foregoing possibilities, but given the objectives and policies of workers' compensation, there should be complete compensation for employment related diseases whenever a solvent contributing employer exists.

CHAPTER 5

THE COVERAGE FORMULA—NECESSITY FOR A "PERSONAL INJURY BY ACCIDENT ARISING OUT OF AND IN THE COURSE OF EMPLOYMENT"

A. THE COVERAGE INQUIRY

Since the inception of workers' compensation legislation, there have been difficulties in fixing and defining the boundaries of coverage. Problems in this area have largely been the result of a failure to properly identify and inquire into the issue of the scope of the risk. The early cases took a tort law, proximate cause approach toward the risk inquiry. Needless to say, a fault based risk analysis is totally incompatible with the objective and policies of workers' compensation. Subsequent decisions developed various doctrines aimed at defining the scope of the risk, e.g., the "peculiar risk" doctrine, see infra.

One can best understand scope of the risk questions by reference to three broad categories of risks. First, there are definite employment related risks, as the loss of limb by a machinery operator; all would agree that this type of injury is within the scope of the risk of employment and covered by workers' compensation. Second, there are personal risks, such as an injury produced by an epileptic seizure while at work, but unrelated to the employment; this injury might be covered by hospital insurance, but not by workers' compensation because the injury arose from a purely personal condition and was unrelated to a risk of employment. Third, there are neutral risks, such as acts of God, or random acts of violence unrelated to one's employment. These risks are neutral because they bear no relation to one's employment, and they cannot be classified as personal risks. Neutral risks are the cause of a great deal of conflict and confusion.

In a further effort to define the boundaries of coverage, an inquiry is made with regard to whether a sufficient relation exists between one's employment and one's injury. Factors such as time, place and circumstances are considered; however, scope of the risk issues with concomitant confusion also arise in this context. For example, an employee traveling to and from work could be excluded from coverage because at the time of injury the employee was not at work and was off the employer's business premises. While time, place, and circumstances may be relevant, the true question in to and from work situations may be whether the perils of such a journey should be within the scope of the risk created by one's employment, given the policies and purposes of workers' compensation.

An additional inquiry which must be made in an effort to define coverage boundaries is that of factual cause. This refers to the necessity for a factual connection between one's activities at the time of injury and the injury of which one complains; i.e., did the employment in which one was allegedly engaged produce the medical complaint for which one now seeks compensation. For example, did one's employment activity contribute to or cause a heart attack that occurred while one was at work.

In summary, the principal elements directed at coverage in workers' compensation cases are:

1. scope of the risk;

2. sufficient relation to employment, and;

3. factual cause.

The preceding issues arise in the context of the statutory language or coverage formula found in workers' compensation legislation. The coverage formula used in the vast majority of workers' compensation acts requires a "personal injury or death by accident arising out of and in the course of employment." The "arising out of" requirement refers to the scope of the risk issue previously discussed in this section and which will be more fully discussed hereinafter. The "in the course of" requirement refers to the sufficient relation to employment issue (time, place, and circumstances factors) which was discussed above and which will be more fully developed later. Factual causation issues will also be discussed.

The coverage formula requirements of "personal injury by accident" have posed problems in cases involving diseases, mental illnesses, and injuries to artificial limbs. Originally, injuries to artificial limbs were not considered "personal injuries," and disabilities from disease that developed over long time periods were excluded from coverage because no personal inquiry "by accident" had occurred.

It should be noted that while the coverage formula speaks in terms of "personal injury," workers' compensation legislation also provides coverage for death cases. Thus, much of what ordinarily is stated with regard to injuries is also applicable to death situations. Therefore, the analysis of various circumstances producing injuries in the following sections is also applicable when those circumstances have resulted in death.

B. THE "ARISING OUT OF" CONCEPT

One can best understand the "arising out of" concept by comparing it to the scope of the risk question asked and resolved by courts on the basis of policy considerations in tort cases. Sometimes this issue is dealt with in tort cases through the use of proximate cause terminology. It is important to remember that this is a question of law and policy exclusively for the court, and certainly scope of the risk issues should be approached in a similar fashion in workers' compensation cases. In light of the objectives and policies of workers' compensation it is submitted that a much broader approach should be taken toward the scope of the risk than is taken in tort cases.

There appears to be five basic risk doctrines employed by the courts to determine the scope of the risk.

1. THE FIVE BASIC RISK DOCTRINES

a. *Proximate Cause*

Originally judges had difficulty divorcing themselves from tort law with its proximate cause and fault concepts, and some early cases, therefore adopted the fault-related proximate cause test for the "arising out of" concept, which required that one's employment be the proximate cause of one's injury. This approach is much too narrow, and it is incompatible and in conflict with the objectives of any statutory no-fault compensation system.

b. *Peculiar Risk*

An early device which resulted in hardship to employees was the peculiar risk doctrine. This risk concept excluded coverage for injuries caused by risks which, admittedly were within the course of one's employment, but which were commonly shared by others, even though the employee was exposed for a longer period of time by virtue of the nature of the employee's employment. For example, an employee who suffered a sunstroke while delivering coal for his employer was viewed as not having been "peculiarly exposed" to the danger of sunstroke because he was not subjected to a materially greater risk of sunstroke than other outdoor workers. Dougherty's Case (1921). The peculiar risk theory is generally rejected in modern compensation cases because it is unrealistic and allows only limited coverage.

c. Increased Risk

A modern approach which provides broader coverage than the peculiar risk test is the increased risk doctrine. This approach includes within the scope of the risk those risks to which an employee has been exposed for a longer period of time than the public, even though the risk is commonly shared by all. If one's employment results in a greater exposure to a risk there would be coverage even though the risk is not one that is qualitatively different from that shared by others. For example, one constantly exposed to extreme heat on the job and who suffers from heatstroke should be entitled to compensation under the increased risk theory.

d. Actual Risk

A liberal approach toward the scope of the risk issue can be found in the actual risk doctrine. The sole question to be answered is whether the risk realized was in fact a risk of one's employment, regardless of whether the risk is commonly shared by the public. For example, heat prostration would be compensable if the nature of the employment exposed the employee to the risk; the fact that the risk is common to all who are exposed to the sun's rays on a hot day would be immaterial. Hughes v. Trustees of St. Patrick's Cathedral (1927).

e. Positional Risk

The positional risk doctrine is the most liberal of the scope of the risk theories, and it has been adopted in a minority of jurisdictions. The only inquiry under a positional risk theory is whether one's employment was responsible for one's being at the time and place where an injury occurred.

Even the most neutral of risks can be included; for example, an employee at work who was accidentally struck by an arrow fired by a small boy next door, would be covered. Gargiulo v. Gargiulo (1953).

2. A MISCELLANY OF RISKS

a. Acts of God

While acts of God such as windstorms, tornadoes, exposure, lightning, floods, earthquakes, etc., would at first appear to be outside the employment risk, it is generally agreed that if one's employment has enhanced or "increased" the risk of injury from these sources, the injury would be compensable. In addition to an increased risk approach to recovery, it may be possible to recover on the basis of "actual risk" or "positional risk" theories. The "proximate cause" or "peculiar risk" approaches would disallow compensation.

b. Street Risk Doctrine

Frequently employees find themselves on the streets and highways in the course of their employment. Early decisions denied recovery to employees who were injured as a result of the realization of risks associated with the use of streets and highways because these were viewed as common risks or hazards to the general public and not risks peculiar to one's employment. The situation is somewhat different today, and an employee who is subjected to a greater exposure to the risks of the street, despite the fact that such risks are common to the public, may be covered. Coverage in these cases can be provided on the basis of the increased risk approach; also, coverage can be had on the basis of the actual risk or positional risk doctrines.

c. Imported Dangers Doctrine

It is not uncommon for employees to be exposed to a risk of harm which they or their fellow employees have imported to the worksite; e.g., matches, explosives, firearms, etc. Traditionally, risks imported by the injured employee were viewed as "personal" and outside of the scope of the risk of employment. A danger imported by one's co-employee, while it may appear to be a neutral risk, could nevertheless give rise to recovery on the basis of increased, actual or positional risk theories. In Ward v. Halliburton Co. (1966), compensation was denied to an employee who was killed when his hunting gun accidentally discharged while he was getting a work uniform from his car;

the court indicated that recovery would have been allowed if the gun had belonged to another employee. Additionally, an employee might be able to recover for the realization of a personal risk that the employee has imported, if it could be established that the employment had increased such a risk.

d. Assault

Assaults are held to be within the scope of the risk and to arise out of one's employment when the nature of the employment (e.g., policeman or security guard) increases the likelihood of such an occurrence, or if the assault has grown out of a controversy that is work related. Ordinarily assaults are not within the scope of the risk if they have been prompted by malice or personal motives; however, even these assaults may be included if in some manner one's work has contributed to the occurrence. Assaults in some cases, such as those by strangers, lunatics, children, etc., may be viewed as neutral risks outside coverage; however, it may be possible for these to be covered through the use of the positional risk doctrine.

Early cases recognized the aggressor defense which denied compensation to an aggressor in work-related assaults. The aggressor defense has been discredited today because it creates a fault based defense in a no-fault system. Despite the rejection of the aggressor defense, a substantial minority of jurisdictions by statute exclude from coverage those who have been harmed as a result of their "willful intent to injure" others. Generally these statutes require a greater degree of fault and wrongdoing than is required for the aggressor defense.

e. Horseplay

Frequently injuries occur in the workplace as a result of horseplay. There is little difficulty in providing coverage for a non-participant who is a victim of a horseplay injury; such an injury is viewed as being within the scope of the risk of one's employment. Difficult problems are posed, however, when one instigates or actively participates in horseplay and receives an injury. These cases may be disposed of on the basis of whether they occurred "in the course of" employment; however, the better analysis is one that focuses on the scope of the risk inquiry with the increased, actual, or positional risk doctrines determining coverage. In any event, an instigator or willing participant may be able to recover on the basis of the longevity and customary nature of the practice.

f. Heart Cases

One of the most problematic areas in the law of workers' compensation is that of heart cases. Commonly these cases are approached on the basis of whether or not a personal injury "by accident" has occurred. This approach requires that "unusual" strain or exertion precipitate the heart attack. This is an impractical and unsatisfactory test for coverage in heart cases; distinctions between "usual" and "unusual" strains are practically impossible to make, and serve to confuse the issue.

The better approach is one that focuses on the scope of the risk; thus if one's employment has contributed to the heart attack because of exertion or other work-related circumstances, the attack may be found to have arisen out of one's employment; otherwise heart attacks occurring on the job would involve personal risks. Professor Larson advocates the utilization of both a legal test and a medical test in heart cases. The legal test would be met on the basis of work-related exertion, and the medical test would simply require proof of a causal connection between such work-related exertion and the heart attack. This inquiry would be the same as that previously characterized as factual cause and would necessitate expert medical testimony.

As a result of the difficulties in this area, some jurisdictions have special provisions directed at heart and exertion cases.

g. *Pre-existing Injury or Disease*

It is certainly not uncommon for employees to bring pre-existing medical problems to the workplace. The difficulty posed in this area stems from the fact that pre-existing medical problems constitute personal risks which would fall outside of coverage; however, if one is able to demonstrate that one's employment exacerbated or aggravated a pre-existing medical problem, then recovery may be permitted. The obvious problem facing employees is that of factual cause and medical proof. One must establish through expert medical testimony the fact of aggravation and a causal connection between one's employment and the claimed injury. Some jurisdictions address this problem area through special provisions in their workers' compensation act.

h. Unexplained Accidents

Coverage questions arise in cases of unexplained deaths, unexplained falls, and idiopathic falls. A strict application of the neutral risk or personal risk theories could result in a denial of coverage, even if a fall or death occurred in the course of employment. An application of the positional risk doctrine can result in recovery even if the cause of a fall or death is unknown, because of the employment relation that existed at the time. The positional risk doctrine could also permit recovery in idiopathic fall situations in which the fall was the result of a purely personal condition, if, for example, the fall occurred at work.

In an effort to resolve the problems posed by an unexplained employee death, courts will generally employ a presumption that the death was one that arose out of employment if the death occurred at the appropriate time and in the appropriate work situation. Given the objectives and policies of workers' compensation legislation every effort should be made to resolve unexplained injury and death cases in favor of the employee or his survivors.

C. THE "IN THE COURSE OF" CONCEPT

1. AN INTRODUCTION AND PERSPECTIVE

The statutory formula for workers' compensation coverage generally requires a personal injury by accident arising out of and "in the course of" one's employment. The "in the course of" requirement refers to the necessity for a sufficiently close relationship between one's employment and injury. This inquiry focuses on considerations of time, place, and circumstances, as they relate to one's employment.

Problems in this area usually occur for two reasons. First, the "in the course of" concept may be confused with the vicarious liability requirement of the same terms used in tort cases to establish liability; for example, a master is liable for the torts of a servant committed in the course of employment. The vicarious liability "in the course of" requirement certainly may be of assistance in many workers' compensation cases in establishing the requisite employment connection or relation; however, it should not be determinative in those cases in which it conflicts with the policies and coverage objectives of workers' compensation legislation. For example, if one's employment has produced an injury which occurs or manifests itself while one is not at work and off the employer's premises, there should still be coverage. In other words, one need not be acting within the course and scope of one's employment when an employment related harm produces injury. The only issue is one of causal connection between one's employment and injury. Rogers v. Allis Chalmers Manufacturing Co. (1949); see 1 A. Larson § 29.22. In Technical Tape Corp. v. Industrial Commission (1974), the inhalation of chemical fumes at work produced residual intoxication causing an employee to have an automobile accident after leaving the workplace; compensation was allowed.

The second cause of difficulties in this area stems from confusing the "in the course of" requirement with the scope of the risk inquiry which is made in conjunction with the "arising out of" requirement. In other words, the time, place, and circumstances considerations involved in the "in the course of" question may be permitted to dictate the answer to the scope of the risk issue. The scope of the risk issue should always be viewed as a question directed at the scope of workers' compensation coverage, with the necessity for a liberal and broad approach toward employment risks. The "in the course of" requirement really should do no more than establish the necessary relation to one's employment required for workers' compensation coverage. The more liberal a jurisdiction's approach toward the selection of a risk theory, then the less that will probably be required to meet the "in the course of" test. If a positional risk theory is employed, little would probably be required to establish the necessary employment relation. For example, a salesman who suffers harm some distance from the employer's place of business, and on the premises of another, could be covered. See Wiseman v. Industrial Accident Commission (1956).

2. COMMON "IN THE COURSE OF" PROBLEMS

a. *Going to and From Work*

Injuries occurring while employees are traveling to and from work have constituted a large portion of workers' compensation litigation, and there is a lack of uniformity in this area. It should be noted at the outset that the problems posed with regard to coverage stem from a failure to recognize that many of these cases should be addressed on the basis of the "arising out of" requirement with its concomitant scope of the risk inquiry.

Generally, those accidents that take place while one is on the way to or from work are viewed as outside the course of one's employment; however, if one is on the employer's premises (having not yet arrived at work or in the process of leaving work) ordinarily there would be coverage. The key issue thus becomes the boundaries of the employer's premises. Various devices have been employed to resolve coverage issues for those injured off of but near the employer's premises; included are: the parking lot exception; the "so-close rule; the "proximity" rule; and the "threshold" doctrine. Some jurisdictions have special provisions in their compensation laws to deal with "going to and from work" problems.

An employee may well be found "in the course of" in the following special circumstances, even if the injury has occurred while going to or coming from work. These special circumstances exist if: the employer provides the transportation or travel expenses; the employer compensates the employee for time spent in travel; or the employee is on call and travel constitutes a significant portion of employment duties. In many situations employees are required, as a regular part of their employment, to spend time away from home or office and difficult questions arise here because of the myriad of circumstances in which one might receive an injury; e.g., sleeping, eating, recreation, etc., in conjunction with work-related travel. Again it must be emphasized that the crux of the "in the course of" problem is to be found in a failure to address many of these cases on the basis of the scope of the risk.

b. *Mixed-Purpose Trips*

An area in which the rules of vicarious liability have created confusion with regard to workers' compensation coverage is that of mixed-purpose trips. On occasion an employee may be injured while on a trip that is both for the employee's benefit and for that of the employer; these are sometimes called "dual purpose" cases. Certainly, if the trip is primarily for the benefit of the employer there should be coverage despite the fact that the trip also involves some personal benefit or personal purpose; this is generally called the dominant purpose rule. Marks' Dependents v. Gray (1929).

Just as in cases of vicarious liability, issues of frolic and detour arise. It should be kept in mind that in vicarious liability situations the issue is one of possible employer liability to a third person, whereas in compensation cases the issue is one of coverage for the injured employee. Given the question in workers' compensation cases a more liberal approach is required and less emphasis should be placed upon the vicarious liability meaning of "in the course of." Little should be required in the way of employment connection, and the major inquiry should focus on the scope of the risk. In some jurisdictions a liberalizing trend is evident in this area. For example, coverage was extended to an employee who, prior to going to work, was injured in an accident while driving his child to school in a company truck; this would certainly appear to have been a personal trip, but the presence of the company's name and address on the truck seemingly determined the outcome. Thomas v. Certified Refrigeration, Inc. (1974).

c. Recreation

Various approaches have been taken toward compensation coverage when accidents have occurred during recreational or social activities.

There may be liability when injuries from these sources have occurred on the employer's premises. Some decisions take a scope of employment approach toward the activity that produced the injury, while others insist upon some kind of benefit to the employer, direct or indirect. Recreational cases may frequently involve "going to and from" work and personal comfort issues (see infra). The more liberal a jurisdiction's risk theory, the greater the likelihood of coverage in recreation cases, and the less that is required for an activity to be "in the course of" employment.

d. Personal Comfort Doctrine

Employees who are injured while engaged in activities aimed at their personal comfort, e.g., drinking, eating, resting, smoking, using toilet facilities, etc., generally enjoy compensation coverage if their activities bear the necessary relationship to their employment. An employee may, however, remove oneself from the course of employment if, in efforts to satisfy personal needs, one abandons one's work or employs means which move the employee outside of the employment relation, thus indicating that a purely personal or neutral risk has been realized. For example, a deliveryman injured while attempting to dislodge a rabbit from a culvert was denied compensation. Ranger Insurance Co. v. Valerio (1977).

e. Emergencies

Employees injured while attempting rescues, or otherwise in emergency situations, are viewed as having acted within the course of their employment if an interest of the employer was furthered by the effort or activity. The good will of the employer alone may constitute a sufficient interest for coverage. As a matter of policy, very little should be required for a finding of "in the course of" when employees receive injuries during rescue attempts. The positional risk theory should be employed to provide coverage when an employee, motivated by common humanity and decency, is injured while attempting to rescue a stranger who bears no relation to the employer's business. See Food Products Corp. v. Industrial Commission of Arizona (1981).

f. *Wilful Misconduct and Violation of Laws, Regulations and Safety Rules*

The question of wilful misconduct on the part of an employee may arise in two important contexts: (1) it may provide the basis for a statutorily created defense in a minority of jurisdictions or, (2) in the absence of such a statute, it may be relevant to the issue of whether an employee was outside of the course of employment at the time of injury. The wilful misconduct defense is usually a difficult one to establish, because employee fault should not bar recovery under workers' compensation theory. The term "wilful" is strictly construed, and gross negligence will not suffice. The issue of wilful misconduct may also arise in the "in the course of" context in conjunction with questions concerning personal comfort, going to and from work, recreation, etc.

Some jurisdictions provide the employer with a statutory defense when an employee has wilfully violated safety rules, regulations, or statutes. The wilful violation defense is in some ways comparable to the assumption of the risk defense in tort cases. The employer must establish actual knowledge of the rule or statute and an appreciation of the risk connected with non-compliance. Additionally, excuses may exist for non-compliance. The justification and wisdom of the wilful violation defense is open to question in light of the no-fault nature of workers' compensation and the inevitability of employee injuries which are in large part the result of human frailty.

g. *Intoxication*

Employee intoxication is addressed statutorily in a majority of jurisdictions, and it may constitute a separate defense to coverage. The key question in employee intoxication cases is one of causation. The "sole cause" approach taken by some statutes appears to be the one most compatible with the policies of workers' compensation legislation; if there has been some work-related contribution to the injury, there should be coverage.

The coverage question in intoxication cases may also be addressed on the basis of a scope of the risk inquiry, an "in the course of" requirement, or as an issue of whether an injury "by accident" has occurred.

h. *Suicides*

Suicides have traditionally posed problems because they may be viewed as the result of a wilful act on the part of an employee, which severs the causal connection between a job related injury and one's death. The minority view, which parallels the traditional tort view, would only allow recovery in those cases in which one committed suicide in a state of delirium or as a result of an uncontrollable impulse evidencing an inability to make a conscious decision with regard to the taking of one's life. Under the minority approach there would need to be medical testimony of a mental disorder sufficiently serious to deprive one of volition.

A more liberal approach is generally taken in many jurisdictions, and if an unbroken chain of causation can be established between a work related injury and a mental condition that leads to a suicide, then compensation may be permitted. See City of Tampa v. Scott (1981).

Given the difficulties involved in establishing the requisite causal relation between employment related injuries and suicides, a better approach would be one requiring simply a demonstration of some contribution to the suicide by an employment related physical or psychic injury. See Lopucki v. Ford Motor Co. (1981). A broad approach should be taken toward the scope of the risk in suicide cases, and such deaths should be viewed as in the course of one's employment when a work relation can be shown.

D. THE NECESSITY OF "PERSONAL INJURY BY ACCIDENT"

1. THE PROBLEMS

Traditionally most workers' compensation acts have required as a part of their coverage formula a "personal injury by accident" or "accidental injury." Difficulties have arisen in interpreting the meanings of "accident" and "personal injury." Historically, problems have existed in this area because of the failure to take a pragmatic and liberal approach toward these requirements as they relate to the scope of the employment risk.

Furthermore, difficulties in this area were compounded by factual causation issues which were disposed of under the guise of "personal injury by accident," and which more appropriately should have been addressed as a part of the employment risk question, with very little required in the way of the cause in fact.

The personal injury by accident requirement has caused confusion and worked hardships in the following three major areas: occupational diseases; mental illness; and diseases, illnesses or injuries that have developed over a gradual period of time. Additionally controversies sometimes exist as to whether injuries to artificial limbs are excluded from coverage by the "personal injury" or "accidental injury" requirement. See Self v. Riverside Companies, Inc. (1980). A growing number of jurisdictions treat artificial limb injuries by special statutory provisions.

Initially occupational diseases were excluded from workers' compensation coverage because it was generally thought that this was an area for private health insurance. There was thus no provision for disease coverage in early compensation legislation, and the courts refused to find coverage because no "personal injury by accident" had occurred; after all, all diseases were considered to be personal or neutral risks commonly shared by everyone. In more modern times the necessity for occupational disease coverage has been candidly recognized either by broad judicial interpretations of the formula wording, or by special occupational disease provisions in the compensation acts.

Another difficulty with the "personal injury by accident" requirement is that presented by mental illnesses. Certainly today, on the basis of medical science, mental illness is recognized as a legitimate form of injury that may be causally connected to a risk of one's employment. The basic employment-related, mental illness fact patterns that commonly arise are: (1) physical trauma producing a nervous disorder; (2) nervous shock producing a physical disorder; (3) nervous shock producing a nervous condition or neurosis; (4) mental distress produced by prolonged work-related stress and anxiety; and (5) compensation neurosis; i.e., an unconscious desire to prolong compensation or a fear that compensation will not be paid. Little difficulty is presented for coverage by the foregoing first two fact patterns; however, coverage issues exist in the latter three. There is authority for compensation recovery in all five areas, and given the current state of medical science, there should be coverage for all the patterns when a mental illness is proven and the requisite employment connection is established. Given the pace and complexity of the modern industrial state with its rapid technological changes, mental disorders may well be within the scope of the risk of one's employment. See generally, Wade v. Anchorage School Dist. (1987).

Originally the formula coverage requirement of an "accident" was generally said to necessitate an "unusual," or "unforeseen," or "unexpected," or "external" event as the cause of an injury. In addition to an "unexpected event," it was also generally said that an injury had to have been sustained on a definite occasion or at a certain time. This approach created insoluble coverage problems because of the apparent necessity of distinguishing between "unexpected" or "unusual" and "expected" or "usual" risks; e.g., was the strain, exertion or hernia caused by an unusual or usual work related event. Furthermore, the definite occasion requirement in "accident" cases resulted in the exclusion of occupational diseases which had gradually developed over a long period of time.

2. THE SOLUTION

The enormous coverage problems caused by the "accident" interpretations in many jurisdictions prompted the National Commission on State Workmen's Compensation Laws to recommend the elimination of this coverage requirement. It should be pointed out that the confusion created by the language "personal injury by accident" can be avoided simply by focusing upon scope of the risk, work connection, and factual cause.

E. OCCUPATIONAL DISEASE

1. COVERAGE SCHEMES

General compensation coverage for occupational diseases is currently provided in all jurisdictions, but the coverage methods vary considerably. The exclusive remedy provisions in the various acts, in recent years, have provided an increasingly important area of employer immunity. See Buford v. American Tel. & Tel. Co. (1989). At least five schemes of occupational disease coverage are identifiable: (1) use of a general definition of occupational disease in the workers' compensation act; (2) use of an expanded definition of "injury" or "personal injury" to include occupational disease; (3) use of a scheduled list of occupational diseases coupled with a general disease catch-all definition;

(4) use of an unrestricted disease coverage provision; and (5) use of a separate occupational disease act. In addition to the foregoing general occupational disease coverage schemes, it is not uncommon to find specific legislative provisions dealing with loss of hearing, hernias, radiation, and various diseases of the lungs. Finally, the area of coal miner pneumoconiosis or "black lung" has virtually been preempted by federal legislation and programs; see supra Chapter 1, E., 5. and infra Chapter 15.

2. COVERAGE PROBLEMS

a. *Occupational Disease versus Accident*

As mentioned previously, early workers' compensation acts contained no provision for occupational disease coverage, and most courts interpreted the formula "personal injury by accident" to exclude all diseases from workers' compensation coverage. As might be expected, the grey area between the definition of personal injury and disease became a conceptually difficult one. With the passage of special occupational disease legislation, however, the distinctions between disease and injury by accident definitions became less important. It should be kept in mind that an occupational disease can in fact occur through accidental means; for example, one can contract many diseases as a result of an accidental cut or skin breakage that is work related. See Wilson Foods Corp. v. Porter (1980).

b. *Occupational Disease versus Common Diseases*

The major problem area today in occupational disease cases is to be found in the identification of those ordinary diseases of life that are said to be common to the public and not distinctively associated with a particular employment. Most jurisdictions attempt to give a detailed definition of the term "occupational disease," and despite the wording chosen, the ultimate issue of coverage is usually decided by the particular jurisdiction's approach to the scope of the employment risk of the disease in question. This is probably the case even though many jurisdictions fail to realize that their decisions are being made on this basis. For example, coverage problems of this nature could easily arise for a delivery man who is regularly exposed to rain, sleet and snow in the winter months, and who claims that his pneumonia is sufficiently work-related to be compensable. Pneumonia may be an ordinary disease of life, common to the public, and certainly not peculiar to his employment; however, deliveries made in winter weather may increase the risk of pneumonia, or make it an actual risk of employment, or place the delivery man in a position to contract the disease.

c. *Occupational Disease and Medical Causation*

In the foregoing example of the delivery man who contracted pneumonia in the winter months, difficulties also arise with regard to medical causation. A medical expert might testify that the employee's exposure because of his working conditions was a minor causative factor in the contraction of the pneumonia, or the expert might testify that the employee was subjected to both employment and non-employment related exposure, either of which could have caused the disease. The key inquiry should be whether the employment exposure caused or substantially contributed to the pneumonia. If the employment relation, as the cause in fact of the disease, is unclear, vague, or uncertain in the medical sense, then there is a likelihood that no coverage will be found. See Florida State Hospital v. Potter (1980).

The medical cause in fact inquiry poses real difficulties because of the frequent merger of the scope of the risk issue with the medical-factual causation question, and the surrounding confusion that this produces. The entire area of occupational disease is confusing and troublesome, and as recognized by the 1972 Report of The National Commission on State Workmen's Compensation Laws, "the determination of the etiology or 'cause' of a disease in a medical sense is often difficult or even impossible."

3. SPECIAL COVERAGE RESTRICTIONS

It has been fairly common for various states to place unique restrictions on recovery for certain occupational diseases. Those diseases which receive restrictive treatment are generally diseases of the lungs, such as silicosis, asbestosis, black lung, etc. Typical restrictions are those that preclude recovery unless death or disability has occurred within a certain number of years from the date of last injurious exposure or from the date of the last employment in a particular area. Another example of restriction is to be found in the denial of benefits to one who has suffered less than total disability as a result of a particular occupational disease. Sometimes one finds that employees are precluded from compensation unless they can demonstrate their exposure to the hazards of a particular disease for a specified period of time. The policies and practices of each jurisdiction should be examined. In some instances there are even special provisions granting greater compensation than normal for certain lung diseases.

CHAPTER 6

DEATH

A. DEATH BENEFITS GENERALLY

Death benefits are provided by workers' compensation legislation to certain classes of beneficiaries. These benefits include burial expenses, with a statutory limit placed on the expenses, and compensation for the beneficiaries that is calculated on the basis of the appropriate statutory formula of the particular jurisdiction. The right to death benefits is a right created by statute, and it is not dependent upon any rights of the deceased worker. Therefore, a worker's release, compromise, or settlement, or unfavorable compensation decision, would be no bar to the claims of beneficiaries. A beneficiary's claim is legally separate and distinct from the worker's claim for compensation during his lifetime, and the worker generally has no right to control or dispose of the claims of the beneficiaries.

B. DEPENDENCY AND PARTIAL DEPENDENCY

As a general proposition only those beneficiaries who are viewed by the compensation act as "dependents" are entitled to death benefits. The acts vary, but generally compensation statutes require

87

a showing of either actual dependency (complete or partial), and/or membership in a designated class or group before there can be recovery. In many instances those bearing certain relationships to the deceased, e.g., wife or child, enjoy a presumption of dependency and need not demonstrate actual dependency.

It is always important at the outset to determine who can be classified as complete or total dependents as opposed to partial dependents, because the former group is given preference and may recover compensation to the exclusion of the latter group. Anyone claiming death benefits other than one who enjoys a statutory presumption of dependency, must prove actual dependency, and membership in the statutory class entitled to compensation. The statutory classes are defined differently from jurisdiction to jurisdiction. Some acts provide fixed lists of persons, e.g., widow or widower, child, parent, brother, etc. Other acts use classes defined by the terms "next of kin," or "member of the employee's family," or "member of the employee's household." While the term "next of kin" may sometimes mean blood relatives only, a liberal approach should be taken toward the classifications, and for example, an unadopted dependent child living in the deceased's household should be included as a beneficiary. See generally Ryan-Walsh Stevedoring Co., Inc. v. Trainer (1979).

In those cases in which one does not receive the benefit of a presumption of total dependency, either total or partial dependency actually must be proven. Generally, total dependency may be proven despite the fact that a dependent had some other minor sources of support; however, one would not be totally dependent if a substantial source of support was received from other than the deceased. Partial dependency is a question of fact, and can be found to exist even if one's own sources provide substantial support. A majority of jurisdictions take a liberal approach toward the definition of "dependent"; see Tabor v. Industrial Accident Fund (1952).

C. WIDOW

In a majority of jurisdictions a widow is conclusively presumed to be totally dependent upon the deceased for workers' compensation purposes. Widowers should receive equal treatment. See Wengler v. Druggists Mutual Insurance Co. (1980). When no legal presumption exists, proof of dependency would be required. A claimant's marital status at the time of the death of the employee is often a key factor because some jurisdictions fix compensation rights as of the time of death. Other jurisdictions, sometimes with inequitable results, fix relationships and dependency as of the time of the accident or injury producing death. For example, widows have been denied death benefits when they married an employee after the date of an injury that ultimately produced death. Tipton v. Industrial Commission (1965).

1. LIVING WITH OR APART

In most jurisdictions a surviving spouse enjoys a presumption of dependency only if living with the deceased employee at the time of injury or death. "Living with" does not necessarily mean residing together; for example, economic necessity or considerations of health might dictate a separation. Additionally, a separation may be the result of desertion or other wrongful conduct on the part of the deceased employee's spouse which does not affect the legal obligation to provide support. If a separation has occurred that relieves the deceased employee's spouse of the legal obligation to provide support, the "living with" requirement would not be met, and there would be no presumption of dependency.

2. COMMON–LAW MARRIAGE

The domestic relations laws of a particular jurisdiction control whether a surviving common-law spouse may recover death benefits. For example, a common-law wife may be viewed as a "widow" or "wife" for workers' compensation purposes. See National Union Fire Insurance Co. v. Britton (1960). Even in jurisdictions in which the relationship is considered illicit, one may be entitled to compensation benefits as an actual dependent member of the deceased's "household." Furthermore, in some jurisdictions an illicit relationship is no bar to recovery if it was entered into in a "good faith" belief in legality by the surviving spouse. See Dawson v. Hatfield Wire & Cable Co. (1971). Bigamous marriage situations are often resolved on the basis of the "last marriage rule," which presumes that the last marriage was the legal one for compensation purposes. See Gibson v. Hughes (1961).

D. CHILDREN

Death benefits are generally provided for the "child" or "children" of a deceased employee on the basis of specific statutory language that includes them within the group conclusively presumed to be dependent. Illegitimate children, stepchildren, posthumous children, and other children who were not the subject of a legal obligation for support on the part of the deceased employee, have posed coverage problems. Coverage has sometimes been afforded under the dependent classifications of "member of the family" or "member of the household," and under specific statutory provisions addressing acknowledged illegitimate children. Today the difficulties previously posed by illegitimate children have been largely eliminated by the Supreme Court decision of Weber v. Aetna Casualty & Surety Co. (1972), in which the Louisiana Workers' Compensation Act was declared unconstitutional in so far as unacknowledged illegitimate children were denied coverage. This was held to be violative of the Equal Protection Clause of the Fourteenth Amendment. Proof problems with regard to paternity still remain.

E. FAMILY AND HOUSEHOLD MEMBERS

While the exact statutory language may vary, many workers' compensation acts permit the recovery of death benefits to one who can qualify as a "member of the family" or "member of the household." On the basis of the creation of these classifications it may be possible for stepchildren, stepgrandchildren, stepmothers, illegitimate children, nephews, mothers-in-law, and even unrelated children, etc., who can establish some dependency upon the deceased to receive death benefits. The liberal approach taken toward these groupings is supported by the humane objectives of workers' compensation.

F. PRIORITIES

Death benefit priorities are statutorily established in workers' compensation acts. Family relationships and/or dependency dictate priorities and benefits. For example, it is sometimes provided that a surviving spouse and minor children are to receive an entire award to the exclusion of others claiming dependency. Ordinarily that class which consists of total dependents are entitled to receive death benefits even if this means no recovery for partial dependents. When more than one wholly dependent claimant exists, there may be an equal division of benefits or statutorily fixed proportions may be allocated. It is possible, however, on the basis of some acts, for both total and partial dependents to receive compensation, but this should only occur after full compensation has been had by total dependents. As a caveat, it should be noted that compensation accrued and due a deceased employee must be paid either to the deceased's estate for distribution, or to the dependents under a compensation act, depending upon the jurisdiction.

CHAPTER 7

MEDICAL EXPENSES, DISABILITIES AND BENEFITS

A. INTRODUCTION TO RECOVERIES

The three broad categories of recovery under workers' compensation are: (1) medical and related expenses; (2) disability benefits; and (3) death benefits. Under the first group, medical expenses, rehabilitation costs, nursing costs, drugs, etc., are recoverable. Disability benefits are designed to provide compensation for the loss of earnings or earning power, and they are usually determined on the basis of either medical loss or wage loss theories, or some combination thereof; these benefits are determined by statutory formulas that may result in weekly, monthly, or sometimes lump sum payments. Death benefits are paid to the dependents of a deceased worker and such benefits are based on a statutory formula; additional amounts are specified for funeral or burial expenses. For reference and comparison purposes, the U. S. Chamber of Commerce compiles, on an annual basis, comprehensive charts of the state, federal and Canadian compensation requirements and benefits. U. S. Chamber of Commerce, Analysis of Workers' Compensation Laws.

B. MEDICAL EXPENSES AND REHABILITATION

At one time workers' compensation acts placed limitations on the amounts recoverable for medical expenses. Today most jurisdictions permit the recovery of unlimited medical expenses so long as a worker's condition necessitates continued treatment and care. A liberal approach is taken toward medical expenses, and commonly the costs of doctors, nurses, specialists, hospitalization, medical equipment, prosthetic devices, psychiatric treatment, drugs, medicines, etc. are included. It should be noted that in those cases in which an injured worker's spouse provides home nursing services, there can be recovery for the value of such services under the heading of medical expenses. See Kushay v. Sexton Dairy Co. (1975).

There is a lack of uniformity among workers' compensation statutes with regard to the recovery of physical and vocational rehabilitation costs. Ordinarily, those costs reasonably necessary for medical rehabilitation are recoverable, however, very few statutes provide complete coverage for the costs of vocational rehabilitation and related expenses necessary for a worker's return to full employment.

It should be remembered that in those cases in which medical complications, bad results, and even greater disabilities from medical malpractice occur, these events can be viewed as a part of the employee's original "injury", and all increased medical costs and benefits should be recoverable. See, e.g., Mallette v. Mercury Outboard Supply Co., Inc. (1959).

It should also be noted that the avoidable consequences rule has been applied to workers' compensation cases by statutes or case law. Employees who unreasonably refuse to submit to medical aid and treatment may jeopardize their rights to benefits. See Commonwealth, Department of Highways v. Lindon (1964).

C. SELECTION OF PHYSICIAN

The right to choose freely one's physician has been the subject of a great deal of controversy under workers' compensation laws. Some acts permit an employee to select a physician and others require that a selection be made from a panel of physicians chosen by the employer. Other acts require that treating physicians be approved by the medical profession for workers' compensation practice.

The physician selection controversy revolves around the need for physician-patient confidentiality and confidence on the one hand, versus the need to control medical costs and to provide effective medical treatment on the other hand. No matter what the physician selection rule of the particular jurisdiction may be, an injured employee cannot generally seek medical assistance without the employer's prior knowledge and consent, except for emergency situations. Of course, if after notice, an employer fails to provide the necessary medical care, an employee is free to procure medical assistance and submit claim for reimbursement. It should be noted that osteopaths and chiropractors may be selected. See Wetzel v. Goodwin Brothers, GMC Truck (1981).

D. MEDICAL LOSS AND WAGE LOSS

The key to understanding compensable disabilities is to be found in medical loss and wage loss theories; both theoretically compensate an injured worker for loss of earnings or earning power, but they achieve this result by different methods. The medical loss theory focuses upon the physical injury or impairment suffered by a worker. Compensation may be based on "pure" medical losses; for example, workers' compensation acts usually contain "schedules" which provide a predetermined amount of compensation for specific enumerated medical losses; i.e., a schedule might provide a specified amount of compensation for the loss of a hand, regardless of the economic impact of such a loss. In other words, certain enumerated medical losses, are clearly recognized as disabilities and a loss of earnings or earning power is conclusively presumed on the basis of the inclusion of the loss in a medical loss schedule.

The wage loss theory attempts to provide compensation for an injured employee on the basis of the employee's actual earnings that have been lost due to an injury. For example, a "pure" wage loss approach might award compensation to an injured employee on the basis of actual lost wages incurred during the period of incapacity. In many jurisdictions wage loss determinations are made by comparing actual earnings prior to the date of injury with one's "earning capacity" after the injury. This "diminished earning capacity" concept permits an injured worker to recover compensation even if there has been no actual loss of earnings. See, e.g., Karr v. Armstrong Tire & Rubber Co. (1953).

No compensation system today employs pure medical loss or pure wage loss theory, rather, one finds that compensation acts utilize both in varying degrees. For example, a compensation act that contains an injury schedule may also provide compensation for an unscheduled injury that has resulted in a medical impairment. The severity of the impairment and the degree of one's disability (i.e., temporary total, permanent total, temporary partial, and permanent partial) commonly are used to determine the duration and amount of the employee's economic losses.

A tremendous amount of controversy exists with regard to the proper use of medical and wage loss theories in the determination of the appropriate amount of compensation for injured workers. See A. Larson, "The Wage-Loss Principle in Workers' Compensation," 6 Wm. Mitchell L.Rev. 501 (1980). While it is desirable for compensation awards to bear a reasonable relation to one's past wages, and to be based upon a reduction in one's earning capacity, rather than on the basis of arbitrary amounts dictated by the type of medical injury sustained, it must be stressed that no wage loss or medical loss approach actually attempts to provide compensation on the basis of the injury's *true* economic impact on the particular worker or on the worker's earning power or earning capacity. All legislation in this area represents compromises which have resulted in a no-fault system of reduced but fairly certain compensation for work-related injuries.

E. THE AVERAGE WAGE AND FORMULAS

The cornerstone of compensation calculations is an employee's average wage, commonly specified as an "average weekly wage" or as some other average wage based upon a unit of time such as months or days. The average weekly wage, average monthly wage or the like represents an average earnings figure, which, when multiplied times a jurisdiction's fixed statutory percentage (ranging from 50 to 66⅔%), produces the employee's basic weekly or monthly benefit. Statutory formulas vary from jurisdiction to jurisdiction, but commonly, compensation benefits are determined on the basis of weeks or months of eligibility. In addition, it is commonly provided that maximums and minimums are to be placed on the amount of the weekly or monthly benefits; further, limitations may be placed upon the number of weeks or months of eligibility.

Frequently, issues arise with regard to the composition of the average weekly wage, and whether, for example, tips, fringe benefits, bonuses, meals, transportation, etc., should be considered. Every effort should be made to make the employee's average weekly wage computation as complete as possible. See Jess Parish Memorial Hospital v. Ansell (1980); but see Morrison-Knudsen Construction Co. v. Director, OWCP (1983).

Difficulties may also arise because of an employee's temporary, irregular, or erratic work history. The average wage may sometimes be calculated with reference to the wages of a comparably situated employee. Most statutes permit calculations of average wages in a discretionary manner, if a just and fair result for the employee cannot be obtained by the use of the normal statutory formulas.

F. DISABILITIES

1. DISABILITIES GENERALLY

Workers' compensation statutes ordinarily provide four classifications of disability. These classifications are determined by the severity or extent of the disability with the disability characterized as either partial or total. Additionally, disabilities are affected by their duration and are characterized as either permanent or temporary. The four common disability classifications are: temporary partial, temporary total, permanent partial, and permanent total. These disability classifications in conjunction with the employee's average wages, and appropriate statutory formulas provide the basis for disability benefit computation.

2. TEMPORARY PARTIAL

A temporary partial disability is present when an employee, who has been injured on the job, is no longer able to perform that job, but for the period of disability is able to engage in some kind of gainful employment. Temporary partial disability compensation is designed to pay an injured worker for lost wages, and thus wage loss theory is generally employed in making awards. Additionally, this classification promotes the prompt return of an injured employee to the workforce. Examples of injuries that commonly produce temporary partial disabilities are sprains, minor fractures, contusions and lacerations.

The critical factor in determining the temporary partial classification may be the impairment of the employee's earning capacity. For example, an employee who has received a minor injury that has resulted in no loss of time at work and who has suffered no actual wage losses, may still be entitled to temporary partial compensation if some impairment to earning capacity can be proven.

3. TEMPORARY TOTAL

The condition of temporary total disability exists when an employee is unable to work at all for a temporary but undetermined amount of time. One may be totally disabled even though not completely helpless or wholly disabled. Examples of injuries that can result in temporary total disability are serious illnesses, heat exhaustion and disabling back injuries. Temporary total disability is designed to provide compensation to an injured worker for the economic losses incurred during a recuperative period.

4. PERMANENT PARTIAL

A permanent partial disability may be found when a permanent and irreparable injury has occurred to an employee, i.e., one that probably will continue for an indefinite period with no present indication of recovery. For example, one who loses a foot on the job will experience a period of temporary total disability during hospitalization and recuperation. At the point in time when maximum medical improvement has been attained, the disability should be classified as permanent partial; a foot has been lost, but the employee is able to perform some gainful work. The purpose of permanent partial disability is to provide compensation for the employee's reduced earning capacity, even though this is often accomplished through the use of a medical loss schedule. It should be noted that the majority view is to the effect that if a scheduled injury produces additional disability to other parts of the body, the employee will be able to recover an amount in excess of that provided in the schedule, for example, loss of a foot could produce traumatic neurosis. See Gonzales v. Gackle Drilling Co. (1962).

5. PERMANENT TOTAL

The condition of permanent total disability exists when an employment related injury renders an employee permanently and indefinitely unable to perform any gainful work. An employee need not be entirely helpless or completely incapacitated in a medical sense. The so-called "odd-lot" doctrine permits the finding of a permanent total disability for workers who are not completely incapacitated, but are handicapped to such an extent that they cannot become regularly employed in any well-known branch of the labor market; the worker is said to have been left in the position of an "odd lot" in the labor market. Cardiff Corp. v. Hall, [1911]. One may receive a permanent total disability on the basis of a scheduled loss; for example, loss of sight in both eyes can be a scheduled loss that requires compensation as a permanent total disability. It is difficult to generalize about permanent total disabilities, but the following factors are generally relevant to such determinations: age; experience; skills and training; education; nature and extent of injury; employment history and nature of employment at the time of injury.

6. DISFIGUREMENT

The great majority of jurisdictions address disfigurement by special provision. Compensation for disfigurement is generally provided in much the same way that compensation is provided for scheduled injuries. In the absence of special disfigurement provisions it may be difficult for a worker to establish an impairment to earning capacity because of disfigurement, scars or the like. These special provisions candidly recognize the need for compensation in disfigurement cases, and thus like medical loss schedules, conclusively presume a wage loss that dictates compensation. Occasionally, the issue may arise with regard to whether an employee may receive compensation both on the basis of a disability classification and disfigurement. It may be possible to obtain compensation on the basis of both. For example, compensation has been awarded for permanent partial disability resulting from burns with additional compensation awarded for disfigurement. Kerr-McGee Corp. v. Washington (1970).

G. MULTIPLE AND SUCCESSIVE INJURIES

Difficulties sometimes arise when multiple injuries are received by a worker from the same accident. Often this problem is addressed statutorily in the particular workers' compensation act. In the absence of a specific provision an approach should be taken that provides the injured employee with the greatest possible coverage and compensation for the most serious degree of disability that can be demonstrated. For example, a worker might receive concurrent injuries to two different fingers on the same hand. These injuries could result in the complete loss of use of both fingers, and the compensation paid could simply amount to twice the scheduled amount for the loss of a finger. This amount might be less than the compensation to which the worker would be entitled on the basis of a percentage disability to the hand as a whole. In other words, an employee should not be confined to an injury schedule when multiple injuries have been sustained and the disability is greater than the sum of the scheduled losses. The reverse should also be the case, and when the sum of the scheduled losses provides greater compensation than the percentage of disability, then the greater amount should be awarded. See Emerson Electric Co. v. Powers (1980); Holcombe v. Fireman's Fund Insurance Co. (1960).

Successive injuries may present problems because the cumulative effect of the injuries may produce a greater degree of disability and dictate greater compensation than the amount that would have been paid on the basis of separate scheduled injuries. For example, an employee who has lost one hand may lose the other hand in another work-related accident. The worker has thus suffered a much greater loss than the sum of single hand losses on a schedule. Three possible approaches are taken to the problem. First, the employer can be required to provide compensation for the entire resulting disability. Second, there may be apportionment statutes requiring the employer to provide compensation on the basis of the disability the employee would have experienced without taking into effect the previous disability. It should be noted that if a greater disability is suffered because of some pre-existing illness, disorder, weakness, or disease on the part of the employee, apportionment may not be permitted; as a general rule, an employer takes an employee as he finds him with regard to latent and pre-existing conditions that result in greater disabilities than otherwise would have been suffered. Third, "second injury funds" may exist (discussed infra) and therefore assure that an employee is fully compensated for an entire disability.

H.   SECOND INJURY FUNDS

Second injury funds (sometimes called "subsequent injury funds") offer the best solution to the problem of the worker who suffers a greater degree of disability, as the result of a work-related injury, because of some pre-existing disability or condition. The second injury fund is designed to encourage the employment and retention of handicapped workers. There is little incentive for their employment if the last employer faces entire liability for a disability in part due to pre-existing causes. The second injury fund provides an equitable solution to the problem of the handicapped employee by allowing the employer to pay only that amount he would have been required to pay in the absence of the pre-existing difficulty. An issue exists in second injury situations with regard to what will qualify as an "injury" or "disability" for purposes of the utilization of the second injury fund. Traditionally employers take their employees as they find them; however, it is questionable whether the last employer of an injured employee should bear the complete burden of an employee's disability that is in part the result of a previous work related injury or disability. It is also questionable whether the last employer should bear the complete burden of an employee's disability that is in part the result of a previous nonwork-related injury. See Lawson v. Suwanee Fruit & Steamship Co. (1949). It should be noted that second injury fund liability cannot be established when the sequence of injuries is reversed; subsequent nonwork-related accidents make no difference in compensation awards.

A liberal approach should be taken toward the utilization of second injury funds because handicapped workers are often the subject of job discrimination. Furthermore, workers' compensation legislation should strive to provide compensation for the entire extent of a disability suffered as a result of a work-related injury regardless of whether that disability has been contributed to by some purely personal condition or previous work-related injury.

I. DEATH AFTER DISABILITY

When death follows disability several issues may arise. In analyzing the problems in this area it should always be remembered that an employee's right to compensation benefits is separate and distinct from the right of an employee's dependents to death benefits. (See supra Chapter 6, A.) For that reason, death benefits should not be reduced by compensation paid to an injured worker prior to the worker's death unless there is a statutory provision to the contrary; for example, some jurisdictions statutorily reduce the dependency period by the period of disability compensation payments. An additional problem area is that of accrued compensation benefits that have not been paid prior to a worker's death. Generally these accrued amounts are paid to the employee's estate or to the employee's dependents, depending on the jurisdiction. Reference should be had to particular statutes that address this issue.

J. DEATH COMPENSATION BENEFITS

In the case of complete or total dependents, death compensation benefits are generally computed on the basis of statutorily fixed percentages of a workers' average wage, just as in the case of computing a worker's disability compensation benefits. The majority of compensation acts place maximum limits on death benefits. Statutes vary considerably with regard to the computation of death benefits for those classified as partial dependents. A popular method of computing benefits for partial dependents is to provide compensation on the basis of the amounts of the deceased worker's contributions. It must be stressed that the formulas and methods employed in computing death benefits for all dependents vary considerably, and generalizations are inappropriate regarding exact computations. Usually, the most important legal issues involved in this area are those mentioned in Chapter 6, supra.

CHAPTER 8

ADMINISTRATION

A. INTRODUCTION

A statutory scheme of no-fault compensation can be no better than its administration. Efficient and effective administration is especially necessary in the workers' compensation context, because a majority of claims are uncontested, and the prompt delivery of compensation benefits is of critical importance to a worker and the worker's family.

According to the 1972 Report of the National Commission on State Workmen's Compensation Laws there are six primary obligations of administration:

(1) to take initiatives in administering the act;

(2) to provide for continuing review and seek periodic revision of both the workmen's compensation statute and supporting regulations and procedures, based on research findings, changing needs, and the evidence of experience;

(3) to advise employees of their rights and obligations and to assure workers of their benefits under the law;

(4) to apprise employers, carriers, and others involved of their rights, obligations, and privileges;

110

(5) to assist voluntary resolutions of disputes, consistent with the law; and

(6) to adjudicate disputes which do not yield to voluntary negotiation.

The National Commission clearly pointed out that the adjudication of disputes should be the least burdensome of the six obligations when the other five obligations are properly executed.

B. COMMISSIONS VERSUS COURTS

Only a few jurisdictions permit the initial judicial adjudication of disputed compensation claims. The great majority of the states have administrative agencies that supervise, administer, and adjudicate workers' compensation matters, subject to subsequent judicial appellate review.

It is generally accepted that the judiciary is ill equipped to administer adequately and effectively compensation matters and accomplish the six primary obligations of administration identified by the National Commission on Workmen's Compensation, supra, Chapter 8, A. Furthermore, the adversary nature of judicial proceedings insures unhealthy conflict between employers and employees and is incompatible with the goals and objectives of workers' compensation. State systems of administration vary, however, the best approach appears to be the one recommended by the National Commission on State Workmen's Compensation Laws. Under its recommendation there would be an executive officer and staff who devote their time solely to administration, with a separate and independent board of compensation appeals. The appellate board would review the decisions of hearing officers in contested compensation cases. An informal procedures unit would handle all claims initially, and those claims that are incapable of voluntary resolution would be forwarded to a hearing officer for a formal determination. Only questions of law from the appellate board would receive judicial review.

C. NOTICES

Almost all workers' compensation acts contain provisions requiring that an employee promptly inform the employer of an injury. Some statutes may require that notice of injury be given within a specified period of time. The purpose of the notice requirement is to facilitate prompt medical treatment and care, and to minimize the extent of an employee's injury. Additionally, notice provides the employer with a timely opportunity to investigate the causes and conditions of injury.

A rigid approach should not be taken, and generally it is not taken toward notice requirements. The employee's failure to comply with the notice requirement should be excused if there is actual knowledge on the part of the employer or one whose knowledge can be imputed to the employer. Certainly, knowledge can be found on the basis of compensation or medical payments to an employee. Additionally, an employee's lack of compliance should be excused if it has not resulted in prejudice to the employer. Many reasonable excuses can exist for non-compliance with formal notice requirements.

D. STATUTES OF LIMITATION

There are generally two types of limitation statutes that govern the timely filing of workers' compensation claims for disability. In one type of statute, the limitation period runs from the date of injury, and in the other type of statute the period commences on the date of the employee's accident. In jurisdictions using date of injury, a liberal approach is usually taken, and the appropriate date may be the time when the injury became apparent or reasonably should have become apparent to the employee. In date of accident jurisdictions, an inflexible and literal approach is sometimes taken toward the time of the accident; this may result in the loss of a worker's claim, because of a personal failure to discover the injury or its work connection prior to the running of the statute. This type of statute of limitations has been the subject of a great deal of criticism. See 3 Larson § 78.42(c).

Generally in death cases, statutes of limitation begin to run at the date of an employee's death; however, some statutes of limitation commence at the time of the accident or injury producing death. A literal approach should not be taken to date of accident or injury statutes in recognition of the fact that dependents' rights do not arise until the date of an employee's death.

The possibility always exists for a finding of a waiver of the limitations period on the part of the employer. A recognition of liability, the payment of compensation or medical benefits, or the failure to raise the defense of the statute of limitations in a timely manner, can result in waiver.

E. WAITING PERIODS

Waiting periods may be found in workers' compensation statutes. These provisions authorize compensation only after the passage of a specific amount of time from the date of an employee's injury. Waiting periods are generally inapplicable to medical benefits and to death benefits. In an effort to discourage malingering and to promote a prompt return to the workforce, many waiting period provisions are directed specifically at temporary total disability claims.

By way of illustration, the Council of State Government's Model Act, Part III, Section 15, proposes a waiting period of three days, with retroactive payment if the total period of disability exceeds fourteen days. This follows the recommendation of the 1972 Report of the National Commission on State Workmen's Compensation Laws. As a general proposition, it should be noted that the longer the waiting or qualifying periods, then the less the costs of workers' compensation programs; however, this results in reduced benefits for workers.

F. HEARINGS, EVIDENCE AND REVIEW

In practically all jurisdictions, disputed workers' compensation cases are handled by an administrative process rather than by the courts. A less formal, more expeditious and more flexible approach is taken than in a normal judicial civil trial. It is always desirable for some part of the administrative machinery to be available for the resolution of contested claims through the use of an informal procedure; however, a formal administrative adjudicative process must be available for those contested claims which cannot otherwise be resolved informally.

The workers' compensation administrative process may vary somewhat from jurisdiction to jurisdiction, and despite occasional commentary to the contrary, the proceedings in contested cases are all marked by a degree of practical formality consistent with the adjudcation of substantive rights. One should exercise some caution when one encounters the often repeated phrase that compensation proceedings are to be informal with the ordinary rules of evidence relaxed.

In every jurisdiction, administrative compensation decisions can ultimately be the subject of judicial review. In most jurisdictions, judicial review is limited to questions of law, and administrative findings of fact will not generally be disturbed.

The common law rules of evidence generally do not apply to compensation proceedings, however, they can serve as a guide. Appellate review sometimes occurs because of the admission of hearsay evidence. Wide discretion is permitted in compensation hearings, and the admission of evidence that would be inadmissible in a court of law is allowed. While the admission of hearsay evidence may not constitute error, if an undue amount of weight has been given to such evidence in the administrative decision, then error may have been committed. A jurisdiction's approach to the treatment of hearsay is particularly important to claimants who are prone to present a great deal of hearsay evidence; indeed, in many cases, only hearsay evidence may be available on key issues. In reviewing compensation decisions, four different approaches have been taken toward the use of hearsay evidence. First, hearsay is admissible and may provide the basis for the decision. Second is the residuum and majority rule which permits administrative decisions to be based upon hearsay evidence, but some of the evidence supporting the decision must have been admissible. Third, the admission of the hearsay is not reversible error; however, if the decision would not have been rendered but for the hearsay evidence, the decision must be reversed. Finally, there is some authority declaring hearsay evidence inadmissible and its admission to be reversible error.

Generally the standard of review in appeals of administratively decided compensation cases is whether there is substantial evidence to support the decision. For variations on the above standard of review, see 3 Larson § 80.26(a)–(i).

G. COMPROMISE, SETTLEMENT, AND LUMP SUM COMMUTATION

The policy considerations in workers' compensation cases differ from those found in the adversary and uncertain environment of the tort system with regard to compromises, agreements, and settlements. As a result of these differences most jurisdictions by statute or by judicial decision deny the claimants the right to settle, adjust, or compromise a claim for less than the statutory amount regardless of whether the claim is disputed or undisputed. See Southern v. Department of Labor and Industries (1951). The minority view would permit compromises and settlements for less than the statutory amounts when disputed questions of liability exist; even so, approval of the compromise, agreement, or settlement would ordinarily be required by the appropriate workers' compensation authority.

It may be possible for a claimant to receive compensation benefits in a "lump sum" rather than by way of periodic payments, depending upon the jurisdiction. This method of payment is subject to criticism given the objectives of compensation benefits to replace lost wages and to provide economic benefits over a period of time. Lump summing generally takes the form of a reduction of periodic benefits to present value with the use of a percentage discount. There may be some situations in which the best interests of a claimant can dictate a lump sum approval, as for example, in the cases of a worker who needs the entire amount for legitimate educational, retraining, or rehabilitation costs. Tremendous potential for harm exists, however, when lump summing is indiscriminately permitted because of the likelihood that the entire award will be quickly and unwisely spent. See Malmedal v. Industrial Accident Board (1959). The use of lump sums and the difficulties that surround their use have been exacerbated by the desire of some claimants' attorneys to obtain their entire fees at once rather than over a period of time.

H. REOPENING, MODIFICATION, TERMINATION, AND REDISTRIBUTION

Statutes vary from jurisdiction to jurisdiction with regard to the details of reopening and modification of compensation awards; however, reopening and modification is usually permitted on the basis of a disabled worker's changed condition. Modification may take the form of increased or decreased benefits, or a cessation of benefits. Time limits for reopening can be found in a majority of jurisdictions. Fraud, mutual mistake of fact, and sometimes "any good cause" can provide grounds for reopening. A minority of jurisdictions permit reopening at any time for changed conditions.

In death benefit cases, the possibility exists for termination or redistribution of benefits based upon certain dependents' changes in status. For example, the remarriage of a widow may result in the termination of benefits; a redistribution could also occur as a result of the death of a minor dependent.

I. INSURANCE

There are three methods of insuring workers' compensation benefits. First of all there is the private insurance system, which provides a majority of the benefits paid in the United States, and which may be utilized in the vast majority of states. Secondly, there is self-insurance, which is also available in a vast majority of states, but which provides a small overall percentage of the benefits paid in the United States. Third, there are state insurance fund systems, which provide almost a fourth of the benefits paid in the United States; six states mandate participation in the state fund, while twelve states permit private insurance competition with their state insurance funds. It is difficult to determine whether any one insurance method is superior to another, and as long as proper controls exist for the adequate protection of compensation claimants, any of the methods accomplish their purposes. Perhaps, lower insurance costs can be achieved through the use of state insurance funds.

It must be stressed that the object of insurance in workers' compensation systems is to provide security for the payment of benefits. If for some reason the insurance carrier or employer is unable to provide insurance or to guarantee benefits, then machinery and resources should be in existence to provide workers and their dependents the benefits to which they are entitled. For example, Michigan has a self-insurer's security fund. See McQueen v. Great Markwestern Packing Co. (1974). Most states do not have direct security systems, but rely upon indirect or administrative supervision of insurance carriers and self-insurers. The Council of State Government's Model Workmen's Compensation and Rehabilitation Law contains special fund provisions which would provide payments in the case of insolvent employers or insurers. See Part IV, Insurance; Section 55, Special Fund.

Workers' Compensation insurance is designed for the benefit and protection of both the employee and the employer. In an effort to maximize the security of the employee and dependent claimants, the defenses which could be used by an insurer against an employer should not be available against claimants. For example, the employer's failure to pay a premium should not provide an effective bar to an otherwise eligible compensation claimant. See Home Life & Accident Co. v. Orchard (1921).

J. REMOVAL

Under 28 U.S.C.A. § 1445, actions brought under the FELA and Jones Act in state court generally cannot be removed to federal court. The same code section also prohibits removal of actions under workers' compensation laws of the state in which the federal district court is sitting. This would include suits for retaliatory discharge for filing a worker's compensation claim. See Wallace v. Ryan–Walsh Stevedoring Co. (1989). The federal statute reflects a Congressional policy of allowing states local control over their workers' compensation systems without federal court interference in the local administrative process. It should be noted that 28 U.S.C.A. § 1332(c), the direct action provision, does not apply to actions initiated in federal court by a workers' compensation insurer; actions against such an insurer initiated in federal court are not allowed. Northbrook National Insurance Co. v. Brewer (1989).

CHAPTER 9

EXTRATERRITORIAL PROBLEMS AND OVERLAPPING COVERAGES

A. CONFLICT OF LAWS

Conflict of laws and full faith and credit problems often arise in workers' compensation cases because of the inevitable multi-state contacts which are encountered by today's employees. For example, an employee may reside in Texas, sign a contract of employment in Oklahoma, work for a company whose home office is in Arkansas, on a job based in Wyoming, and receive a compensable injury while on company business in Louisiana. Conflicts questions ordinarily are concerned with which state's workers' compensation statute is applicable. As a general rule, the rights provided by the workers' compensation act of one state cannot be enforced in other states. See 4 Larson § 84.20.

The following fact patterns usually give rise to most conflicts problems: (1) the accident is local and the employment contract is foreign; (2) the employment contract is local and the accident is foreign; (3) both the accident and the employment contract are foreign; and (4) the accident is foreign to the state of the employer's principal place of business or legal residence. Most states have specific statutory provisions which address conflict of laws issues. Normally, if a compensable injury has taken place within a state, that fact alone may provide a basis for the utilization of local law.

State statutes addressing out of state injuries commonly provide for the application of the law of the forum on the basis of the contract of employment being entered into within the forum state, or on the basis of employment connections, relations, or contacts with the forum state. Where both the employment contract and state of injury are foreign, a proceeding under the law of an unrelated forum is generally inappropriate. Finally, the domicile or residence of the claimant, and/or the location of the employer's home office or legal residence, can affect the application of a particular state's workers' compensation act. In order to avoid the conflicts difficulties in workers' compensation cases, the Report of the National Commission on State Workmen's Compensation Laws recommended that a worker or dependents have the choice of claiming compensation in the state where the injury or death occurred, or where the employment was principally localized, or where the employee was hired. This recommendation would probably eliminate the problem of the employee who could be without compensation coverage in any state, because of multi-state contacts. The Restatement (Second) of Conflicts § 181 takes a liberal and expansive approach toward the circumstances that may bring the workers' compensation law of the forum into play. It is suggested that resort should be had to this restatement section when statutes of a forum state fail to address a workers' compensation conflict problem. This restatement section is compatible with the objectives and policies of workers' compensation legislation.

B. FULL FAITH AND CREDIT

The full faith and credit clause has posed two major problems for workers' compensation: (1) the extent to which the workers' compensation laws of one state should be recognized and given weight in the decisions of another state; and (2) to what extent should successive compensation awards be permitted from state to state for the same injury or death.

The primary difficulties created in the first situation were the result of Bradford Electric Light Co. v. Clapper (1932), in which the Supreme Court held that New Hampshire was forced to recognize the Vermont workers' compensation statute under the full faith and credit clause. A subsequent series of Supreme Court decisions have virtually abolished the *Clapper* doctrine, and the full faith and credit clause's requirement of the recognition of foreign law, now presents few problems when the forum state wishes to apply its own workers' compensation act. See Carroll v. Lanza (1955); Kelly v. Guyon General Piping, Inc. (1989) (Virginia would apply North Carolina exclusive remedy provision to bar tort claim arising out of accident in South Carolina).

The full faith and credit clause has been the source of a great deal of controversy because of the difficulties posed when more than one state awards compensation to a claimant for the same injury or death. The Supreme Court resolved a major area of controversy in Thomas v. Washington Gas Light Co. (1980). This case held that one jurisdiction has no legitimate interest in preventing another jurisdiction from awarding supplemental compensation, when that second jurisdiction had the power in the first instance to apply its compensation law and to make an award. The full faith and credit clause is not to be construed in such a way as to bar another state's successive award of workers' compensation, so long as credit is given for the prior state's award. In other words, a worker is entitled to receive the largest single amount of compensation to which one would be entitled under the applicable compensation acts.

C. THE PROBLEM OF OVERLAPPING COVERAGE

The coverage boundaries between state workers' compensation acts and certain federal remedies and programs are unclear. These vague boundaries create difficulties for claimants because of the possibility of federal preemption, and an improper election of remedies which could result in a denial of compensation or in a lesser award than that to which a claimant could be entitled. The federal remedies that pose potential problems in this area are: the Longshoremen's and Harbor Workers' Compensation Act (LHWCA); personal injury and death actions by seamen or their survivors based upon Jones Act negligence, general maritime law unseaworthiness, and maintenance and cure; and personal injury and death actions based upon the Federal Employers' Liability Act.

In LHWCA situations the "twilight zone" doctrine has been recognized by the Supreme Court. Davis v. Department of Labor & Industries (1942). This doctrine eliminates the risk of an initial mistake on the part of a claimant, by allowing a presumption of coverage under the first act providing a basis for the claim. Additionally, the Supreme Court has indicated that concurrent jurisdiction may exist in borderline cases, particularly in regard to injuries or deaths occurring on land. Sun Ship, Inc. v. Pennsylvania (1980). The possibility of successive and supplementary awards exists in the LHWCA area by analogy to the policies contained in Thomas v. Washington Gas Light Co., supra, even though the constitutional bases would be different. Certainly, no double recovery should be permitted. It should be noted that the LHWCA generally provides more generous benefits than the various state compensation acts.

The coverage problems of seamen involving either the LHWCA or state workers' compensation acts usually depend upon a factual determination of one's status as a seaman. The LHWCA specifically excludes from coverage a master or member of the crew of a vessel. Borderline cases involving state compensation acts may also receive "twilight zone" doctrine treatment. See Maryland Casualty Co. v. Toups (1949). But see Anderson v. Alaska Packers Association (1981). Successive awards are sometimes allowed on the basis of concurrent jurisdiction theories when federal seamen's remedies are pursued after an acceptance of state workers' compensation benefits. See Manuel Caceres v. San Juan Barge Co. (1975).

The Federal Employers' Liability Act (FELA) provides a negligence remedy for all interstate railway workers whose jobs affect interstate commerce, including employees engaged in auxiliary activities related to interstate railroads. Motor carrier, airline, and other interstate transportation workers are not covered by the FELA. If an employee is covered by the FELA, then it is said to be the exclusive remedy because of federal preemption in the field of interstate commerce, and thus state compensation acts have no application. The LHWCA provides the exclusive remedy for covered workers and bars actions under the FELA. See Chesapeake & Ohio Railway Co. v. Schwalb (1989).

As a final note on overlapping coverages, it should be remembered that the payment of workers' compensation benefits may have a direct impact upon one's social security benefits, because the Social Security Act provides for the reduction of benefits to the extent that they are duplicated by state or federal workers' compensation payments. See 42 U.S.C.A. § 424a. The FELA is not considered a workers' compensation law or plan for these purposes. In addition, approximately one-half of the states treat workers' compensation payments as disqualifying income for unemployment compensation purposes. There is a lack of uniformity on this issue. See Page v. General Electric Co. (1978).

CHAPTER 10

THIRD PARTY ACTIONS

A. EXCLUSIVE NATURE OF COMPENSATION ACT

Workers' compensation legislation provides employees and their dependents with their exclusive remedy against the employer and insurance carrier for all injuries and deaths which arise out of and in the course of employment. The exclusivity provisions of workers' compensation acts have generally withstood constitutional attacks for the most part in recent times, and their continued vitality remains the keystone of compensation legislation. Constitutional questions concerning exclusivity may, however, be of importance in certain areas. See Chapter 3, B., supra. See also Fleischman v. Flowers (1971). Generally, the immunities provided to the employer and others are difficult to avoid. Kimball v. Millet (1988).

The exclusive nature of the workers' compensation remedy can sometimes result in a denial of compensation in cases in which damage has clearly occurred. For example, injuries to sexual organs, the senses, the psyche and sometimes disfigurement, and non-disabling pain and suffering may go uncompensated, if the injuries producing these results fall within the workers' compensation formula, because most workers' compensation acts fail to provide compensation for these results.

It should always be remembered that an employer may be sued in tort despite the exclusivity provision, on the basis of intentional tort theories and in situations giving rise to nonphysical torts. Lopez v. S.B. Thomas, Inc. (1987) (emotional distress under 42 U.S.C.A. § 1981). See Chapter 3, B., supra.

B. WHO ARE THIRD PARTIES

The exclusivity provision of workers' compensation legislation applies only to employers and others who may be so treated, such as insurance carriers and co-employees. Generally the rights of employees and survivors to pursue common law and statutory remedies against a "third party" whose conduct has caused or contributed to an injury or death, remain intact. Frequently issues arise with regard to who are "third parties" subject to separate actions for damages. One of the most troublesome groups, is that of co-employees. A majority of jurisdictions, either on the basis of statute or judicial decision, have extended the employer's immunity to co-employees. A minority of jurisdictions view co-employees as "third persons" outside of the immunity enjoyed by the employer.

It is difficult to generalize about who are third parties, however, third parties have from time to time been found among the following: physicians, product manufacturers, co-employees (including possibly corporate officers, directors, or stockholders), supervisory employees, compensation carriers and their safety inspectors, unions and their safety inspectors, governmental entities, owners and occupiers of land, etc. See chapter 3, supra.

C. THIRD PARTY ACTIONS AGAINST THE EMPLOYER

Questions of contribution and indemnity may arise when third parties attempt to recover over against the employers of injured or killed employees. Most jurisdictions deny a third party the right to contribution from an employer whose negligence has played a part in an employee's harm, because of the general common law rule that there can only be contribution from one who is liable to the plaintiff. The exclusivity provision of workers' compensation legislation relieves the employer of tort liability for injuries or deaths falling within the coverage formula; thus, generally employers cannot be the subjects of contribution actions. Third party indemnity actions present a problem for all workers' compensation jurisdictions. Prof. Larson describes this issue as an evenly-balanced controversy in workers' compensation law. Larson, "Third Party Action Over Against Workers' Compensation Employer," 1982 Duke L.J. 483, 484. Despite the exclusivity provisions in workers' compensation acts, and despite the necessity of inquiries directed at fault in non-contractual indemnity situations, the possibility of employer liability certainly exists under substantive indemnity law. See Lockheed Aircraft Corp. v. United States (1983). Additionally, in appropriate cases, indemnity may be obtained from an employer on the basis of an express or implied agreement, or on the basis of a separate and independent duty owed by the employer to the third person. See Carneiro v. Alfred B. King Co. (1975).

D. DEFENSES OF THIRD PARTIES

Normally third parties who are defendants in actions brought by employees, employers, or insurance carriers, may employ any defenses which could be utilized against the employee. Thus, regardless of whether or not the action is one for damages on the part of the employee, or a subrogation action brought by an employer or insurer, the employee's negligence or the statute of limitations may be used as defenses. Since the action, even in subrogation cases, is that of the employee, the contributory fault of an employer, may not generally be raised as a defense. Mermigis v. Servicemaster Industries, Inc. (1989) (jury not allowed to consider employer negligence in order to reduce award). See Baker v. Traders & General Insurance Co. (1952).

E. SUBROGATION

It is difficult to generalize about subrogation rights and procedures, but almost all jurisdictions have subrogation statutes that affect workers' compensation cases. The common-law background of subrogation arose out of duties that are no longer popular. See Seavey, "Liability to Master for Negligent Harm to Servant," 1956 Wash. U.L.Q. 309. There appears to be a common-law basis for subrogation in some compensation cases. See Federal Marine Terminals, Inc. v. Burnside Shipping Co. (1969). A variety of statutory approaches may be found. Some statutes grant employees priority in actions against third parties, and if the employee fails to take advantage of the priority, then the subrogee may maintain the action. Other statutes provide the employer or carrier with priority to proceed against third parties. Still other statutes grant no priority and allow both to proceed against third parties independently or jointly. A few jurisdictions deny subrogation rights altogether, while others bestow all rights upon the subrogee.

The central policy issue to be found in the subrogation area centers on the conflict between the desire for full and adequate compensation, and the potential problem of double recovery if subrogation is not allowed. Additional policy issues involve the following: the possibility of workers' compensation payments inuring to the benefit of a wrongdoer; the desire to impose liability on a third party at fault; and the need for a third party to indemnify those who have been required to pay workers' compensation benefits. See Malone, Plant, and Little, Workers' Compensation and Employment Rights, pp. 440–44 (West 2d Ed. 1980).

F. UNINSURED MOTORIST INSURANCE AND NO–FAULT INSURANCE

Special problems have been created by the off-set provisions contained in uninsured motorist and no-fault insurance policies when claims also involve workers' compensation benefits. No uniform solution to these problems has been found, and each state's insurance statutes and public policy must be examined.

Where there is uninsured motorist insurance, some courts have held the off-set provisions invalid or void as being contrary to public policy because the insurance provision reduces effective coverage below that required by statute. Continental Ins. Co. v. Fahey (1987). Other courts have held that insurance contracts are valid which allow insurers to reduce uninsured motorist liability by the amount of workers' compensation paid. Ullman v. Wolverine Ins. Co. (1970). In those states which allow the off-set for workers' compensation, there are divided authorities on the issue of whether reduction should be made from an insured's total damages or from the amount of insurer liability under the insurance policy; see, e.g., Waggaman v. Northwestern Security Ins. Co. (1971); American Ins. Co. v. Tutt (1974); Michigan Mutual Liability Co. v. Mesner (1966).

No-fault insurance creates a similar off-set problem when a workers' compensation claim is involved. Some courts have held that the exclusive remedy provision in the workers' compensation act precludes any recovery of no-fault benefits regardless of statutes that would require workers' compensation benefits to be off-set. IML Freight, Inc. v. Ottosen (1975). Other courts have decided that the exclusive remedy provision does not bar receipt of no-fault benefits and that due process and equal protection are not violated. Mathis v. Interstate Motor Freight System (1980). In jurisdictions where reduction or off-set is allowed, it is generally held that workers' compensation benefits are to be deducted from the total loss of earnings rather than from the no-fault policy limits or statutory ceiling. See e.g., Shipes v. Hanover Ins. Co. (1989); In re Maldonado (1984).

CHAPTER 11

FUTURE OF WORKERS' COMPENSATION

A. THE NATIONAL COMMISSION ON STATE WORKMEN'S COMPENSATION LAWS

The Occupational Safety and Health Act of 1970, (29 U.S.C.A. § 651 et seq.) Section 27, established a National Commission on State Workmen's Compensation Laws and authorized "an effective study and objective evaluation of state workmen's compensation laws in order to determine if such laws provide an adequate, prompt, and equitable system of compensation for injury or death arising out of or in the course of employment." Section 27(a)(2). The National Commission submitted its report to the President and Congress on July 31, 1972, in which it made 84 recommendations for minimum state standards. The report indicated that 19 of its proposed state standards were "essential," and that the states should comply with these by July 1, 1975, or else congressional action should be taken in the form of a national minimum standards law. The National Commission found five major objectives for modern workers' compensation programs:

(1) Broad coverage of employees and work-related injuries and diseases;

(2) Substantial protection against interruption of income;

(3) Provision of sufficient medical care and rehabilitation services;

(4) Encouragement of safety; and

(5) An effective system for delivery of benefits and services.

Some of the National Commission's recommended "essential" elements of workers' compensation laws were:

(1) Compulsory coverage;

(2) No Occupational or Numerical Exemptions to coverage;

(3) Full coverage of work-related diseases;

(4) Full medical and physical rehabilitation services without arbitrary limits;

(5) Employee's choice of jurisdiction for filing interstate claims;

(6) Adequate weekly cash benefits for temporary total, permanent total, and death cases; and

(7) No arbitrary limits on duration or sum of benefits.

To date the 19 "essential" recommendations of the National Commission have not been adopted by any state, but many states have used the recommendations as a basis for the improvement of their particular workers' compensation acts. In 1976, an Inter-Agency Workers' Compensation Task Force reported in its findings that there was a need to reform state workers' compensation programs. The recommendations of both the National Commission and the Task Force have been used as a basis for a proposed National Workers' Compensation Standards Act.

B. NATIONAL WORKERS' COMPENSATION STANDARDS ACT PROPOSALS

Neither the National Commission nor the Inter-Agency Task Force (later merged with the Division of State Workers' Compensation Standards within the Department of Labor's Office of Workers' Compensation Programs) recommended the replacement of state workers' compensation laws with an overall federal program, but both emphasized the overall need to reform state programs. As a result of these studies, several bills have been introduced in Congress from time to time to set federal "minimum standards" for all state workers' compensation systems with one overall federal program. For example, Senate Bill 420 was introduced in the 96th Congress in an effort to create the "National Workers' Compensation Standards Act of 1979" (see Appendix I).

C. ALLOCATION OF FUTURE ECONOMIC AND SOCIAL BURDENS FOR INDUSTRIAL ACCIDENTS AND DISEASES

Despite the many justifiable criticisms of state workers' compensation laws, these acts will probably continue to serve as the chief vehicles for compensating workers for employment related injuries and deaths. The Report of the National Commission on State Workmen's Compensation laws indicates that workers' compensation is preferable to tort actions because of the fact that: (1) in many cases both employee and employer fault and causation produce industrial accidents; (2) the tort process is expensive, lengthy, and uncertain in nature with an assurance of no compensation to some victims; and (3) the tort system contains an inherent deterrence to rehabilitation.

The National Commission also indicated that presently it would be impracticable and unbeneficial to attempt to disassemble the present workers' compensation system and place its various branches under other social programs. The report further noted that it is unlikely that acceptable medical program alternatives to workers' compensation with regard to medical care will be established in the foreseeable future. Furthermore, the report observed that no other delivery system is more effective than workers' compensation. In summary, the conclusion of the National Commission was to the effect that workers' compensation systems, with recommended changes, should continue. See Report of the National Commission on State Workmen's Compensation Laws, pp. 119–121 (1972).

It is certainly likely that in the future there will be federal and state social programs which, to some extent, may overlap with workers' compensation.

Every effort should be made to avoid a duplication of benefits and to insure the coordination of complementary systems. See 4 Larson §§ 96, 97.

It is possible that tort reform in the future will look to the workers' compensation model for guidance, particularly in the areas of medical malpractice and catastrophic injuries.

It should be noted that in 1989, the Federal Courts Study Committee, appointed under the Judicial Improvements and Access to Justice Act of 1988, made tentative recommendations that Congress repeal the FELA and the Jones Act. Railway workers would be left to state workers' compensation systems, and the LHWCA would be amended to include seamen. Also recommended was the creation of a new Article I court, the Court of Disability Claims, that would hear social security disability appeals and appeals from federal workers' compensation programs.

PART 3

EMPLOYEE PROTECTION LEGISLATION

CHAPTER 12

UNEMPLOYMENT COMPENSATION

A. BACKGROUND

In 1935, an unemployment insurance system was established in order to provide economic security for workers during periods of temporary unemployment. The original system was created by Title IX of the Social Security Act of 1935. In 1939, the tax provisions of Title IX became the Federal Unemployment Tax Act, under the Internal Revenue Code. Today the Social Security Act, the Federal Unemployment Tax Act, and numerous amendments to these acts provide the statutory basis for federal unemployment compensation programs in the United States. Constitutional challenges to the system have met with little success. Chas. C. Steward Machine Co. v. Davis (1937); Carmichael v. Southern Coal and Coke Co. (1937); W.H.H. Chamberlin v. Andrews (1936). Recent constitutional challenges have generally been unsuccessful. See McKay v. Horn (1981). This is not to say that the unemployment insurance system is free from all constitutional problems. For example, payment or nonpayment of compensation during labor disputes creates a federal preemption question under the Supremacy Clause; see Nash v. Florida Industrial Commission (1967). First Amendment rights can also pose problems. Frazee v. Illinois Dept. of Employment Security (1989). See Sherbert v. Verner (1963).

The principal federal statutes comprising the basis of the unemployment insurance system today are: the Federal Unemployment Tax Act (I.R.C. §§ 3301–3311); the Social Security Act, Titles III, IX, and XII; 5 U.S.C.A. §§ 8501–8508, 8521–8525; the Wagner-Peyser Act; the Social Security Amendments of 1960; the Manpower Development and Training Act of 1962; the Federal State Extended Unemployment Compensation Act of 1970; the Employment Security Amendments of 1970; the Disaster Relief Act of 1970; the Emergency Unemployment Compensation Act of 1971; the Disaster Relief Act of 1974; the Trade Act of 1974; the Emergency Unemployment Compensation Act of 1974; the Emergency Jobs and Unemployment Assistance Act of 1974, as amended; the Emergency Compensation and Special Unemployment Assistance Act of 1975; the Unemployment Compensation Act Amendments of 1976; the Emergency Unemployment Compensation Act of 1977; the Omnibus Reconciliation Act of 1980; the Omnibus Budget Reconciliation Act of 1981; the Tax Equity and Fiscal Responsibility Act of 1982; and the Social Security Amendments of 1983. In addition to the foregoing, each state, the District of Columbia, Puerto Rico, and the Virgin Islands have separate unemployment compensation laws.

The unemployment insurance system relies on cooperative federal-state programs. Federal laws provide general guidelines, standards, and requirements, with administration left to the states under their particular unemployment legislation. The unemployment compensation system is generally funded by unemployment insurance taxes or "contributions" imposed upon employers. The federal taxes are generally applied to the costs of administration, while the state taxes provide trust funds for the payment of benefits. Federal taxes are paid into a Federal Unemployment Trust Fund from which administrative costs and the federal share of extended benefits are paid. The Fund is also used to establish a Federal Unemployment Account from which the states can borrow if their state trust funds become depleted. Unemployment taxes should not be confused with the separate Social Security taxes imposed by the federal government, or with the separate disability benefits taxes imposed by some states. It should be noted that unemployment benefits are taxable as ordinary income.

B. FEDERAL UNEMPLOYMENT INSURANCE PROGRAMS

1. REGULAR STATE PROGRAMS

a. *Overview*

The principal vehicle for providing weekly unemployment benefits is referred to as the regular state program. Subject to federal guidelines, the states determine: (1) qualifying requirements; (2) amounts of benefits; (3) duration; and (4) grounds for disqualification.

While state unemployment compensation laws can vary, ordinarily qualification requires a demonstration of: employment by an employer subject to the unemployment tax of a particular jurisdiction, and employment during a "base period" (a recent 12 month period); and generally one must have been employed in more than one quarter.

Payments usually take the form of weekly benefits. The weekly amount is calculated on the basis of a particular jurisdiction's formula. Commonly an employee's average weekly wage provides the basis for the weekly benefit amount, and this average amount is determined by dividing one's high quarter wages by the 13 weeks in a quarter; one-half of the result is the weekly benefit amount paid to the worker. There may be a waiting period prior to the initial payment of benefits. In some jurisdictions this may be referred to as the "waiting week;" however, not all jurisdictions impose an unemployment period of one week prior to the payment of compensation. Normally, claimants have a "benefit year" of a designated 52 weeks within which to receive or "draw out" all compensation entitlements.

The duration of unemployment compensation benefits varies with the particular jurisdiction; however, the vast majority of jurisdictions determine duration on the basis of the length of employment or the amount earned (variable duration approach). The longer the length or the greater the amount, the more weeks of benefits one can receive. A minority of jurisdictions consider an employee's work history to be irrelevant, and all claimants who qualify for benefits are treated in the same manner; i.e., each uniformly receives the same number of weeks of benefits on the theory that benefits should be tied to that period of time necessary to secure new employment (uniform duration approach).

Workers are denied compensation benefits if certain grounds for disqualification exist. Unemployment compensation policy dictates payment only to those employees who have lost their jobs through no fault on their part. In all jurisdictions an employee is disqualified from benefits if the worker: (1) voluntarily quits employment without good cause; or (2) is discharged for employment related misconduct. Additionally, disqualification can occur at any time if a claimant or benefit recipient refuses to accept suitable employment without good cause. Finally, in order for benefits to continue, a claimant must: (1) register for employment with the jurisdiction's Employment Service; (2) be able to work; (3) be available for work; and (4) seek work on one's own.

b. *Procedures and Appeals*

Representatives of the state employment agencies, who may be called deputies or claims examiners, make initial findings of fact (usually on the basis of interviews) which lead to a grant or a denial of unemployment compensation benefits. The appellate rights of a dissatisfied claimant are generally guaranteed by Title III of the Social Security Act, Section 303(a), which requires administration by the states in a manner "reasonably calculated to insure full payment of unemployment benefits when due," and which requires an "opportunity for a fair hearing before an impartial tribunal for all individuals whose claims for unemployment are denied." See Graves v. Meystrik (1977). It should be noted that employers have appellate rights as well, and they frequently exercise these rights because an employer's unemployment experience rating affects the amounts that an employer is required to contribute. Appellate procedures vary from state to state, but all jurisdictions allow access to the state judicial system for appellate review, once administrative remedies have been exhausted (usually after a hearing before an appeals tribunal whose decision may or may not be then reviewed by a board or some other state administrative body). A state administrative practice of permitting the automatic suspension of benefit payments upon the filing of an appeal by an employer was enjoined by the Supreme Court. California Department of Human Resources Development v. Java (1971). See Jenkins v. Bowling (1982).

c. Extended and Supplemental Benefits

In recent times, certain amendments have provided extended, supplemental or special unemployment benefits, thus increasing unemployment compensation for many unemployed persons in the United States. The Federal-State Extended Benefits Program pays "exhaustees" (individuals who have exhausted their regular program entitlements) further unemployment compensation, with the costs shared equally by the federal and state governments. The Omnibus Budget Reconciliation Act of 1981, repealed the national "on" and "off" triggering indicators which automatically regulated the extended benefits program. The Federal Supplemental Compensation Act of 1982 made additional unemployment benefits available in states experiencing periods of "higher unemployment;" these benefits are funded out of general federal revenues. The Social Security Amendments of 1983 extended the Federal Supplemental Compensation program.

2. FEDERAL EMPLOYEES AND EX–SERVICEMEN

In 1956, unemployment compensation coverage was extended to federal employees. The state law of the jurisdiction in which a claimant worked as a federal employee usually determines an employee's eligibility. This eligibility may also be determined by the law of the state in which a claimant subsequently worked in privately covered employment, or by the law of the state in which a claimant resides at the time of the filing of the claim. The amount of benefits is determined by state law. The conditions and eligibility requirements for compensation are also governed by state law, but findings of fact provided by the employing federal agency with regard to federal employment, wages, and the reasons for separation (which have been made under U.S. Department of Labor procedures) are binding upon the states.

In 1958, unemployment compensation coverage was extended to ex-servicemen. The state law of the jurisdiction in which a claimant first files an unemployment compensation claim which establishes a benefit year after the claimant's most recent separation from active duty, determines eligibility. A U.S. Department of Labor schedule prescribes applicable wages for benefit purposes. These are based upon a claimant's pay grade at the time of one's latest discharge or release from federal service. If a claimant is eligible for certain

Veterans Administration benefits (subsistence or educational), the claimant is not entitled to unemployment compensation during these periods of eligibility.

3. DISASTER UNEMPLOYMENT ASSISTANCE

Those employees who suffer unemployment as a result of major disasters are entitled to unemployment benefit assistance. The President makes disaster area declarations. The states generally administer the payment of benefits, and these are strictly derived from federal revenues. Individual benefits are payable for the period of unemployment caused by the disaster, or until suitable reemployment is obtained, but in no event longer than the prescribed disaster assistance period.

4. TRADE ADJUSTMENT ASSISTANCE

Direct assistance is provided to employees who find themselves unemployed because of foreign competition. These benefits are provided only to those employees whose terminations are the result of foreign imports. These imports must be a substantial cause of actual or threatened termination. Assistance is paid out of federal revenues and is generally administered by the states. This assistance takes the form of weekly benefits, training allowances, relocation allowances, and job search allowances.

C. STATE FINANCED PROGRAMS

1. EXTENDED AND ADDITIONAL BENEFITS

A few states have enacted supplemental unemployment programs. These programs are financed completely by the particular jurisdiction, and they are usually aimed at providing extended benefits during high unemployment periods. California, Connecticut, and Puerto Rico have state extended benefit programs. Hawaii has enacted an Additional Unemployment Compensation Benefits Law that provides benefits for unemployment resulting from disasters.

2. UNEMPLOYMENT COMPENSATION DISABILITY BENEFITS

Six jurisdictions in the United States have enacted special disability benefit programs to assist workers who are ineligible for either unemployment compensation or workers' compensation. Workers' compensation generally excludes disabilities arising out of nonwork-related diseases or injuries; benefits are not payable through unemployment insurance programs to disabled workers because the ability to work is a condition of eligibility. California, Hawaii, New Jersey, New York, Rhode Island, and Puerto Rico have special unemployment disability benefit programs that fill the gap between workers' compensation and unemployment compensation laws. A branch of the particular jurisdiction's labor agency administers the program. Contribution by employers to state funds, private insurance, or self-insurance finance the programs. Some states make distinctions between the employed and the unemployed in their benefit formulas, while other jurisdictions do not.

CHAPTER 13

FAIR LABOR STANDARDS ACT

A. INTRODUCTION

The federal attempt to regulate the wages and hours of employees began in 1892 with the passage of the Eight-Hour Law. Later, the Supreme Court in Hammer v. Dagenhart (1918), held that Congress could not properly exercise its power under the Commerce Clause to prohibit the shipment of goods produced by child labor in interstate commerce. The Fair Labor Standards Act of 1938, 29 U.S.C.A. § 201 et seq. (hereinafter referred to as "FLSA") was enacted to regulate wages and hours (set minimum wage and overtime requirements) and child labor. The FLSA was upheld as constitutional in United States v. Darby (1941), in which the Hammer v. Dagenhart case, supra, was overruled. Over the years Congress has amended the FLSA and added major and minor acts to the federal wage-hour laws. The Equal Pay Act of 1963 was an important amendment to the FLSA; it generally prohibits sex-based wage discrimination by requiring equal pay for equal work regardless of sex. The Congressional extension of wage and hour coverage to public schools and hospitals was upheld as constitutional in Maryland v. Wirtz (1968), but this decision was overruled in National

League of Cities v. Usery (1976). In this latter case, the Supreme Court held that the attempted Congressional regulation of wages and hours of employees of state and local governments constituted an unconstitutional infringement on state sovereignty. Constitutional issues again reached the Supreme Court in Garcia v. San Antonio Metro. Transit Authority (1985), in which a divided court upheld the application of the FLSA to state and local governments, overruling *National League of Cities v. Usery.* Congress passed the Fair Labor Standards Amendments of 1985 in order to lessen the impact of *Garcia* by authorizing the use of compensatory time in the place of overtime for state and local government employees.

The FLSA may be applied to a nonprofit religious organization that derives income largely from commercial business, despite constitutional challenges based upon the First Amendment. Tony and Susan Alamo Foundation v. Secretary of Labor (1985).

Today the FLSA, as amended, provides compensation standards and regulation in four basic areas: (1) minimum wages; (2) overtime compensation; (3) sex-based wage discrimination (equal pay for equal work); and (4) child labor. The FLSA, as amended, is liberally construed by the courts, and, with certain exceptions, it applies generally to interstate commerce and industry. Other federal acts apply compensation standards to federally financed public works contracts (Davis-Bacon Act), government service contracts (Service Contract Act), and government supply contracts (Walsh-Healey Public Contracts Act). Some states have enacted higher compensation standards than those existing under federal law. These higher state standards are not superseded or preempted, and the federal standards cannot be used to excuse noncompliance with the higher state ones. If employees are covered by both federal and state compensation standards, then the stricter federal or state standards are applicable.

B. STANDARDS AND REQUIREMENTS

1. MINIMUM WAGE

Congress changes the minimum wage rate from time to time, and as of January 1, 1981, the FLSA established the minimum hourly rate for all covered employees at $3.35. This means, for example, that employees who are paid on a monthly basis and who are working 40 hour weeks, must be paid at least $580.67 per month; employees who are paid semi-monthly must be paid $290.33; employees who are paid weekly must be paid $134.00 per week. The foregoing are monthly, semi-monthly, and weekly average standards; the FLSA does not require an employer to pay these amounts each period, but the *average standards* must be met (based upon 8 hour work days; 40 hour work weeks; and 2,080 work hours in a year). In 1989, Congress voted to increase the minimum wage to

$3.80 on April 1, 1990, and to $4.25 a year later; workers under 20 years of age, in some instances, could be paid a training wage of $3.35 in 1990, and $3.61 after April 1, 1991.

It must always be remembered that the work-week is the longest unit of time over which wages can be averaged in order to determine whether the minimum wage has been paid. This does not mean that all employees must be paid solely on an hourly rate basis; they can be paid on a salary, commission, or piecework basis that is monthly, semi-monthly, or weekly, but the minimum hourly rate must be received by them. If employees are paid solely on an hourly rate basis, then the minimum hourly rate must be met.

Problems sometime arise because certain deductions may be legally made from an employee's wages. Wages must be paid in cash or "facilities furnished," and thus the reasonable costs of board, lodging or other facilities can be used in meeting minimum wage requirements. Payment in scrip, tokens, coupons, etc., are prohibited. Gifts, talent fees, discretionary bonuses, and certain other payments are excluded from wage calculations. The application of the minimum wage to particular employees requires detailed research, because of the complexity and exceptions contained in the FLSA and related wage and hour laws.

2. OVERTIME COMPENSATION

The federal wage and hour laws do not limit the number of hours that an employee can work in a workweek, but the employee must be paid time and one-half the employee's regular rate of pay for each hour worked over 40 in a workweek. It should be noted that an employee's regular rate of pay can be higher than the minimum hourly rate set by law for these purposes. The workweek is the longest period over which earnings may be averaged in arriving at an employee's regular hourly rate of pay. For example, if an employee works 45 hours in one week and 35 in the next week, the employee must be paid overtime for five hours in the first week, despite the fact that the employee's hourly average over two weeks is 40 hours per week. Time lost on the job must be made up in the same workweek, or else overtime must be paid for all hours subsequently worked over 40 in any other workweek. Overtime exceptions and exemptions exist that must be researched in particular cases.

Many disputes arise because employers and employees fail to agree on what activities are to be considered "working time." For example, time spent on call may or may not be considered as working time. The Portal-to-Portal Act of 1947, excludes preliminary and postliminary activities from working time not otherwise compensable by contract, custom, or practice. Premium pay can also create overtime calculation difficulties. This is pay received in excess of basic straight-time wages, and it can take the form of holiday pay, contracted overtime, gifts, bonuses, sick pay, etc. If premium pay is considered to be part of an employee's regular earnings, then FLSA overtime is increased, otherwise premium pay may be offset against the statutory overtime pay.

3. SEX–BASED WAGE DISCRIMINATION

The Equal Pay Act of 1963 amended the minimum wage provisions of the FLSA, and prohibited wage discrimination based upon sex. The provisions require equal pay for equal work for men and women doing equal work on jobs requiring equal skill, effort and responsibility and that are performed under similar working conditions. Minimum, overtime, and premium wages for men and women must be equal if the work is equal, and the wages of one sex cannot be lowered in order to comply with the law. Exceptions are allowed for: (1) seniority systems; (2) merit systems; (3) systems measuring earnings by quantity or quality of production; and (4) factors other than sex. The act prohibits sex-based wage discrimination only in "any establishment" operated by an employer. The act does not cover discriminatory rates as between an employer's two or more legitimate "establishments." It should be noted that wage differences authorized by the Equal Pay Act are valid pay practices for the purposes of the Civil Rights

Act of 1964, Title VII; however, it is possible for sex-based discrimination involving pay practices, beyond the reach of the Equal Pay Act, to be remedied under Title VII. In order for equal pay coverage to exist, an employee generally must be covered by the FLSA minimum wage provisions. It should also be pointed out that amendments in 1972, placed executive, administrative, and professional employees within equal pay coverage.

4. CHILD LABOR

The FLSA prohibits "oppressive child labor" in commerce or in the production of goods for commerce. There is a "hot goods" ban that prohibits the interstate shipment of goods from establishments that have employed oppressive child labor. Enterprise coverage is used to prohibit the use of oppressive child labor, regardless of whether the work of children has an interstate impact or is purely local in nature. The FLSA defines "oppressive child labor" through the use of age restrictions. Essentially, minors under 14 cannot be employed, except in agriculture; minors 14 to 16 can work limited hours outside of their school hours in a limited class of jobs; and minors 16 to 18 cannot be employed in certain hazardous occupations. Employers generally obtain age or permit certificates for each minor in accordance with Department of Labor regulations and state guidelines.

C. COVERAGES

Compensation standards have been imposed by Congress through the exercise of its powers to regulate interstate commerce and through it powers to control federal government contracts and federally financed projects. All geographical areas under the jurisdiction of the United States, including possessions and leased bases in foreign countries, are subject to the FLSA. Two forms of coverage are provided by the FLSA: (1) "enterprise" coverage; and (2) "individual employee" coverage. Enterprise coverage generally exists if an employer has two or more workers engaged in interstate commerce, or in the production of goods for interstate commerce, while meeting a requirement of business volume. If enterprise coverage exists, then all employees of the enterprise are covered. Individual employee coverage can exist even if an employer's business does not qualify for enterprise coverage. An individual employee can be covered if the employee is engaged in commerce or in the production of goods for commerce, or is employed in a closely related process or occupation directly essential to the production of goods. The FLSA contains a number of exemptions based upon the type of industry or the type of employee. Once FLSA coverage is found to exist, the minimum wage, overtime, equal pay and child labor provisions are applicable, unless a specific exemption governs.

In those situations in which government contract laws impose compensation standards, the particular transaction and the appropriate federal act must be considered. For example, the Walsh-Healey Act imposes employee compensation standards through the terms and conditions of federal government supply contracts.

D. ENFORCEMENT AND REMEDIES

The administration and enforcement of federal compensation standards primarily rests with the U.S. Department of Labor, Employment Standards Administration. The Wage and Hour Division performs inspections and investigations, makes compliance determinations, and issues rules and regulations. The Equal Employment Opportunity Commission is now charged with the enforcement of the equal pay provisions.

The Secretary of Labor is authorized to file suit on behalf of employees to collect wages and overtime, plus liquidated damages in an equal amount. The Secretary is also empowered to file suits enjoining or restraining employer violations; the Secretary can also seek civil contempt citations against employers for continued violations of decrees. It should be noted that a "clearly erroneous" standard of review is to be used by courts of appeal in reviewing the application of an exemption to the FLSA. Icicle Seafoods, Inc. v. Worthington (1986). The U.S. Department of Justice can prosecute wilful violators in criminal proceedings.

Employees are authorized to file suit for reinstatement, back wages, liquidated damages in an equal amount, reasonable attorney's fees, and costs. A three year statute of limitations exists for wilful violations, while a two year statute exists for other violations. McLaughlin v. Richland Shoe Co. (1988) (definition of "willful" in connection with 3 year statute of limitations). It should be noted that employees generally do not have the right to release employers for less than the full amounts owing or to waive their rights to compensation. See D.A. Schulte, Inc. v. Gangi (1946); Brooklyn Savings Bank v. O'Neil (1945).

CHAPTER 14

OCCUPATIONAL SAFETY AND HEALTH ACT

A. BACKGROUND AND SCOPE

In 1970, Congress enacted the Occupational Safety and Health Act, 29 U.S.C.A. § 651 et seq., for the purpose of assuring as far as possible that safe and healthful working conditions exist for all workers in the United States. The basic act has withstood constitutional challenge; Atlas Roofing Co. v. OSHRC (1977); but some procedural difficulties have been encountered. See Marshall v. Barlow's, Inc. (1978). The act extends geographically to all areas under U.S. jurisdiction, including territories, possessions, and the outer continental shelves. The act provides coverage and applies to all employers engaged in a business that affects interstate commerce, and the act's jurisdictional scope has been broadly construed. See Usery v. Lacy (1980). State and local governments are excluded from coverage. Federal employees are not covered, but special safety and health programs are required by Executive Order 12196.

Essentially, the act imposes a twofold obligation upon all employers: (1) there is a "general duty" clause requiring employers to furnish a workplace free from recognized hazards that are likely to

162

cause serious injury or death to workers, and (2) there are safety and health standards that employers must meet. Employers are required by the act to keep records of accidents, illnesses, deaths, and particular hazards. The posting of OSHA information and citations for violations are also required under the act. Finally, employers are required to make reports to OSHA.

Of increasing importance to both employers and employees is OSHA's Hazard Communication Program. 29 C.F.R. § 1926.59. The purpose of this program is to give employers and employees vital information about chemical hazards through product container labeling and dissemination of "material safety data sheets." Some states have enacted "right to know" legislation that may be preempted by OSHA unless the particular state is operating under an approved plan.

Several federal agencies administer and enforce the act. Safety and health standards are usually recommended on the basis of research by the National Institute for Occupational Safety and Health, and they fall under the responsibility of the Secretary of Health and Human Services. The Occupational Safety and Health Administration (OSHA) of the U.S. Department of Labor promulgates and enforces standards. An independent agency, the Occupational Safety and Health Review Commission adjudicates contested cases through the use of administrative law judges. Judicial review of commission decisions rests with the federal circuit courts of appeal.

The act provides that the states may assume responsibility for workplace safety and health by adopting a plan of standards and enforcement that is at least as effective as the federal one. All state plans must receive approval from the Occupational Safety and Health Administration. Upon approval, the states are entitled to enforce their own laws. A minority of states have adopted these plans.

It should be kept in mind that no private rights of action are created against employers for violation of standards under the act. See Russell v. Bartley (1974). Citations and standards, however, can have a significant impact on private damage actions. The safety and health standards can be evidence of an employer's standard of care in tort actions. See Donovan v. General Motors (1985) (standard of care issue); Schroeder v. C.F. Braun & Co. (1974). See also, Hines v. Brandon Steel Decks, Inc. (1989) (use of OSHA reports as evidence in civil trial).

B. STANDARDS AND VARIANCES

There are three types of safety and health standards, and two types of variances that come into play under the act. First of all, there are interim or "start-up" standards based upon existing federal and national consensus standards. The existing or already established federal standards originate from the Service Contract Act, the Longshoremen's and Harbor Workers' Compensation Act, the Construction Safety Act, and the Walsh-Healey Act. The consensus standards originate from national standards organizations such as the American National Standards Institute, the National Fire Protection Association, and the American Society for Testing and Materials. Consensus standards also originate from federal procedures permitting consideration of opposing views or from designated standards of the Secretary of Labor after consultation with particular federal agencies.

A second type of standard is called a permanent standard. Permanent standards are designed to replace or supplement the interim ones, and they generally come into being after advisory committee recommendation, publication in the Federal Register, receipt of comment by interested parties, and public hearing. The Secretary of Labor then makes a permanent standard determination.

The third type of safety and health standard is called a temporary emergency standard, which the Secretary of Labor establishes when the Secretary determines that new safety and health findings demonstrate that employees are exposed to grave dangers.

All of the three foregoing types of safety and health standards are subject to judicial review by the U.S. Circuit Courts of Appeal upon petition by any person affected by the standard, within 60 days of a standard being set. The development and promulgation of safety and health standards can be the subject of serious judicial scrutiny. See Industrial Union Department, AFL–CIO v. American Petroleum Institute (1980).

An employer may obtain either a permanent or a temporary variance from the safety and health standards in certain circumstances. A permanent variance is obtained after application and a showing that an employer's working conditions, practices, methods, etc. are as safe and healthful as those provided by the standards. Applications are filed with the Assistant Secretary of Labor for Occupational Safety and Health. Temporary variances may be obtained from the Secretary of Labor if an employer can demonstrate either that necessary equipment or personnel are not immediately available or that the construction or alteration of required facilities or controls cannot be completed by a standard's effective date. Economic hardship is not a consideration in these determinations, and temporary variances are only good for a limited time period.

C. ENFORCEMENT AND PROCEDURES

The enforcement of the act usually involves OSHA inspections, and citations of employers for: (1) breach of the general duty obligation; (2) breach of specific safety and health standards; or (3) failure to keep records, make reports, or post notices required by the act.

Upon the presentation of appropriate credentials, OSHA inspectors are authorized to enter without delay and at reasonable times an employer's premises. These investigations are to occur at reasonable times, within reasonable limits, and be conducted in a reasonable manner. OSHA inspectors are entitled to private interviews with employers, owners, agents, employees or operators. If an OSHA inspector is denied entry, a search warrant may be obtained from a U.S. District Court by the Solicitor of Labor. The probable cause requirements are less stringent than those in criminal cases. See Marshall v. Barlow's, Inc., supra. Ex parte warrants are obtainable under OSHA regulations. It should be noted that it is unlawful to discriminate against employees or to discharge them for OSHA inspection requests, testimony in OSHA inspection requests, testimony in OSHA proceedings, or for the exercise of any rights under the act.

When a violation is discovered, a written citation, proposed penalty, and correction date are furnished to the employer. Citations may be contested, and in such cases, administrative law judges are assigned by the Occupational Safety and Health Review Commission, to conduct hearings. The commission may or may not grant review of an administrative law judge's decision; commission review is not a matter of right. If commission review is not undertaken, then the judge's decision becomes the final order of the commission 30 days after receipt. In any event once a decision is final, it may be appealed by any aggrieved party to the appropriate U.S. Circuit Court of Appeals within 60 days.

Civil and criminal penalties exist for various violations. Penalties can be as high as $1,000 per violation per day, and a $10,000 criminal penalty can be imposed for certain wilful violations. In cases involving civil penalties, it is important, as a matter of practice, to distinguish between serious and nonserious violations. Serious violations require that a penalty be proposed. In nonserious violation cases, penalties are rarely proposed.

The Secretary of Labor is further empowered by the act to obtain temporary restraining orders shutting down business operations that create imminent dangers of death or serious injury. This procedure is available when imminent dangers cannot be eliminated through regular OSHA enforcement procedures.

CHAPTER 15

FEDERAL BLACK LUNG
BENEFITS LEGISLATION

A. BACKGROUND AND SCOPE

The Federal Coal Mine Health and Safety Act of 1969, 30 U.S.C.A. § 801 et seq., was enacted in an effort to provide standards for safety and health for coal mines in the United States. It also provided compensation benefits for coal miners and their dependents, or survivors, when a miner's disability or death was the result of pneumoconiosis, otherwise known as "black lung," a chronic dust disease of the lungs, which is more fully defined in the act. This act has been the subject of several important amendments: the Black Lung Benefits Act of 1972; the Black Lung Benefits Reform Act of 1977; the Black Lung Benefits Review Act of 1977; the Black Lung Benefits Revenue Act of 1981; the Black Lung Benefits Amendments of 1981 and the Consolidated Omnibus Budget Reconcilation Act of 1985. The constitutionality of federal black lung legislation was upheld in Turner Elkhorn Mining Co. v. Usery (1976).

The original federal black lung legislation attempted to place the responsibility for compensation and medical expenses on responsible mine operators whose identities could be determined, but

169

the federal government assumed these obligations when no responsible mine operator could be determined. Various devices have been employed by the federal government to insure the payment of black lung benefits. Reforms in 1977, created a Black Lung Disability Trust Fund which is administered jointly by the Secretaries of Labor, Treasury, and Health and Human Services. This fund is financed primarily by excise taxes on mined coal. The Black Lung Disability Trust Fund has suffered from a chronic lack of funding, and this resulted in amendments in 1981 aimed at preserving the fund through increased excise taxes and through benefit limitations.

Originally, claims were processed by the Social Security Administration; however, the Department of Labor has assumed this responsibility. This was logical, in light of the fact that the Department of Labor is the responsible agency for mining health and safety. Claims filed up to July 1, 1973, continued to be under the Social Security Administration's jurisdiction, but claims filed after July 1, 1973, are administered by the Department of Labor. The Black Lung Benefits Reform Act of 1977, broadened entitlement and provided review for some previously denied claims, either by the Social Security Administration or the Department of Labor. Current claims procedures are set forth in detail in 20 C.F.R. § 410.101 et seq. and in 20 C.F.R. § 718.1 et seq.

B. ELIGIBILITY AND BENEFITS

Monthly cash benefits are payable under the federal black lung program to past and present coal miners who are totally disabled as a result of pneumoconiosis; a miner's compensation increases if there are dependents. Additionally, in miner death cases, widows, children, surviving divorced wives, parents, brothers and sisters may receive benefits. If a widow was entitled to benefits at the time of her death, her children may receive benefits.

The basic benefit for a disabled coal miner is equal to $37\frac{1}{2}$ percent of the monthly pay of a federal employee in the Grade of GS–2, step 1, who is totally disabled. A surviving widow is paid the same benefit. Any single surviving child would receive the same benefit that a surviving widow would have received. Single surviving children are entitled to a full widow's benefit, if a widow dies while receiving benefits. Miner's benefits and the benefits of dependents are increased based upon the number of dependents. Benefits are reduced by state workers' compensation, unemployment compensation, state disability insurance, or excess earnings under the Social Security Act.

In order to be eligible for benefits under the federal black lung program, a coverage formula must be met. See Mullins Coal Co. v. Director (1987). The formula requires: (1) a "miner," who is (2) "totally disabled due to pneumoconiosis." In order to qualify as a "miner," a person must have worked as an employee in a coal mine whether underground or above ground, performing functions in extracting the coal or preparing the coal so extracted. The definition of "miner" has undergone several statutory changes since the original act, and in 1977, it was expanded to provide coverage for self-employed miners, and certain others in the coal mine construction and transportation industries. See Baker v. United States Steel Corp. (1989) (liberal construction given to the term "miner"). Once "miner" status is established, a claimant must prove total disability due to pneumoconiosis. In proving total disability due to pneumoconiosis, claimants traditionally enjoyed the assistance of certain rebuttable and irrebuttable presumptions. The 1981 amendments effectively eliminated some presumptions, however, two important ones remain: (1) a miner with pneumoconiosis who was exposed for 10 or more years is rebuttably presumed to have pneumoconiosis that arose out of employment; and (2) a miner with complicated pneumoconiosis receives an irrebuttable presumption of the necessary total disability, or in death cases, that death was due to the pneumoconiosis; or additionally in death cases that total disability from pneumoconiosis existed at the time of death. See generally, Pittston Coal Group v. Sebben (1988).

The 1981 amendments also addressed the issue of proof and provided that after the effective date of the 1981 amendments, the Secretary of Labor need not accept a radiologist's interpretation of chest x-rays, and could consider second interpretations. Furthermore, the Secretary need not accept as binding the affidavits of interested persons who are eligible for benefits in death cases.

C. PROCEDURES

Claims for black lung benefits may be filed at certain offices of the Department of Labor, Social Security district offices, or Foreign Service offices of the United States by mail or presentation. The Department of Labor's Office of Workers' Compensation supervises the claims procedures, and once a claim has been forwarded to them, a deputy commissioner conducts an initial investigation which is designed to determine a claimant's eligibility for benefits, and if a responsible operator exists.

Deputy commissioner decisions in contested cases are assigned to Administrative Law Judges for formal hearings in accordance with the Administrative Procedure Act. See Pyro Mining Co. v. Slaton (1989). Appeals from these hearings are lodged with the Benefits Review Board, which may enter a final decision or remand the case either to the Administrative Law Judge or to the deputy commissioner. Final decisions of the Benefits Review Board may be appealed to the U.S. Circuit Court of Appeals in the circuit where the miner was last employed.

CHAPTER 16

SOCIAL SECURITY

A. INTRODUCTION

The federal Social Security system began in 1935 in an effort to provide limited retirement or death benefits for workers in commerce and industry. Since 1935, the system has greatly expanded, and benefits have increased dramatically.

Historically significant changes occurred as follows: in 1954, coverage became almost universal; in 1956, disability insurance benefits were added; in 1958, disability eligibility was liberalized, and benefits were added for dependents of disability insurance recipients; in 1961, early but reduced retirement was permitted for men at age 62; in 1965, medicare benefits were added; in 1972, automatic cost-of-living-adjustments (COLA) were added to the benefit system; in 1977, substantial increases in tax rates were enacted to cover projected long term deficits; and in 1981, short term deficits were financed by interfund borrowing.

Amendments in 1983 resulted in the taxation of certain social security benefits for the first time; called for the normal retirement age to be gradually changed from 65 to 67; established mandatory coverage for employees of nonprofit organizations; resulted in some federal workers to being covered by social security rather than by civil service; established deferred compensation plan taxation for social security purposes; prohibited states from terminating coverage of state and local government employees; altered cost-of-living-adjustment computation methods; and eliminated several gender-based distinctions previously made by the social security laws. The Disability Reform Act of 1984 changed the standard of review for terminating disability benefits and, among other changes, provided for the evaluation of pain. Technical amendments were passed in 1986 and 1987. Catastrophic health care coverage and financing was enacted under the Medicare Catastrophic Coverage Act of 1988, however, Congress voted to repeal this Act in 1989.

Today, the Social Security system contains the following benefit programs: (1) Retirement and survivors benefits (Old-Age and Survivors Insurance-OASI); (2) Disability benefits (Disability Insurance-DI); (3) Medicare benefits (Hospitalization Insurance-HI; a separate Supplementary Medical Insurance (SMI) program requires enrollment and premium payments); and (4) Supplemental Security Income benefits (SSI). With the exception of state and local governments, and certain non-profit organizations, coverage is generally mandatory; election of coverage is permitted, however, for these groups.

For the most part, Social Security benefits are financed by taxes or "contributions" collected from employers, employees, and self-employed persons who work in employments covered by Social Security. The Federal Insurance Contributions Act (FICA) which falls within the Internal Revenue Code, governs taxation and collection. The maximum employee contribution for 1988 was $3,379.50. The 1988 FICA withholding rate was 7.51% on wages up to $45,000.00. These collected taxes pay for retirement, survivors, disability, and hospital insurance benefits. In the case of certain persons, however, hospital insurance benefits are paid from the general revenues of the United States, and it should also be noted that supplementary medical insurance benefits are generally financed through the collection of monthly premiums. The general revenues of the United States pay for supplemental security income benefits.

Three basic trust funds hold Social Security contributions: (1) the Old-Age and Survivors Insurance Trust Fund; (2) the Disability Insurance Trust Fund; and (3) the Hospital Insurance Trust Fund (this fund also receives general revenues in order to pay benefits to uninsured persons 65 and older). The Supplementary Medical Insurance Trust Fund receives premium collections and general revenues that have been appropriated for the fund. A Board of Trustees, consisting of the Secretaries of Health and Human Services, Treasury, and Labor, hold these funds, and amounts not currently needed are invested in federal securities that bear interest.

The Department of Health and Human Services, through its Social Security Administration, basically administers the retirement, survivors, disability, hospital and medical insurance, and supplemental security income programs. Other public assistance and welfare services programs are financed separately, and they are generally administered by the states in cooperation with the federal government; these include: aid to needy families with children; medical assistance, maternal and child-health services; crippled children services; child support and welfare services; food stamps; and energy assistance.

B. RETIREMENT AND SURVIVORS INSURANCE (OASI)

1. ELIGIBILITY FOR OASI

Eligibility for retirement and survivors benefits depends upon the "insured status" of an employee. Generally, an employee's insured status is established by the number of "quarters of coverage" that have been earned in work covered by Social Security. A worker and family can become "fully insured" with as little as 31 quarters (eight years) of work. The requisite age and quarters of coverage can vary. 20 C.F.R. § 404.115 (chart of age and quarters). If a worker is "currently insured," benefits can be paid to survivors upon the worker's death; six quarters of coverage in the 13 quarters preceding death gives rise to this "currently insured status." OASI benefits are conditioned upon the attainment of retirement age or death. Full OASI benefits are payable at age 65; reduced benefits are available at 62. The 1983 amendments will gradually increase the retirement age to 67. Other OASI benefits have age eligibility variations. OASI benefits are in the form of monthly benefit payments.

2. OASI BENEFIT CALCULATIONS

The past earnings of covered workers generally determine the benefit levels which are to be paid to retired employees, disabled workers, dependents and survivors. Four basic concepts govern benefit calculations: (1) computation years; (2) index earnings; (3) average indexed monthly earnings (AIME); and (4) primary insurance amount (PIA). The "computation years" is essentially the number of years worked in employment covered by Social Security. The "index earnings" represents the earnings of each year which have been converted to reflect increases in wage levels over the years; this indexing creates an earnings record. The "average indexed monthly earnings" (AIME) is the result of having divided the total indexed earnings by the number of months in the "computation years." Finally, a "primary insurance amount" (PIA) or basic benefit level is obtained by applying a percentage formula to the AIME; the 1989 percentage formula is: 90% of the first $339.00 or less of AIME, plus 32% of any AIME over $339.00 to $2,044.00, plus 15% of any AIME over $2,044.00.

All benefit levels are subject to periodic cost-of-living-adjustments (COLA).

3. OASI BENEFITS

The figure which provides the basis for almost all benefit amounts is the primary insurance amount (PIA). Lump sum death benefits are fixed; special benefits are sometimes paid without reference to the PIA. The OASI types of benefits payable and the percentage of the primary insurance amount (PIA) receivable in 1988 for retirees, disabled workers, dependents and survivors are as follows:

(1) *Full retirement*—100% of PIA (eligible at age 65); reduced benefits available at 62.

(2) *Widowed spouses*—100% of PIA (eligible at age 65); reduced benefits available at 60.

(3) *Spouses*—50% of the PIA (eligible at age 65 or younger if caring for a disabled child, or child under 16); reduced benefits available at 62.

(4) *Divorced spouses*—50% of PIA (eligible on the same basis as spouses, supra, but 10 years of marriage also required).

(5) *Children*—50% of PIA (eligible until age 18 if a child of a retired or deceased insured employee; eligible while attending full-time elementary or secondary school).

(6) *Surviving children*—75% of PIA (eligible on the same basis as children, supra).

(7) *Parents*—82½% of PIA if one parent entitled; 75% of PIA if more than one parent entitled.

(8) *Maximum family benefits*—175% of PIA.

(9) *Lump sum death benefit*—$255 payment to survivors (not a percent of PIA).

(10) *Transitionally insured benefits*—Not a percent of PIA (eligible if over 65 with insufficient quarters of coverage).

(11) *Special age 72*—Not a percent of PIA (eligible if over 72 with insufficient quarters of coverage to permit retiree benefits; must not receive public assistance).

(12) *Special minimum*—Not a percent of PIA (eligible are workers with low average earnings).

(13) *Currently insured*—OASDI benefits (eligible if survivor of worker not fully insured so long as deceased employee worked at least 6 of the 13 quarters in covered employment preceding death).

It should be noted that there can be reduction in all benefits based upon a beneficiary's annual earnings. See 20 C.F.R. Subpart E. This reduction can vary, but generally all benefits are charged on the basis of $1.00 of excess earnings for each $1.00 of monthly benefits.

C. DISABILITY INSURANCE (DI)

1. ELIGIBILITY

In general, the test for disability benefit eligibility employs the same "insured status" concept used by OASI, supra. Disability eligibility requires that an employee be both: (1) "fully insured" under OASI; and (2) "disability insured." The disability insured requirement is met if a worker has 20 quarters of coverage in the 40 quarters immediately preceding disability. A waiting period of 5 months exists before these benefits can be paid. At age 65, disability benefits cease, and regular full retirement benefits are paid. In making eligibility determinations, "disability" is generally defined as the inability to engage in gainful activity by reason of any medically determinable physical or mental impairment that can be expected to last at least 12 continuous months or to result in death. Social Security disability benefits are generally offset by any other disability benefits.

2. DI BENEFITS

There are five fundamental types of disability insurance benefits:

(1) *Disabled worker*—100% of PIA (eligible 5 months after disability if fully insured under OASI and disability insured).

(2) *Disabled surviving spouse*—100% of PIA (eligible at age 60; benefits available at age 50, if disabled).

(3) *Disabled surviving divorced spouse* —50% of PIA (eligible at age 60; benefits available at age 50 if disabled).

(4) *Disabled child*—50% of PIA (eligible at age 18).

(5) *Disabled surviving child*—75% of PIA (eligible at age 18).

It must be pointed out that the Disability Insurance Trust Fund only pays benefits to disabled workers and their dependents. The benefits payable to "disabled surviving spouses" and "disabled surviving children" are paid from the Old-Age and Survivors Insurance Trust Fund. The 1980 amendments provided for the review and assessment of eligibility every three years with the exception of cases of permanent disability. This policy generated a great deal of controversy and litigation, and resulted in the Disability Reform Act of 1984.

3. DI EVALUATION

There is a stepped sequential approach to disability determinations. 20 C.F.R. § 404.1520 (20 C.F.R. § 416.920 for supplemental security income disability determinations). The claimant must initially demonstrate physical and/or mental impairments that are severe and meet the duration requirements. There is a five-step evaluation that asks and answers certain key questions. Favorable disability determinations for claimants can be made at steps three and five. (1) Is the claimant working in a substantial gainful activity; if so, then no disability will be found regardless of medical condition or age, education and work experience. (2) Does the claimant have a severe impairment; if there is no impairment or combination of impairments that significantly limit physical or mental ability, then no disability will be found. If a severe impairment(s) does exist, then the following question is necessary. (3) Does the claimant's impairment or impairments meet or equal the "listings," contained in 20 C.F.R. Part 404, Subpart P, Appendix 1, containing specific medical criteria; if so, then a finding of disability will be made without considering age, education and work experience. (4) If a claimant does not meet the "listings," then inquiry is made whether the claimant's impairment(s) prevents the claimant from performing past relevant work. A review of residual functional capacity and the physical and mental demands of past work are evaluated at this point. If the claimant is found able to perform past relevant work, then a finding of no disability will be made. (5) If the claimant cannot perform past relevant work because of severe impairment(s), then the burden shifts to the agency to prove the claimant capable of performing other gainful employment. The question of residual functional capacity to perform other work is therefore evaluated, considering the age, education and past work experience of the claimant. At this point, vocational-expert testimony or Medical–Vocational Guidelines contained in 20 C.F.R. Part 404, Subpart P, Appendix 2 (commonly known as the "Grids") may be used to aid in the ultimate determination of disability. See Bowen v. Yuckert (1987) ("severity regulation" upheld); Heckler v. Campbell (1983) (medical-vocational guidelines are valid).

It should be noted that a constitutional tort challenge to the continuing disability review program was made in Schweiker v. Chilicky (1988), but the Court rejected the cause of action by a narrow margin.

D. MEDICARE—HOSPITAL INSURANCE (HI) AND SUPPLEMENTARY MEDICAL INSURANCE (SMI)

Certain disabled and aged persons are entitled to the benefits of a national health insurance program called Medicare. Most persons over 65 are eligible automatically; if not eligible, coverage can be purchased for an annual premium. There are two basic medicare programs: (1) Part A, Hospital Insurance (HI), which is fundamentally financed through special payroll taxes similar to FICA taxes, and which are held in the Hospital Insurance Trust Fund; and (2) Part B, Supplementary Medical Insurance (SMI), which is fundamentally financed through individual medical premiums and general revenues of the United States, and which are held in the Supplementary Medical Insurance Trust Fund. Both Part A and Part B benefit programs contain cost-sharing measures, usually in the form of coinsurance and deductibles. The Department of Health and Human Services administers both programs. Part A (HI) payments are generally tied to "benefit periods." If a patient has not been hospitalized for 60 consecutive days, a benefit period is available; there are no limits on the number of benefit periods that patients can have during their lifetime. Each benefit period under Part A pays for: (1) inpatient hospital care (subject to 90 days of coverage and other limitations); (2) extended care services up to 150 days during any calendar year; (3) home health services; and (4) in lieu of certain other benefits, hospice care, subject to limitation periods. Part B (SMI) was designed as a voluntary program that essentially pays 80% of reasonable charges for doctors, osteopaths, chiropractors, psychiatrists, independent therapists, and most medical, outpatient, and laboratory services that Part A does not cover. The elderly and disabled pay only portions of program premiums and the difference is paid by the federal government from general revenues.

Congress passed the Medicare Catastrophic Coverage Act of 1988 to aid the elderly, by expanding the benefits contained in the HI and SMI programs. The basic features expanded HI or Part A benefits by abolishing most of the time limits and cost-sharing requirements contained in the old program. The "spell of illness" concept was also abolished, thus, inpatient hospital services could be allowed for an unlimited number of days per year. Nursing home services, home health services and hospice care would also be significantly expanded. It should be noted that coverage was not provided for long-term nursing home care. For Part B benefits, the Act placed a cap on the amount of cost-sharing charges an individual must pay per year.

Financing of the new provisions was accomplished by increased income taxes for the elderly (program beneficiaries), called "supplemental premiums" for Part A benefits. Increased premiums, called "flat premiums" were to be charged for Part B benefits. Political controversy arose concerning the new catastrophic coverage program, and Congress voted to repeal it in 1989.

E. SUPPLEMENTAL SECURITY INCOME (SSI)

The Supplemental Security Income (SSI) program provides financial assistance to U.S. citizens and lawfully admitted aliens who meet income and resource criteria. They must be aged, blind, or disabled. The SSI program provides a "floor of income" for these persons, and it is financed by general tax revenues. SSI benefits are paid monthly to persons who are: (1) age 65 or older; or

(2) blind; or (3) disabled. These persons must be U.S. citizens or lawful residents of the 50 states, the District of Columbia or the Northern Mariana Islands. "Federal Benefit Rates" (FBR) help determine the eligibility of individuals and couples. These rates are increased periodically and the FBR is employed on a per month basis in order to compare the income and resource criteria in an effort to determine eligibility. The periodic redetermination of eligibility is required for all recipients. The receipt of Social Security insurance benefits does not necessarily disqualify persons from receiving SSI benefits, but Social Security insurance benefits are included in the income determinations that must be made before SSI benefits can be paid.

F. PROCEDURE

The claims procedure for most Social Security benefits under retirement, survivors, disability, medicare insurance programs and under the supplemental security income program, is initiated on special forms provided by the Social Security Administration. These claim forms are usually filed with a local Social Security office which makes an initial determination of eligibility. If there is a dispute, the claimant or the claimant's representative must request a reconsideration of the initial decision. A claimant who is dissatisfied with a reconsideration decision is entitled to a hearing before an administrative law judge. The adminis-

CHAPTER 17

FEDERAL AND STATE ANTI-DISCRIMINATION LAWS IN GENERAL

A. BACKGROUND AND SCOPE

Federal and state laws provide workers with significant safeguards against discrimination in the workplace. The First, Fifth, Thirteenth, and Fourteenth Amendments to the U.S. Constitution, together with the Commerce Clause, form the foundation for most federal anti-discrimination measures.

Comprehensive and effective legislative and judicial efforts began only in the 1960's, most notably with the enactment of Title VII of the Civil Rights Act of 1964, 42 U.S.C.A. § 2000e et seq. Title VII is easily the most far-reaching of the federal statutory prohibitions against employment discrimination. As will be discussed in detail in Chapter 18, that statute constructs a comprehensive administrative and judicial framework to deter and provide compensation for discrimination on grounds of gender and religion as well as race and national origin. Further, it condemns discrimination through the whole spectrum of the employment relationship, touching all "terms and conditions" of employment from hire to termination.

In the same decade judges revitalized post-Civil War Congressional legislation, Congress passed other important anti-discrimination laws, and new Presidential Executive Orders broadly prohibited discrimination by the U.S. government and federal contractors. During much of the 1970's, too, the Supreme Court expansively construed the protections of Title VII and fashioned anti-discrimination remedies from the U.S. Constitution and other federal statutes. But apart from some permissive affirmative action decisions, the 1980's has been an era of retrenchment and, most recently, retreat from this vigorous enforcement orientation. The decade began with such decisions as Texas Dept. of Community Affairs v. Burdine (1981) and General Telephone Company of the Southwest v. Falcon (1982), which, respectively, increased the difficulty of proving intentional discriminatory treatment and impeded employees' efforts to assert their grievances as a class. The decade closed with a decision that impairs a Title VII plaintiff's capacity to prove unlawful discrimination without proving prohibited motive. Wards Cove Packing Co. v. Atonio (1989). Two others (Patterson v. McLean Credit Union (1989) and Jett v. Dallas Independent School District (1989)) eviscerate one of the reconstruction-era statutes, 42 U.S.C.A. § 1981, just two decades after the Court began to revive it.

Several bills have been introduced in Congress to overturn one or more of these recent decisions. If recent history is any guide, at least some of the proposed legislation will likely be enacted. The Civil Rights Attorney's Fees Awards Act, a 1976 amendment to 42 U.S.C.A. § 1988, overruled the Court's limitations on fee awards in civil rights cases announced in Alyeska Pipeline Service Co. v. Wilderness Society (1975). In 1978, Congress overrode Supreme Court decisions that had narrowed statutory protections against sex and age discrimination. See, respectively, The Pregnancy Discrimination Act, overruling General Electric Co. v. Gilbert (1976), and the 1978 amendment to the Age Discrimination in Employment Act of 1967, 29 U.S.C.A. § 621 et seq. (ADEA), overruling United Air Lines, Inc. v. McMann (1977). And in 1988, Congress, overriding a presidential veto, overturned a decision restricting a statutory ban on sex discrimination by educational institutions. Civil Rights Restoration Act, overruling Grove City College v. Bell (1984).

B. FEDERAL LAWS

In addition to Title VII and the Reconstruction Civil Rights Acts, federal laws, rules, regulations, and remedies affecting employment discrimination include: the Equal Pay Act of 1963 ("EPA"); the Age Discrimination in Employment Act of 1967 ("ADEA"); the Civil Rights Act of 1964, Title VI; Title IX, Education Amendments of 1972; the Civil Rights Attorney's Fees Awards Act of 1976; the Rehabilitation Act of 1973; the Immigration Reform and Control Act of 1986; the Civil Rights Act of 1968, Title I; the Intergovernmental Personnel Act of 1970; the Vietnam Era Veterans Readjustment Act of 1974; the Age Discrimination Act of 1975; the Foreign Boycott Laws (Export Administration Act of 1969, as amended); the Labor Management Relations Act; Executive Order 11246 (Government Contractors and Subcontractors); Executive Order 11141 (Age Discrimination); and the U.S. Constitution and its amendments as interpreted by the Supreme Court. Summaries of the more important federal anti-discrimination laws are provided in Chapters 18 and 19. For a fuller treatment of these protections, see M. Player, Employment Discrimination Law (West 1988).

C. STATE LAWS

Most of the states have enacted anti-discrimination statutes that supplement the remedies available under federal law. The federal laws, standards, and programs do not generally preempt these state efforts unless the state laws are in conflict. For the most part, state laws prohibiting employment discrimination are called "Fair Employment Practices" laws. But Michigan has a Civil Rights Act; California has a Fair Employment and Housing Act; New Mexico has a Human Rights Act; and New York's employment discrimination prohibitions are part of its Executive Law.

The state legislation usually forbids discrimination based upon race, creed, color, ancestry, national origin, sex, age, or marital status. Still, there is considerable variation in prohibited grounds. Alabama, for example, has no fair employment practices laws, while California has enacted laws specifically covering race, age, sex, national origin, religious, arrest record, and blindness discrimination. California also regulates equal pay, pregnancy benefits, and employee records, as well as the employment uses of lie detector tests and voice stress analyzers.

The states, in reliance upon their police powers, could enact a broader range of anti-discrimination measures than the federal government. But many states lack the resources and political support necessary to ensure the effective administration and enforcement of anti-discrimination laws. Federal law will therefore probably remain the chief bulwark against employment discrimination and bias.

CHAPTER 18

TITLE VII OF THE 1964 CIVIL RIGHTS ACT

A. SCOPE AND COVERAGE

As observed in Chapter 17, Title VII of the Civil Rights Act of 1964 is the most broadly based federal statute prohibiting discrimination in employment. Title VII's prohibition on race, sex, religious and national origin discrimination sets it apart from single-focus statutes that ban only sex discrimination (EPA and Title IX), age discrimination (ADEA), or handicap discrimination (the Rehabilitation Act of 1973). Further, its sweeping embrace of all terms, conditions and privileges of employment distinguishes Title VII from statutes, like EPA, that prohibit employment discrimination solely with respect to one term or condition of employment, such as pay.

Title VII applies to employers, employment agencies, apprenticeship programs and labor organizations whose activities affect interstate commerce. Employers are exempt if they have fewer than 15 employees for each working day in 20 or more calendar weeks in the current or prior calendar year. Private membership clubs exempt from taxation under the Internal Revenue Code are also exempt from Title VII. Indian tribes, members of

194

Congress, and employers with respect to the employment of aliens outside the United States are also excluded from the "employer" definition.

State and local governments are considered employers, and the constitutionality of Title VII as applied to those defendants is settled. Even before *Garcia v. San Antonio Metro Authority* determined that the Tenth Amendment does not supersede Congress' Commerce Clause authority to regulate the wages and hours of state employees, the Supreme Court had held in Fitzpatrick v. Bitzer (1976), that Title VII's grounding in Section 5 of the Fourteenth Amendment empowered Congress to override the Eleventh Amendment barrier to state liability in federal court.

Religious organizations are also viewed as Title VII employers, but they are specifically permitted to make certain employment decisions on the basis of religion. Two related and somewhat overlapping provisions insulate employers from any liability for religious discrimination or demand no more than "reasonable accommodation" to employee religious beliefs.

Section 702 exempts a "religious corporation, association, educational institution, or society" from Title VII "with respect to the employment of individuals of a particular religion to perform work connected with the carrying on" of the institution's activities. Although this section has been construed to shield even the secular, non-profit activities of a genuinely religious institution, it has withstood challenge as an unconstitutional establishment of religion. Corporation of Presiding Bishop v. Amos (1987). On the other hand, Section 702 does not protect a religious institution from Title VII liability with respect to discrimination on some basis other than religion, for example, sex, race, or national origin. McClure v. Salvation Army (1972); EEOC v. Pacific Press Publ. Association (1982).

Educational institutions insufficiently "religious" to qualify for Section 702 exemption may nevertheless avoid liability for hiring discrimination under § 703(e)(2) if they are "in whole or in substantial part, owned, supported, controlled or managed by a particular religion." See Pime v. Loyola University (1986).

As used in Section 703(a)(1), the phrase "terms, conditions or privileges of employment" includes intangible as well as tangible job detriments. For example, if harassment by an authorized employer representative is sufficiently severe or pervasive to create an "abusive working environment," sexual and, almost assuredly, racial harassment are actionable under Title VII. Meritor Savings Bank v. Vinson (1986). The circuit courts are divided, however, on whether Title VII affords any remedy for proven harassment that precedes a lawful discharge. Contrast Huddleston v. Roger Dean Chevrolet, Inc. (1988) (approving nominal damages) with Swanson v. Elmhurst Chrysler Plymouth, Inc. (1989) (no nominal damages).

B. THE BASIC SUBSTANTIVE PROHIBITIONS: FOUR MODES OF PROOF

The most critical and frequently litigated questions under Title VII concern the theories on which liability may be predicated and the corresponding modes of proof.

The basic, deceptively simple substantive prohibitions of Title VII are contained in Section 703(a). Section 703(a)(1) declares it an "unlawful employment practice" for a covered employer

"to fail or refuse to hire or to discharge any individual, or otherwise to discriminate against any individual with respect to his compensation, terms, conditions or privileges of employment, because of such individual's race, color, religion, sex, or national origin."

Similarly, Section 703(a)(2) forbids limiting the employment "opportunities" of an applicant or incumbent employee on any of the same grounds. The case law controversy has centered on two related questions. First, what types of employer conduct constitute forbidden discrimination; second, what nexus must exist between prohibited employer conduct and harm to a plaintiff's employment status. Four modes of proof have been developed to address these issues.

1. INDIVIDUAL DISPARATE TREATMENT—"DIRECT" EVIDENCE

The most obvious way of showing an unlawful employment practice is to produce evidence of an epithet or slur uttered by an authorized agent of the employer, or of an employer policy framed squarely in terms of race, sex, religion, or national origin. Cases presenting such "direct," "express" or "facial" evidence are relative rarities now that employers are familiar with the requirements and penalties of the statute and consequently more apt to comply or better skilled in disguising noncompliance. Nevertheless, when produced, such evidence will without more ordinarily suffice to show that an adverse employment condition, or limitation on an employment opportunity, was imposed "because of" the plaintiff's protected group characteristic.

The only available employer defense if the plaintiff persuades the trier of fact of the existence of such a facially discriminatory policy or practice is evidence of a "bona fide occupational qualification," or BFOQ. Section 703(e)(1) relieves an employer of liability if it can establish that a classification or distinction based on sex, religion, or national origin—but not, it should be noted, race— is a "bona fide occupational qualification reasonably necessary to the normal operation of that particular business or enterprise . . .." ADEA contains a similarly worded BFOQ defense, and the Court has construed the corresponding provisions of the two statutes virtually identically.

The federal courts have given the BFOQ defense very limited application. BFOQ is treated as a typical affirmative defense, so that the employer bears the burdens of pleading, producing evidence, and persuasion. There are two basic elements. First, the job qualification or employee trait for which the employer's practice or policy screens must be closely related to the "essence" of the business. For example, the psychological reassurance or sexual titillation ostensibly afforded airline passengers by a requirement that flight attendants be female cannot justify the exclusion of males if the essence of the business is defined as safe transportation rather than maximum profit. See Diaz v. Pan American World Airways, Inc. (1971).

Second, even if an exclusion of members of a particular protected group is designed to further a critical element of the business, the employer's evidence must demonstrate that "all or substantially all" members of the excluded group would be unable adequately to perform key job functions. See Weeks v. Southern Bell Telephone and Telegraph Company (1969). This second requirement will eliminate most BFOQ defenses rooted in the assertion that only members of a particular gender have the strength or endurance required by the job. Alternatively, an employer may justify an express discrimination by proving that significant numbers of the excluded gender, religion or national origin lack the requisite job traits and it would be highly impracticable to determine by individualized testing which ones do. Western Air Lines v. Criswell (1985). In any event, the qualifications the employer relies upon must pertain to the particular position for which those qualifications are required. Trans World Airlines, Inc. v. Thurston (1985).

Given the stringency of the BFOQ defense, its principal remaining utility is in resisting claims of age discrimination, especially in cases where an employee's deteriorating physical capabilities correlate strongly with aging and would impair safe hands-on performance. See Usery v. Tamiami Trail Tours, Inc. (1976), cited with approval in *Criswell.* It is scarcely conceivable, moreover, that the BFOQ defense could ever justify a slur, as opposed to an employer policy. Nevertheless, in exceptionally exigent circumstances involving physical safety, the BFOQ defense may avail an employer even if it fails to demonstrate that almost all members of the excluded group are incapable of performing a critical aspect of an essential job. Dothard v. Rawlinson (1977) (upholding exclusion of women from contact positions as guards in unusually dangerous maximum security prisons). Lower courts have also upheld relaxed applications of the defense to allay employer concerns about customer privacy, Fesel v. Masonic Home of Delaware, Inc. (1978) (nursing home attendants), and EEOC guidelines recognize an exception to further employer interests in authenticity. See 29 C.F.R. § 1604.2 (1979) (actors and actresses).

2. INDIVIDUAL DISPARATE TREATMENT—INFERENTIAL PROOF

Because direct evidence of intent is so uncommon, courts have recognized alternative ways of establishing unlawful discrimination. The inferential method of proving "individual disparate treatment" owes its origin to McDonnell Douglas Corp. v. Green (1973), and was later elaborated in several other Supreme Court decisions culminating in *Burdine.*

The plaintiff makes a *McDonnell Douglas prima facie* case, and thereby survives a Federal Rule of Civil Procedure 41(b) involuntary dismissal motion at the close of her case in chief, by offering evidence that she (1) belongs to a protected group; (2) applied for or continued to desire the position in question; (3) met minimum uniform qualifications to receive or retain the position; and (4) was rejected. The first of these elements is *pro forma,* since anyone, even a white male, can claim protected group status by contrasting himself in racial, religious, national origin, or gender terms to the group he claims was preferred. See *McDonald,* supra. A final element, sometimes relaxed or waived by lower courts, is evidence that the employer, after rejecting the plaintiff, continued to seek applicants with her general qualifications or selected a person from outside her protected group. See *Patterson,* supra.

If a plaintiff survives involuntary dismissal, the defendant can prevent the resulting inference of discrimination from becoming conclusive by offering evidence that it had one or more "legitimate, nondiscriminatory reasons" for an employment decision. Although the opinion in *McDonnell Douglas* suggested that the employer need only "articulate" that reason, the Court, definitively determined in *Burdine* that the employer's burden, while not onerous, may be discharged only through evidence rather than argument. But the Court insisted that the burden is one of production only and that the burden of persuasion for intentional discrimination resides with the plaintiff throughout.

Finally, even if a court should conclude that a defendant's asserted reason is nondiscriminatory and "legitimate," a plaintiff can still prevail by rebutting the bona fides of defendant's evidence. To do this the plaintiff must persuade the court that the defendant's purported legitimate reason is a smokescreen or "pretext" for intentional discrimination. The plaintiff may make this showing in either of two generic ways: by demonstrating that the employer, in reaching its decision, explicitly relied on plaintiff's protected group status, rather than on its proffered legitimate reason; or, less directly, by convincing the court that the proffered reason is an implausible explanation for the challenged decision. United States Postal Service Bd. of Governors v. Aikens (1983). There are no categorical limitations on the types of evidence that may establish pretext. For example, a plaintiff is not required to demonstrate that she was better qualified than a successful applicant, but may alternatively or additionally present evidence that the employer had previously practiced unlawful discrimination against her or her group. See *McDonnell Douglas; Patterson* (1989).

The preliminary question whether plaintiff established a *prima facie* case loses all significance once a Rule 41(b) motion is denied and defendant presents its proof. After both sides rest, the trier of fact must evaluate all admitted evidence, including the *prima facie* evidence from plaintiff's case in chief, to decide if plaintiff has carried the ultimate burden of demonstrating intentional discrimination. *Aikens.* The trial judge's ultimate determination about discriminatory intent—whether shown through direct or indirect evidence—is one of fact and may therefore be overturned on appeal only if "clearly erroneous." Anderson v. City of Bessemer (1985); Federal Rule of Civil Procedure 52(a).

The classic evidentiary structure erected by *McDonnell Douglas* and *Burdine,* while furnishing a workable matrix for inferentially finding intentional discrimination, is also often unrealistic because it assumes that an employer's motivation was grounded *entirely* on a prohibited reason *or* a legitimate one. In fact, employers commonly advance more than one asserted legitimate reason for a challenged employment decision, and courts often conclude that an employer relied on one or more of those reasons as well as a reason condemned by Title VII.

The Supreme Court has recently come to grips with the reality of "mixed motive." In Price Waterhouse v. Hopkins (1989), a plurality concluded that once a plaintiff establishes, through the *McDonnell Douglas/Burdine* formulation, that a prohibited reason played "a motivating part" in an employer's decision, the defendant may avoid liability only by proving, as an affirmative defense, that it would have reached the same decision even absent the prohibited reason. But two concurring justices, whose votes were necessary to the judgment, insisted that this employer persuasion burden arises only if the *Burdine* foundation evidence establishes that the unlawful motive was a "substantial factor" in the adverse employment decision. (Opinions of White and O'Connor, concurring).

3. SYSTEMIC DISPARATE TREATMENT

Intentional discriminatory treatment may also be demonstrated in the aggregate. "Systemic disparate treatment" proof depends primarily upon statistical evidence of gross disparities between the actual and expected representation of the plaintiff's group in one or more levels of an employer's workforce. According to the underlying theory, an employer that does not routinely discriminate should over time achieve within its employee complement an incidence of protected group representation not significantly less than the group's representation in an available pool of qualified applicants. International Brotherhood of Teamsters v. United States (1977).

A continuing difficulty in applying this theory has been to define the pool of minority applicants or employees from which the expected percentage of minority representation should be calculated. While protected group representation in a recruiting-zone population or local workforce may suffice where the jobs in question are largely unskilled, *id.*, the fair measurement of disparities in highly skilled positions demands refinement for availability, interest, and, above all, qualifications. Hazelwood School District v. United States (1977); cf. *Wards Cove Packing Co. v. Atonia,* supra.

Whatever comparison is used, plaintiff must establish a statistically significant "gross" disparity between observed and expected protected group representation. The magnitude of this disparity must be sufficient to show that discrimination was an employer's routine operating procedure and that relief should be granted to the entire underrepresented class. This generally requires expert testimony concerning the statistical technique of binomial distribution and its key measure of "standard deviation." The Supreme Court has indicated that a disparity between expected and observed protected group representation of greater than minus "two or three" standard deviations will generally suffice as evidence of gross underrepresentation. *Hazelwood.*

A more sophisticated statistical technique, multiple regression analysis, will usually be required to establish the requisite disparity when variations in the particular term and condition of employment at issue—for example, compensation—are explainable by reference to a large number of factors. The Court has indicated, however, that a plaintiff's multiple regression analysis need not eliminate all potential nondiscriminatory explanations of disparity, only the most significant.   Bazemore v. Friday (1986).

The employer's principal defense in these cases is to present evidence that casts doubt on the logical, legal, or statistical probative value of plaintiff's evidence.   For example, an employer may avoid the force of evidence of disparity by showing infirmities in the presumed qualified availability pool; by demonstrating that a protected group's underrepresentation is attributable largely to hiring that took place before the employer became subject to Title VII; by disputing the very existence of a disparity with "applicant flow" statistics which establish that among actual applicants the employer hired at least as great a percentage of protected group members as of others; or by quarreling with the magnitude of a disparity or the statistical significance of the sample in which a disparity is found.   *Hazelwood.*

An employer unable to prevent a finding of gross underrepresentation may nevertheless justify by presenting a neutral explanation for the disparity.

This might be done, for example, by offering evidence that a neutral practice with disproportionate adverse impact accounts for an underrepresentation. This puts the employer in the odd position of becoming its own accuser, since such a practice may independently give rise to Title VII liability even without proof of discriminatory intent. See part 4. immediately following. In effect, the employer argues that one unlawful employment practice (a facially neutral test or experience requirement that disproportionately affects the protected group) explains another (the significant underrepresentation of the protected group in the job level for which the test or experience requirement screens). By undertaking this showing the employer may limit its liability to those members of the protected group who were personally affected by the neutral practice. In addition, the court may conclude that the neutral practice which accounts for an underrepresentation is itself justified under the standard pertaining to that mode of proof.

Courts that have permitted employers to defend a gross underrepresentation by pointing to such a neutral practice have required them to bear the burden of persuasion on the neutral practice justification. See Griffin v. Carlin (1985); Segar v. Smith (1984). It is unclear whether these decisions will survive a recent ruling of the Supreme Court that reduces the employer's burden in defending neutral practices to one of production only. (See part 4., immediately following.)

Given the ease of establishing a prima facie case of individual disparate treatment, and the expense and difficulty of gathering and analyzing the data necessary to establish a case of systemic disparate treatment, solo plaintiffs usually proceed with "direct" or *McDonnell Douglas/Burdine* evidence alone. Nevertheless, there is a complementary relationship between evidence of individual and systemic disparate treatment. An individual plaintiff may fortify "direct" evidence, or evidence that raises the *McDonnell Douglas/Burdine* inference of intentionally discriminatory treatment, with evidence of statistically discriminatory patterns. Similarly, a plaintiff class may bolster a case of systemic discriminatory treatment with anecdotal evidence of discrimination against its individual members.

Systemic treatment trials are conducted in distinct liability and remedial phases. First, from statistics alone or a combination of statistical and anecdotal evidence, the court determines whether the employer has discriminated against the plaintiff's protected group as a whole. If so, individual members of the plaintiff class may then attempt to establish their eligibility for relief. Evidence of gross, unexplained statistically significant disparities between the expected and observed numbers of protected group members gives rise to a presumption that each class member who unsuccessfully sought hire, promotion, or retention during the established liability period was rejected because of his or her protected group status.

The employer may rebut this presumption and avoid liability to individual "applicant" class members by persuading a court that they were not in fact victims of discrimination. For example, the employer may demonstrate that there were no vacancies in the pertinent position at the time a particular class member applied or that a successful applicant was better qualified. Franks v. Bowman Transportation Co. (1976). Even class members who did not apply for a position during the proven liability period may sometimes receive individual relief; but they carry the heavy burden of persuading that it was futile for them to apply because of an employer's notorious and widespread practice of excluding their protected group. *Teamsters.*

4. NEUTRAL PRACTICES WITH DISPROPORTIONATE ADVERSE IMPACT

The federal courts have at times struggled to clarify the evidentiary frameworks for proving individual and systemic disparate treatment, but there has been no real question that such intentional conduct constitutes unlawful discrimination "because of" a protected group characteristic. By contrast, neutral employer practices that in operation fall with disproportionate adverse impact on the plaintiff's protected group have proven far more troublesome.

Initially a strong judicial consensus emerged that Congress intended to eradicate such practices on much the same terms as intentional acts of discrimination. Writing for a unanimous Court in Griggs v. Duke Power Co. (1971), Chief Justice Burger wrote that practices fair in form but discriminatory in effect may violate Title VII even though the employer's motivation in adopting the practice is neutral or benign. The early cases developing this theory considered the lawfulness of "objective" employer practices such as educational requirements or standardized aptitude or psychological tests, see *Griggs* and Albemarle Paper Co. v. Moody (1975); height and weight requirements, *Dothard;* or rules prohibiting the employment of drug addicts, New York City Transit Authority v. Beazer (1979); arrestees, Gregory v. Litton Systems, Inc. (1972); convicts, Green v. Missouri Pacific R.R. Co. (1975); or debtors whose wages have been frequently garnished, Wallace v. Debron Corp. (1974). Occasionally, however, disproportionate adverse impact analysis was applied to a "subjective" employer process such as the unstructured evaluation of black employees by white foremen, Rowe v. General Motors Corp. (1972). The Supreme Court recently approved the use of impact analysis to scrutinize these subjective promotion decisions. Watson v. Fort Worth Bank and Trust (1988).

Measuring whether an employer's neutral practice has a "disproportionate" adverse impact on a protected group is generally simpler than determining whether a protected group is so grossly underrepresented in a workforce as to suggest systemic disparate treatment. Courts often adopt as a measure of disproportion the "eighty percent rule" from EEOC's Uniform Guidelines on Employee Selection Procedures. These provide that a protected group's selection rate which is less than 80 percent of the rate for the group with the greatest success will be regarded by the Commission for enforcement purposes as evidence of adverse impact. 29 C.F.R. § 1607.4. See Connecticut v. Teal (1982); *Watson.*

In *Teal,* the Supreme Court clarified that a single component of an employer's multi-stage selection process may have unlawfully discriminatory adverse impact on the particular protected group members it screens out even if the protected group as a whole fares better than a non-minority group in the overall process. The Court explained that the "principal focus" of Title VII is "the protection of the individual employee," rather than of minority groups, and that Section 703(a)(2) is concerned not just with the "bottom line" of jobs or promotions, but also with any "limitations" or "classifications" that deprive individuals of opportunities to advance. In sum, a racially balanced workforce does not immunize an employer from liability for a specific act of discrimination, whether intentional or neutral.

Changes in the Court's commitment to the neutral practice theory were visible as early as *Griggs* itself, when the Court wrestled with inventing a judge-made defense to the judge-made *prima facie*

case. If balanced "bottom line" hiring or deploy-
ment of the work force does not serve as a defense
to a practice's disproportionate adverse impact,
what does? The Court wrote in *Griggs* that an
employer could avoid liability if the challenged
requirement were related to the job in question.
But elsewhere in *Griggs* and in later cases, the
Court confusingly described the defense, in increasing order of rigor, as requiring evidence that the
employer practice be "demonstrably" or "manifest-
ly" related to the job in question (*Griggs*); that the
practice be a matter of business "necessity" (id.);
and that the necessity relate to "safe and efficient
job performance." *Dothard.*

These variable formulations generated two
thorny interpretative problems. First, what is the
content of the defense; second, which party bears
the burden of persuasion? On the first question,
the suggestion that an employer must show a neutral practice to be necessary or essential to its
business, rather than just desirable, was inconsistent with a third phase of the "neutral practice"
case, elaborated in *Albemarle.* There the Court
explained that even if an employer (by whatever
standard) justifies the adverse effect of its practice
by reference to a business reason, the plaintiff may
still prevail by demonstrating that the employer
could have met its needs with a "less discriminatory alternative." But if the plaintiff does show such
an alternative, it necessarily demonstrates that the
employer's chosen practice was not a matter of

strict necessity. By the same token, if the employer's own, second-stage evidence must prove business "necessity," the third stage becomes superfluous. On the quantum of evidence question, the Court sometimes suggested that the employer defense, whatever its content, is an affirmative one on which the employer bears the burden of persuasion. See, e.g., *Dothard.*

The Court has recently resolved both these questions—the nature of the employer defense and the allocation of the burden of persuasion—so as to undermine severely the *Griggs* neutral practice mode of proof. Ironically, this resolution began with *Watson,* the case which extended the application of disproportionate adverse impact analysis to subjective employer practices. A plurality there also wrote that an employer may defend adverse impact merely by producing evidence that its practice is "based on legitimate business reasons." As the dissent complained, this description renders the employer defense to a neutral practice case virtually indistinguishable from the easily established "legitimate non-discrimination reason" defense to a *McDonnell Douglas/Burdine* case of individual disparate treatment.

This position of the *Watson* plurality has now commanded a majority in *Wards Cove Packing,* which also apparently extends the holding to cases that challenge the more traditional "objective" neutral practices. A neutral practice will now survive Title VII challenge if it simply "serves, in a significant way, the legitimate employment goals of the employer." The practice need not be " 'essential' or 'indispensable' to the employer's business. . . ." The *Wards Cove* opinion is equally explicit that the employer carries only the burden of producing evidence, the burden of persuasion remaining with the plaintiff.

Finally, as though to confirm the *Watson* dissent's view that the Court was improperly equating the disproportionate adverse impact case with a case of individual disparate treatment, the *Wards Cove* majority writes that a plaintiff who rebuts by showing a lesser discriminatory alternative a la *Albemarle* thereby demonstrates that the employer's chosen practice was merely a "pretext" for discrimination. In this way the Court suggests that a method of demonstrating unlawful discrimination which *Griggs* developed precisely for cases where discriminatory intent could *not* be shown turns, in the end, on employer intent.

Removing any doubt about its hostility to the neutral practice case, the Court then cautions the judiciary against too readily adopting a plaintiff's proposed lesser discriminatory alternative. The alternative must be "equally effective" as the employer's chosen practice, and such factors as "cost or other burdens" are "relevant in determining whether they would be equally as effective. . . ." Moreover, if the Court's use of "pretext" terminology implies a state of mind element, a plaintiff may be able to overcome an employer's justification for an adversely impacting neutral practice only by proving that the employer selected the greater discriminatory alternative *for the purpose* of harming the protected group.

C. RELIGIOUS DISCRIMINATION

Employers not qualifying for immunity from liability for religious discrimination under § 702 or § 703(e)(2) (see A., above) are subject to a special affirmative obligation somewhat distinct from the normal duty not to discriminate. Section 703(a)(1) forbids an employer from discriminating because of "religion"; and Section 701(j), added in 1972, in turn defines "religion" to include "all aspects of religious observance and practice as well as belief, unless an employer demonstrates that he is unable to reasonably accommodate to an employee's . . . religious observance or practice without undue hardship. . . ."

The prima facie case consists of evidence that an employer practice conflicts with the employee's exercise of a bona fide religious belief. See Ansonia Board of Education v. Philbrook (1986). But the resulting employer obligation to reasonably accommodate the religious practice has been eased by the Supreme Court's conclusion that an accommodation works "undue hardship" whenever it results "in more than a *de minimis* cost." Trans World Airlines, Inc. v. Hardison (1977). In *Ansonia,* the Court suggested that if an employer's schedule conflicts with the plaintiff's religious need to refrain from secular employment on holy days, the employer would satisfy its accommodation obligation by offering the employee additional unpaid leave. The employer would violate Title VII only if it overtly discriminated by providing paid leave for all non-religious reasons. Largely because the duty to accommodate has thus been substantially diluted by judicial construction, Section 701(j) has survived establishment clause challenge. Protos v. Volkswagen of America, Inc. (1986).

D. PARTICULAR PRACTICES TREATED SPECIALLY UNDER TITLE VII

1. WAGE DISCRIMINATION AUTHORIZED OR NOT PROHIBITED BY EPA

As discussed in Chapter 19, B, the EPA only prohibits sex-based pay differentials for "equal work," jobs involving substantially the same skill, effort, and responsibility. EPA also contains four listed affirmative defenses to a claim of unequal pay for equal work.

The "Bennett Amendment" to Title VII, the last sentence of Section 703(h), attempts to harmonize the two statutes' treatment of sex-based wage discrimination. It provides that a successful affirmative defense to an EPA claim does double duty as a defense to liability under Title VII. Lower courts are divided, however, on the converse question, whether EPA liability automatically means Title

VII liability as well. Compare EEOC v. White and Son Enterprises (1989) and Kouba v. Allstate Insurance Co. (1982) (automatic Title VII liability) with Fallon v. Illinois (1989) (Title VII liability standard is higher, since plaintiff bears burden of persuasion throughout).

On the other hand, intentional sex-based wage discrimination violates Title VII even if no member of the opposite sex performs "equal work" within the meaning of EPA. County of Washington v. Gunther (1981). But the related "comparable worth" theory has generally been rejected. An employer does not violate Title VII merely by observing market norms that result in its paying more for male-dominated jobs than for female-dominated jobs that have similar value to the employer but would not be considered "equal" under EPA. See American Federation of State, County and Municipal Employees v. State of Washington (1985).

2. RESTRICTIONS RELATIVE TO PREGNANCY AND ABORTION

Since only women become pregnant, it might seem that a distinction on the basis of pregnancy would be tantamount to express or facial discrimination because of gender. The Supreme Court held otherwise, however, in General Electric Co. v. Gilbert (1976), when it concluded that a pregnancy exclusion from an otherwise comprehensive disability insurance plan distinguished on a gender-neutral basis between pregnant women and non-pregnant persons. Congress legislatively overruled this result with the Pregnancy Discrimination Act of 1978, or PDA, which added to Title VII a new § 701(k). This amendment defines the sex discrimination prohibited by § 703 to include distinctions "on the basis of pregnancy, childbirth or related medical conditions . . .."

The PDA does not require an employer to provide leaves or benefits for pregnancy that it does not provide to male employees for comparable conditions; the amendment's motivating principle is nondiscrimination, not positive protection. But neither does the Act preempt state legislation that affirmatively requires employers to offer such benefits to pregnancy-disabled employees. California Federal Savings & Loan Association v. Guerra (1987). Similarly, an employer is not forbidden from offering greater health insurance benefits for pregnancy than for other medical conditions as a matter of contract. Aubrey v. Aetna Life Ins. Co. (1989).

In addition, although the legislative history of PDA focused on the health and medical requirements of female employees, a majority of the Court has held that the amendment also prohibits employer-sponsored health insurance provisions that exclude spousal pregnancies and thereby offer male employees inferior total coverage than their female co-workers. Newport News Shipbuilding and Dry Dock Co. v. EEOC (1983). PDA also proscribes discriminating against an employee for undergoing an abortion, either by terminating her or, apparently, denying her sick leave available for other medical disabilities. But PDA explicitly relieves employers from subsidizing abortions through health insurance benefits, except in cases of "medical complications" or "where the life of the mother would be endangered if the fetus were carried to term."

3. FETAL VULNERABILITY RULES

Since the PDA effectively equates pregnancy discrimination with discrimination "because of sex," a violation of its terms is ordinarily treated as express or facial gender discrimination, defensible only by establishing a BFOQ. Policies designed to protect employees' fetuses or offspring through rules that discriminate on the basis of pregnancy are unlikely to pass muster under traditional BFOQ standards, since offspring protection would not normally be essential to the operation of an employer's business. In order to uphold these rules as a matter of public policy, therefore, courts have sometimes modified the BFOQ requirements or permitted the policies to be defended as though they were neutral practices. See International Union, UAW v. Johnson Controls (1989); cf. Hayes v. Shelby Memorial Hospital (1984) (invalidating employer policy despite relaxed standards). EEOC now also takes the position that even though the discrimination resulting from fetal protection policies is expressly gender based, employers should not be restricted to the BFOQ defense but should be permitted to justify those policies under the somewhat less stringent standard of "business necessity." EEOC Policy Statement on Reproductive and Fetal Hazards Under Title VII (October 3, 1988).

4. GENDER–BASED CALCULATION OF PENSION CONTRIBUTIONS AND BENEFITS

Relying on the *Gilbert* reasoning, employers have contended that pension plan provisions requiring greater contributions by female employees or awarding them lesser benefits upon retirement are geared to the neutral factor of greater average female longevity rather than to gender. The Supreme Court, however, has found gender an inadequate proxy for greater female longevity, noting that a significant part of the differential might be explainable by other factors, such as the heavier incidence of smoking among men. In any event, again stressing Title VII's focus on the individual, the Court expressed concern that even an accurate generalization about greater female longevity obscures the fact that many women will live less long than many men, and each such woman is entitled to benefits calculated without regard to gender-based averages.

Accordingly, the Court has invalidated plans that require women to make greater contributions or that award them lesser benefits. See, respectively, Los Angeles Department of Water & Power v. Manhart (1978); Arizona Governing Committee v. Norris (1983). These decisions have revolutionized the employer-sponsored pension industry, forcing many insurers to offer plans featuring gender-neutral annuity assumptions.

5. SENIORITY SYSTEMS

Two unarguably neutral practices are singled out for special treatment by the text of Title VII. Section 703(h) provides that "notwithstanding any other provision" of Title VII, an employer does not commit an unlawful employment practice by imposing different terms or conditions of employment pursuant to a bona fide seniority or merit system. The employer is immune from liability even if the effect or impact of these systems falls more heavily on the plaintiff's protected group. Judicial construction of these provisions, however, has afforded far greater protection for seniority and merit systems than for professionally developed ability tests.

Unless the plaintiff is able to prove that a seniority system was initially adopted or maintained with a specific discriminatory purpose, and is thus not "bona fide," a seniority system cannot be the basis of employer liability. *Teamsters.* A bona fide seniority system is lawful, whether adopted before or after the enactment of Title VII, even if it perpetuates the effects of independently unlawful employer conduct—for example, hiring or promotion discrimination. American Tobacco Co. v. Patterson (1982); United Air Lines, Inc. v. Evans (1977). Further, the Court has broadly interpreted the kinds of collectively bargained arrangements that qualify as "seniority systems" entitled to the special protection of § 703(h). For example, a requirement that an employee work for a specified time before entering the permanent employee seniority ladder has itself been held to constitute part of a protected seniority system. California Brewers Association v. Bryant (1980).

The intensity of the Supreme Court's commitment to insulate seniority systems from injunction was most recently evidenced by a decision that the limitations period for a claim attacking the bona fides of a seniority system runs from the date a system is adopted, even if the plaintiff could not then have anticipated harm from the system or for that matter first became employed thereafter. Lorance v. AT & T Technologies, Inc. (1989). And the strong presumption that a system covered by § 703(h) is bona fide is buttressed by treating trial court determinations about the adopters' intent as unmixed findings of fact, reversible under Federal Rule of Civil Procedure 52(a) only if "clearly erroneous." Pullman–Standard v. Swint (1982).

6. PROFESSIONALLY DEVELOPED ABILITY TESTS

Section 703(h) also permits employers to act upon the results of a "professionally developed ability test." But in sharp contrast to the great deference shown seniority systems, the judicial protection accorded these tests has been inconsistent and pallid. In a sense it has even been *more* difficult for an employer to defend the adverse impact of a paper-and-pencil test than to avoid liability for other neutral practices; and this may be even truer today since the general defense to such practices has been so greatly relaxed by *Wards Cove.*

Soon after Title VII became effective, the EEOC issued "guidelines" on employee selection procedures that require employers to conduct highly technical and demanding "validation" studies of ability tests to demonstrate that they reliably pinpoint desired employee traits essential to a particular job. The Supreme Court's deferral to those guidelines in *Albemarle* required employers to incur considerable expense in validation efforts before they could safely hinge employment decisions on the results of tests having significant differential adverse impact.

Lower courts have since somewhat eased validation requirements, holding that employers need not slavishly adhere to the difficult and complex EEOC guidelines. Instead employers may defend more generally with evidence that tests are "predictive of or significantly correlated with important elements of work behavior . . . relevant to the job . . . for which candidates are being evaluated." Contreras v. City of Los Angeles (1981). Nevertheless, even this version of the validation defense places a considerably greater burden on an employer than merely producing evidence that "a challenged practice serves, in a significant way," one of many possible "legitimate employment goals." *Wards Cove.* This is the somewhat ironic result of a provision in § 703(h) which on its face appears designed to make it easier for employers to act on the result of professionally developed ability tests.

E. RETALIATION

To protect employees who seek to vindicate their rights under Section 703, a separate provision, Section 704(a), broadly prohibits retaliation. Two basic species of conduct are protected: 1) participation in any administrative or judicial investigation, proceeding, or hearing to enforce Title VII rights; and 2) less formal opposition in good faith to practices that an employee reasonably believes to be prohibited by the Act. Once conduct is characterized as protected, the prima facie case is straightforward. The plaintiff must produce evidence that (1) she participated in proceedings authorized by Title VII or opposed one or more apparently prohibited practices; (2) she sustained an adverse term or condition of employment; and (3) the adverse employment action and the statutorily protected participation or opposition were causally connected. The case is then analogized to one of individual disparate treatment, with the employer obliged to produce evidence of a legitimate nondiscriminatory reason and the plaintiff permitted to rebut by demonstrating pretext.

The "participation" protection, designed to assure free access to the administrative and judicial bodies empowered to investigate and adjudicate Title VII violations, is virtually unlimited. The "opposition" right has been subject to a number of fact-sensitive qualifications, developed case by case, concerning the lawfulness or reasonableness of the manner and means of opposition. Employee protests that constitute both opposition to practices made unlawful by Title VII as well as violations of established, legitimate work rules have posed especially difficult problems. When a court adjudges an employee's manner of opposition to have gone beyond what is necessary for effective protest—when, for example, she gratuitously embarrasses a superior—employee discipline will likely be upheld. At the same time, however, an employer's unilateral sense of diminished loyalty resulting from the opposition will not by itself be considered a legitimate, nondiscriminatory reason for discipline. See Jennings v. Tinley Park Community Consolidated School District No. 146 (1988).

F. UNION LIABILITY

Labor unions are not excluded from the general definition of "employer," and consequently may be liable for violations of Section 703(a) on the same terms as any other employer. In addition, Section 703(c) declares distinct unlawful practices applicable to labor organizations alone. One is to "cause or attempt to cause an employer" to discriminate in violation of Section 703. Another is to rely on prohibited grounds in segregating or classifying union members or applicants, or in failing to refer individuals for employment, so as to deprive them of employment opportunities. Finally, wholly apart from any effect on employment opportunities, labor organizations are prohibited from excluding applicants from membership or otherwise discriminating against them. Construing this last prohibition quite broadly, the Supreme Court has held that a union commits an unlawful employment practice by refusing to file grievances presented by black members, even when it does so in order to avoid antagonizing the employer and in turn to improve its chances of success on other collective bargaining issues. Goodman v. Lukens Steel Co. (1987).

G. TITLE VII PROCEDURES

Although 1972 amendments gave EEOC the right to seek judicial relief in the first instance, most judicial action takes the form of private suits in federal district court. The path to court contains a series of intricate and time-consuming administrative procedures at the state and federal levels. These requirements are designed to give state or local antidiscrimination agencies and EEOC opportunities to obtain voluntary resolution of discrimination disputes, as well as to promote federal-state comity.

Charges must be filed directly with EEOC, within 180 days of an alleged unlawful employment practice, in states that do not have fair employment practices legislation and enforcement agencies that EEOC deems adequate. In states that do meet EEOC's standards, a charge must be filed with EEOC within 300 days, and with the state or local "deferral" agency within 240 days, of the alleged unlawful employment practice. Unless it dismisses a charge earlier, the deferral agency must be given 60 days in which to attempt to resolve the dispute before EEOC may proceed. See generally Section 706 of Title VII. But a state or local filing later than 240 but still within 300 days of the alleged unlawful practice will also be considered timely if the state or local agency terminates its proceedings before day 300. See Mohasco Corp. v. Silver (1980).

The state or local administrative filing will be considered adequate even where the complainant has filed a charge only or initially with EEOC, if EEOC itself refers the charge to the local agency and suspends its proceedings for the required 60 days or until local proceedings terminate. Love v. Pullman (1972). Further, under "work sharing" agreements with EEOC, state or local agencies may waive the right to process the charge initially; EEOC may proceed to investigate without waiting 60 days; and the state or local agency retains jurisdiction to process the charge thereafter if it chooses. EEOC v. Commercial Office Products (1988). Finally, filing with the state agency on the 240–day "plus" schedule approved by *Mohasco* will satisfy Title VII even if that filing would be untimely under state law. Id.

Although Section 706 appears to require that the state or local filing precede the filing of a charge with EEOC, it is apparent from the *Love* deferral practice and the *Commercial Office Products* approval of work-sharing agreements that in practice EEOC is often the first agency to investigate and conciliate charges, even in deferral states. Nevertheless, where the state or local agency has made a prior determination, the statute directs EEOC to give it "substantial weight."

Federal employees claiming violations of Title VII are required to seek administrative relief within their own agency, starting with designated Equal Employment Opportunity Counselors and Directors. The head of an agency is the final authority for agency decisions. Claimants can appeal these decisions to the Office of Review and Appeals of EEOC or they may file an action in federal district court with a trial de novo on all issues. Chandler v. Roudebush (1976). This comprehensive scheme has persuaded the Supreme Court that Congress impliedly intended to make Title VII the sole remedy for discrimination in federal employment, to the exclusion of the Reconstruction Civil Rights Acts. *Brown.*

For purposes of administrative charge-filing deadlines, the date of an alleged unlawful employment practice is usually the date on which the complaining applicant or employee should be aware of the consequences of employer conduct, not thereafter when those consequences become manifest. Delaware State College v. Ricks (1980). Arguments that the filing deadlines should be extended because the consequences of alleged unlawful employment practices persist—the "continuing violation" theory—have met with little success in the Supreme Court. See *Evans, Lorance.* And pursuing a grievance under a collective bargaining agreement will not toll the time to file a charge with EEOC. International Union of Electrical Workers v. Robbins & Myers (1976). But the 180–day and 300–day EEOC charge-filing deadlines are not jurisdictional; they are simply procedural preconditions to suit, analogous to statutes of limitations, and thus may be waived, estopped, or equitably tolled. Zipes v. Trans World Airlines, Inc. (1982).

When EEOC takes jurisdiction, it conducts an investigation and ultimately arrives at one of two basic conclusions. The Agency may find "reasonable cause" to believe that the Act has been violated, and will then undertake conciliation; or it may find "no reasonable cause" and issue a notice of dismissal. In either event, a complainant is entitled upon demand to receive a "right-to-sue" letter from EEOC no later than 180 days after the effective date of the filing of a charge with the agency. Since EEOC not infrequently takes years to process charges, the question has arisen how long a prospective Title VII plaintiff may wait beyond 180 days before demanding a right-to-sue letter. Courts have occasionally barred Title VII actions in these circumstances on grounds of laches, when a delay of several years in demanding a suit letter was deemed unreasonable and caused tangible prejudice to the defendant.

The right to bring a federal lawsuit does not turn on EEOC's evaluation of the probable merits of a charge, so the judicial action may be commenced even if EEOC concludes that there is no reasonable cause to believe that the employer has violated Title VII. *McDonnell Douglas.* Nor does resort to a grievance or arbitration procedure bar a later action under Title VII even after an unfavorable disposition. Alexander v. Gardner–Denver Co. (1974). A complainant who wishes to sue in federal court must commence an action by filing a complaint within 90 days after receipt of the EEOC "right-to-sue" letter or notice of dismissal. The 90–day deadline is generally strictly enforced, although it, like the administrative charge-filing deadline, is probably amenable to tolling, estoppel, or waiver. See Baldwin County Welcome Center v. Brown (1984). Related actions under the Reconstruction Civil Rights Acts may be commenced even before Title VII charges have been administratively processed, but the limitations periods and administrative deadlines of the respective statutes must be satisfied independently. Johnson v. Railway Express Agency, Inc., supra.

Title VII actions in federal court are limited by statutory requirements concerning parties and allegations. The EEOC charge which forms the predicate for a Title VII action may be filed either "by or on behalf of" an aggrieved person. Section 706(f)(1). Thus named plaintiffs who have filed charges may prosecute the action on behalf of class members (in a Federal Rule 23 class action) or co-plaintiffs (joined under Federal Rule 20) who have not. A second parties requirement, that the action be brought "against the respondent named in the charge," § 706(f)(1), has sometimes been construed to authorize jurisdiction over a defendant improperly named, or not formally named in the charge at all, if its identity is sufficiently revealed in the substance of the charge or it is closely related to a named respondent. See, e.g., Evans v. Sheraton Park Hotel (1974) (international union must defend when charge named two of its locals).

Since the EEOC charge is the necessary foundation for a Title VII action, the issues that may be litigated in federal court will be tied to some degree to the contents of the charge. But recognizing that EEOC charges are often drafted by unrepresented employees ill-equipped to craft them with care, courts have permitted Title VII plaintiffs to try claims "like or related to allegations contained in the charge and growing out of such allegations during the pendency of the case before the Commission." Sanchez v. Standard Brands, Inc. (1970). The widespread adoption of the *Sanchez* rule puts a premium on defendants' efforts to limit the scope of EEOC proceedings. Generalizations about the meaning of "like or related" are particularly hazardous. But it may be ventured that allegations in a Title VII judicial complaint that add a new ground of discrimination (race or sex, for instance) are less likely to be entertained than are allegations that touch on additional terms or conditions of employment or implicate other potential plaintiffs in different departments or divisions. In any case, the EEOC determination of "reasonable cause" or "no reasonable cause" will at trial be given only such weight as the federal court believes it deserves.

H. CLASS ACTIONS

Claims of systemic disparate treatment or of neutral practices having a disproportionate adverse impact will often be advanced through class actions. In theory, maintenance of actions in class form should expedite the presentation of evidence on behalf of large numbers of claimants. In fact, after receiving class actions quite hospitably in the early years of the Act, courts have recently erected substantial barriers to class certification through interpretations of Federal Rule 23.

The most formidable obstacle was declared by a Supreme Court decision construing the "commonality" and "typicality" requirements of Rule 23(a) (2). General Telephone Company of the Southwest v. Falcon, supra, precludes named plaintiffs complaining of discrimination in one term and condition of employment (for example, promotion) from representing persons complaining about the same kind of discrimination with respect to other terms and conditions of employment (for example, hiring). The Court stressed that the requisite commonality and typicality must extend to defendant employer practices, not merely the general type of discrimination—race, gender, religion, or national origin—alleged.

The Court in *Falcon* did note that named plaintiffs complaining of one term or condition of employment could represent class members complaining of another where the employer used a common testing procedure or where different kinds of employees could be shown to have suffered discrimination "in the same general fashion," e.g., through "entirely subjective decision making processes" or at the hands of the same employer personnel. See also *Bazemore*. Nevertheless, many lower courts have taken a grudging approach to class action certification since *Falcon*.

Plaintiffs' counsel have tried to comply with the Court's strictures by assembling class-representative complements composed of applicants, employees and former employees complaining of varied terms and conditions of employment, with each named plaintiff offering to represent a discrete subclass. Defendants routinely reply with objections and motions asserting the existence of conflicts among the proposed subclasses and challenging plaintiffs' adequacy to represent them. When these motions succeed and class certification is denied, they may preclude the class action as a practical matter, since orders denying certification are not ordinarily appealable on an interlocutory basis. Instead, the named plaintiffs must incur the expense and delay of proceeding to trial on their individual claims; only later, on appeal, may they challenge the denial of certification. Even when defendants' objections are not sustained, they usually necessitate extensive discovery and briefing about the propriety of certification that can rob the class action of its intended expedition and efficiency.

I. REMEDIES AND "REVERSE DISCRIMINATION"

The range of judicial remedial authority is prescribed by § 706(g). This section provides for injunctions and "such affirmative action as may be appropriate," including orders directing reinstatement or hire, back pay, and other equitable relief. It also limits a defendant's back pay liability retrospectively to no earlier than two years before the filing of a charge with EEOC. Back pay awards are reduced by amounts the plaintiff earned, or with reasonable diligence could have earned, since the date of a discharge or failure or refusal to hire.

Because each species of Title VII relief is considered equitable, jury trials are not available unless a Title VII claim is joined with a claim for legal relief—for instance, a claim under § 1981. The "equity" characterization also limits monetary relief to an award of back pay, precluding more generous measures such as compensation for emotional distress or punitive damages. A reasonable attorney's fee may be recovered as part of the costs by a prevailing party under a separate provision, § 701(k).

Prevailing plaintiffs are routinely awarded injunctions against continuing violations and back pay, since each of these remedies serves both of the Act's remedial goals: to restore discrimination victims to the approximate status they would have enjoyed absent discrimination (the "make whole" purpose), and to deter employer violations. Accordingly, the Supreme Court, while recognizing that federal judges enjoy some discretion to withhold any Title VII remedy in particular circumstances, has held that back pay may be denied only for unusual reasons which, if applied generally, would not impede those remedial objectives. For example, the "neutral practice/disproportionate adverse impact" case dispenses with evidence of discriminatory intent, and a general good faith exception to back pay liability would therefore seriously erode the advantages of that mode of proof. The Court has consequently rejected such an exception. *Albemarle.*

More complex is the availability of retroactive remedial seniority, which is vital to those plaintiffs who secure orders directing their hire, promotion or reinstatement. Awards of seniority that enhance the measure of employer-paid compensation or benefits and thus help restore discriminatees to their "rightful place" serve both Title VII remedial objectives, deterrence as well as compensation. Retroactive remedial seniority for those economic purposes is therefore presumptively available on the same terms as back pay. *Franks*. On the other hand, retroactive seniority that serves the alternative or additional purpose of improving the discriminatee's position relative to other employees in competing for scarce job resources—better-paying positions, more favorable hours, or, most critically, protection against demotion or layoff—furthers only the goal of compensation, not employer deterrence. For this reason, even though such protection is usually necessary to make a proven victim of discrimination whole and is therefore not a "preference" prohibited by § 703(j), the *Albemarle* presumption favoring retroactive seniority for "benefits" purposes does not attach to retroactive "competitive" seniority. Rather, in considering whether to award retroactive competitive seniority, a court must balance a number of unweighted equities, including the number of protected group and non-protected group persons interested in the scarce resource, the number of current vacancies, and the economic prospects of the industry. *Teamsters*.

Although the Supreme Court has implied that § 706(g) provides discretion to "bump" an incumbent employee in order to reinstate a proven victim or "discriminatee," lower courts have displayed great reluctance to do so and instead have sometimes awarded the discriminatee "front pay." Front pay, squarely endorsed by only one member of the Supreme Court, see *Franks* (Burger, C.J., concurring), leaves the incumbent in place and orders the employer to pay the discriminatee an amount equivalent to what he would earn if actually reinstated. Front pay is fraught with computational difficulties, and it is usually awarded only when reinstatement would be inequitable.

"Voluntary," "benign" employer affirmative action, and reverse discriminatory remedies imposed by court order or consent decree, raise similar yet legally distinct questions of fairness as between minority and majority group employees. Strictly speaking, employer affirmative action in the form of self-imposed quotas or goals does not really implicate the judiciary's remedial authority under § 706(g) at all. An employer simply institutes racial or gender preferences, without court compulsion, typically to avoid lawsuits by the group benefiting from the preference or to preserve federal contracts that require affirmative action. The employer plan operates to prefer members of defined minority or female groups or classes, rather than individuals proven to have suffered discrimination at the hands of the defendant employer. As a result, these preferences are suspect under § 703 as ordinary unlawful employment practices directed against any majority group members or males who are denied employment opportunities by the plan. The jeopardy would seem considerable because the Court has regularly emphasized that the statute seeks to protect individuals from discrimination on the basis of group characteristics, rather than groups as such. See, e.g., *Teal, Manhart.*

Nevertheless, in an opinion that expressly elevated a supposed legislative "spirit" over statutory text, the Supreme Court has given qualified approval to "voluntary," "benign" racial preferences. United Steelworkers v. Weber (1979). A majority held that the employer there had lawfully taken race into account in preferring black employees as a group for admission to an on-the-job training program—a preference that on its face violated the specific terms of § 703(d). Further, the Court wrote that an employer could justifiably adopt race-conscious programs of this type whenever it found a manifest underrepresentation of blacks in a traditionally segregated job category; the employer need not first uncover evidence of its own prior discrimination in filling those positions. See Johnson v. Transportation Agency (1987). Finally, the employer plan in *Weber* was approved despite being only doubtfully voluntary: the plan was adopted after the Office of Federal Contract Compliance Programs had threatened the employer with debarment from federal contracts under Executive Order 11246 if it did not increase its skilled minority representation.

Perhaps to ease its misgivings about approving a form of race discrimination that the text of § 703(d) expressly prohibited, the *Weber* majority listed a number of sanitizing factors to circumscribe the scope of lawful "benign" discrimination. It observed that the employer plan before it did not require white employees to be discharged and therefore did not "unnecessarily trammel" their interests; that it did not absolutely bar white employees from the skilled positions, but merely limited their numbers; and that it was a temporary measure, intended not to maintain a racial balance but to eliminate a manifest imbalance in the skilled job categories. The Court satisfied itself on these points again in *Johnson,* when it extended the *Weber* principle by upholding an explicit gender preference for promotions.

Affirmative action plans have fared less well when challenged as violations of equal protection. For example, the Court has concluded that a public employer, before instituting such a program, must have "convincing evidence" of its own prior discrimination and must employ means narrowly tailored to rectify that conduct. Wygant v. Jackson Board of Education (1986). The collective bargaining agreement in *Wygant* required the layoff of non-minority teachers with greater seniority than minority teachers who were retained, a feature that might also have offended the *Weber* sanitizing factor of "unnecessary trammeling." In any event, the *Wygant* plurality's broader approach recently commanded a majority of the Court in a decision striking down a municipal program to set aside a minimum amount of subcontracting work for minority business enterprises. City of Richmond v. J.A. Croson Company (1989).

Unlike "voluntary" affirmative action, judgments directing preferential treatment for a minority or gender group, issued after litigated findings of discrimination or upon the parties' consent, squarely test the limits of a court's remedial authority under § 706(g) to "order such affirmative action as may be appropriate. . . ." In the case of public employers, these judgments may also deny disfavored racial or gender groups equal protection.

The justices are deeply divided over the propriety under § 706(g) of consent judgments that afford relief to minority group members who are not themselves proven victims of discrimination. The degree of "trammelling" appears important. An opinion that in dictum declared such relief beyond a court's authority concerned a consent judgment modification that would have required more senior non-minority firefighters to be laid off before their more junior minority counterparts. Yet a subsequent decision, also involving firefighters, upheld a court's authority to approve a consent judgment that established promotion quotas but did not compel layoffs or terminations. Compare Firefighters

Local Union No. 1784 v. Stotts (1984), with Local No. 93, International Ass'n of Firefighters v. City of Cleveland (1986).

The Court has been more united in upholding group-based remedies judicially ordered after litigated findings of persistent, egregious discrimination. Local 28, Sheetmetal Workers International Ass'n v. EEOC (1986) (membership goal for defendant union); United States v. Paradise (1987) (quota promotion plan). In operation the membership goal approved in *Local 28* would have absolutely excluded certain whites from union membership, in turn precluding their employment. But the Court had stressed in *Wygant* that the burdens of hiring goals are "diffused to a considerable extent among society generally" and do not "impose the same kind of injury" as layoffs.

The Court may be retreating from its approval of consent judgments that embody group-based or quota remedies, and perhaps also from voluntary employer affirmative action programs. A 5–4 majority held in Martin v. Wilks (1989), that nonminority employees who object to a consent judgment adverse to their interests are not required to intervene in a Title VII action but instead may collaterally attack the judgment in independent actions. Since the Court had several times recognized that employers are principally motivated to adopt "voluntary" affirmative action programs, or settle pending lawsuits by consent agreements, in order to avoid the costs of extended litigation, the

Martin decision appears designed to remove much of the incentive for these arrangements.

The Court's increasing solicitude for the innocent white or male incumbent who is harmed by a preferential, group-based remedy is further reflected in another recent decision. The Court has held that nonminority intervenors who unsuccessfully oppose Title VII consent decrees that threaten them with personal injury will ordinarily not be liable for the fees incurred by plaintiffs in resisting their objections. Independent Fed. of Flight Attendants v. Zipes (1989). After *Croson, Martin,* and *Zipes,* the Court may eventually respond to one justice's call to overrule *Weber* itself. Johnson v. Transportation Agency, supra (Scalia, J., dissenting).

J. ISSUE AND CLAIM PRECLUSION

An increasingly important procedural issue is the extent, if any, to which court actions will be barred by prior agency or court determinations. EEOC reasonable cause determinations, as observed above, cannot prevent timely filed Title VII actions from being heard on the merits. Nor will the decisions of state or local deferral agencies have any preclusive effect on subsequent Title VII actions: it would make no sense to preclude a federal court when EEOC is merely required to give those decisions "substantial weight." University of Tennessee v. Elliott (1985). On the other hand, when a state administrative determination is appealed to a state court, a judgment of non-liability will bar a Title VII action in federal court by force of the Full Faith and Credit Act, 28 U.S.C.A. § 1738, at least where the judicial review was sought by the employee. Kremer v. Chemical Construction Corp. (1982). Prospective Title VII plaintiffs who are exhausting state administrative processes must therefore be aware that seeking judicial review of an adverse agency determination may preclude an independent action under Title VII.

In one area, class actions, the Court has somewhat lessened the impact of an adverse federal court decision. Although judgments rejecting pattern-type discrimination claims enjoy *res judicata* or collateral estoppel effect in subsequent actions asserting the same theory, they do not bar the claims of individual class members alleging disparate treatment à la *McDonnell–Douglas/Burdine.* Cooper v. Federal Reserve Bank of Richmond (1984). Moreover, when a court denies class action certification, individual class members' claims may still be timely, since the filing of a class action tolls the 90–day period for filing suit until certification is denied. Crown, Cork & Seal Co. v. Parker (1983).

CHAPTER 19

OTHER FEDERAL ANTIDISCRIMINATION LAWS

A. CIVIL RIGHTS ACTS OF 1866, 1870, AND 1871

The Civil Rights Acts of 1866, 1870, and 1871 are generally referred to as the Reconstruction Civil Rights Acts, and they were originally intended to enforce the 13th and 14th Amendments in the post-Civil War era. The provisions most relevant to employment are codified in 42 U.S.C.A. §§ 1981, 1983, and 1985. These acts remained dormant for many years but were resurrected in the 1960's. See Jones v. Alfred H. Mayer Co. (1968).

Although the Reconstruction Civil Rights Acts do not reach gender or religious discrimination as such and offer only limited protection for most employment terms after initial hire, they hold several potential attractions over Title VII. For one, no administrative exhaustion is required. See Patsy v. Board of Regents of the State of Florida (1982) (§ 1983). Second, the applicable limitation periods borrowed from state law are normally longer than Title VII's short string for filing charges with state or federal agencies. Third, there is no minimum-employee numerical threshold for employer liability. Perhaps the greatest allure of the nineteenth-century statutes is the availability of jury trial and compensatory and punitive damages. These features contrast markedly with the sparse typical relief of injunction and "back pay" awarded a prevailing plaintiff after a bench trial under Title VII. See Johnson v. Railway Express Agency (1975). Small wonder, then, that many employees sought to avail themselves of a revitalized § 1981, even before the Supreme Court, in *Johnson,* formally recognized its application to contracts of employment.

1. SECTION 1981

Section 1981 secures equal rights under the law without regard to race. It has been construed to provide a private civil damages remedy for racial discrimination in employment. See *Johnson;* McDonald v. Santa Fe Trail Transportation Co. (1976). It affords "all persons" in the United States "the same right . . . to make and enforce contracts . . . and to the full and equal benefit of all laws . . . as is enjoyed by white citizens. . . ." The "white citizens" caveat has been construed to describe the racial (as opposed to, say, gender) character of the prohibited discrimination, rather than to limit the class of appropriate plaintiffs to nonwhites. Accordingly, while the lower courts are in agreement that the statute does not prohibit discrimination because of gender, it is also settled that whites as well as blacks may assert contract

denial claims under § 1981 on the basis of race.
McDonald.

Section 1981 also embraces discrimination on the
basis of ancestry, construed to mean membership
in an "ethnically and physiognomically distinctive
sub-grouping." St. Francis College v. Al–Khazraji
(1987) and Shaare Tefila Congregation v. Cobb
(1987) (protection for Arabs and Jews, respectively).
Although neither statute prohibits discrimination
on the basis of alienage *per se,* aliens may complain
of race or ancestry discrimination under § 1981, or
of race, gender, religious, or national origin discrimination under Title VII. Espinoza v. Farah
Mfg. Co. (1973) (Title VII); Bhandari v. First National Bank of Commerce (1987) (en banc) (§ 1981).
Limited protection from discrimination on the basis of non-citizenship status is now provided by the
Immigration Reform and Control Act of 1986 (discussed in Chapter 19).

Significant judicial limitations on the utility of
§ 1981 began with General Building Contractors
Assn. v. Pennsylvania (1982). There the Supreme
Court held that a showing of disparate impact does
not suffice to prove a § 1981 employment violation,
which requires instead a direct or inferential demonstration of discriminatory intent.

By far the most significant limitation on the
scope of § 1981 has been worked by the Supreme
Court's decision in the 1988–89 term in *Patterson.*
The Court initially requested rebriefing and rear-
gument as to whether it should reconsider the

holding of Runyon v. McCrary (1976), that § 1981 reaches purely private conduct. *Patterson* ultimately did reaffirm *Runyon* in this respect, but, in tandem with *Jett*, it also yielded the somewhat ironic conclusion that § 1981 reaches *only* private conduct, as explained below.

At the same time, *Patterson* sharply restricts the scope of the § 1981 claims that still remain viable. The Court continues to recognize that § 1981 protects the right to "enforce" contracts, so that an employer is prohibited from discriminating on the basis of race or national origin so as to impede the enforcement of contract rights. But five justices also ruled that the statutory prohibition on racial or ethnic discrimination in the "making" of private employment contracts does not extend to conduct occurring after the employment relation is established. In particular, the Court held employer racial "harassment," fostering or tolerating a discriminatory work environment, outside the ambit of the statute.

The majority opinion's broad language classifies as non-actionable "postformation conduct" any "conditions of continuing employment." Yet the opinion also suggests that one species of "postformation conduct"—a promotion decision which "rises to the level of an opportunity for a new and distinct relation"—may still be actionable. The Court cited the example of a law firm's refusal to admit an associate attorney to partnership, but lower courts have since had difficulty applying the "new and distinct relation" exception to other in-house opportunities for advancement. It is also unclear whether the opinion precludes a claim of discriminatory discharge, which arguably goes to the very existence of a contract and not just the way it is performed. Lower courts since *Patterson* have also divided on this question.

The Supreme Court has directed the lower federal courts to borrow analogous state statutes of limitations in actions under § 1981, but has also held that pursuing Title VII administrative procedures does not toll the § 1981 statute of limitations. *Johnson.* The Court has since clarified that in actions under any of the Reconstruction Civil Rights Acts, the forum state's "personal injury" statute of limitations should apply, see Wilson v. Garcia (1985) (§ 1983) and Goodman v. Lukens Steel Co. (1987) (§ 1981); and the federal court should borrow the limitations period from a state's general or residual statute rather than, for example, a statute geared specifically to intentional torts. Owens v. Okure (1989).

2. SECTION 1983

Section 1983 authorizes actions at law or suits in equity against any "person" for the deprivation of rights, privileges or immunities secured by the federal Constitution or laws, so long as the defendant acted "under color of" state law, custom or usage.

For most employment discrimination claimants, Section 1983 is of less utility than § 1981, for two basic reasons. First, it provides remedies for deprivations only of rights independently secured by the federal constitution or statutes; second, even those deprivations are actionable only if imposed "under color of" state law. The Supreme Court has held that municipalities and other local governments are "persons," and hence appropriate defendants, for purposes of § 1983. Monell v. New York City Department of Social Services (1978). *Monell* also held, however, that municipalities are not subject to liability merely vicariously; for example, *respondeat superior* will not suffice to hold local entities accountable for every federal constitutional or statutory violation committed by their employees. Instead, the Court has repeatedly insisted that local government entities are responsible only for official policies or the acts of those employees with "policy making authority," a question of law to be decided by reference to local laws, customs, and usages. Pembaur v. Cincinnati (1986) (plurality opinion); St. Louis v. Praprotnik (1988) (plurality opinion); and *Jett* (5–member majority opinion).

3. SECTION 1985(3)

Section 1985(3) prohibits employment-related conspiracies to interfere with federally secured constitutional or statutory civil rights. Great American Federal Savings & Loan Association v. Novotny (1979). The statute has been further narrowed by construction. *Novotny* held that the remedy created by § 1985 is displaced if the particular right asserted is also actionable under Title VII.

4. RECENT RESTRICTIONS

On its face, § 1981 appears to reach any employer, including federal, state and local governments. But a series of Supreme Court decisions has rendered § 1981 largely unavailable in actions against government employers. In Brown v. General Services Administration (1976), the Court held that the detailed procedural provisions of § 717 of Title VII, which pertain to federal employees, impliedly repealed § 1981 with respect to actions against the federal government. Title VII therefore affords the exclusive remedy for discrimination based on race (or national origin or ancestry) in federal employment.

More recently, the Court has eliminated § 1981 as a source of rights in actions against local and state governments as well. To circumvent the rigors of the § 1983 "official policy" limitation declared by *Monell,* and thereby invoke vicarious liability, employees sometimes sued state and local government entities under Section 1981. But the Supreme Court has recently held that municipalities, and presumably states as well, are not subject to § 1981 liability on any theory. *Jett.* The Court considered it unlikely that Congress, in enacting what is now § 1981 in 1866 or re-enacting it in 1870, intended that statute to reach state instrumentalities, when only a year later, in 1871, it enacted § 1983 and thereby provided a civil remedy expressly reaching actions taken under state authority. In fact, the Court had never held municipalities (the kind of state instrumentality defending in *Jett* itself) amenable to liability under § 1983 until more than a century later, in *Monell.* Moreover, in the same week it decided *Jett,* the Court held that states are *not* liable under § 1983, in either state or federal court, other than for prospective relief against state officials acting in an official capacity. Will v. Michigan Dep't of State Police (1989).

These decisions sharply constrict the reach of § 1983, as well as § 1981. *Will* precludes any § 1983 remedy against states as such, as well as compensatory relief in actions against state officials. And in *Jett,* after holding municipalities immune under § 1981, a majority adopts the restrictive "policy" limitation on § 1983 liability previously embraced only by pluralities in *Pembaur* and *Praprotnik.* Thus damages under § 1983 are now apparently available in only two general classes of employment cases: First, actions against a local government or its authorized agents proven to have acted pursuant to an official policy, or an established custom recognized as official policy under principles of state law; second, actions against the relatively unusual private employer shown to have acted "under color of" state law.

Section 1981 has been even more drastically reduced in scope. After *Jett,* it is no longer available at all as an avenue of relief against government employers. Moreover, even within its newly confined sphere of actions against privately acting private employers, § 1981 no longer is of great utility. For the most part, *Patterson* limits § 1981 liability to claims concerning contract formation.

Discrimination claims by state employees, other than § 1983 claims seeking purely prospective relief against state officials, should now generally be barred under *either* statute by the combination of *Jett* and *Will.* Further, it has been clear since *Brown* and *Novotny* that Title VII, where available, displaces all other remedies for discrimination against federal employees and for conspiracies affecting employment. In sum, unless Congress overrules one or more of these decisions, only municipal or other local government employees will now normally be able to take advantage of the jury trials and more generous remedies afforded by the Reconstruction Civil Rights Acts; and even those employees will no longer have access to § 1981, only to Title VII and § 1983.

When a private employer intentionally refuses for reasons of race, national origin or ancestry even to execute an employment contract, the unsuccessful applicant will still have a claim under § 1981. But most other discrimination claims against private employers, as well as almost all claims against state and federal employers, will now be remitted to the maze of administrative exhaustion, trial by judge, and limited remedial relief afforded by Title VII.

The federal courts' role in enforcing the Reconstruction Civil Rights Acts has also been diminished by liberal application of the doctrines of *res judicata* and collateral estoppel. The Supreme Court has found no policy of § 1983 that warrants denying state judgments their normal preclusive effect in federal court under the Full Faith and Credit Statute, 28 U.S.C.A. § 1738. These judgments now therefore bar civil rights claims from relitigation to the same extent as in the forum state's courts. Allen v. McCurry (1980) (prior state criminal proceeding); Migra v. Warren City School District Board of Education (1984) (prior state civil action). Indeed, relying on federal common law, the Supreme Court has even approved the preclusion of Civil Rights Acts claims by unreviewed quasi-judicial determinations of state administrative agencies. University of Tennessee v. Elliott (1986).

B. EQUAL PAY ACT OF 1963

The Equal Pay Act of 1963, 29 U.S.C.A. § 206(d), (EPA) requires "equal pay for equal work" within the same establishment regardless of sex. The concept of "equal work" lies at the heart of the Act. General comparisons between two jobs carrying unequal pay will not suffice to establish that work is "equal"; rather, demonstrating an EPA violation demands specific showings of equivalent skill, effort, and responsibility, as well as performance under similar working conditions. Once an inequality is found, however, it cannot be remedied by a reduction in the wages of the higher paid sex.

EPA allows exceptions to the equal pay for equal work principle when differentials are pursuant to: (1) seniority systems; (2) merit systems; (3) systems which measure earnings by quantity or quality of production (incentive systems); or (4) factors other than sex.

Corning Glass Works v. Brennan (1974), illustrates the judiciary's relatively vigilant enforcement of EPA. First, the opinion notes that job equivalence, as measured by skill, effort, responsibility, and working conditions, need not be precise, only substantial. Second, the Court, reviewing legislative history, determined that the time of day or night during which work is performed does not constitute the kind of difference in working conditions that renders jobs "unequal." Finally, while the Court recognized that time of performance might constitute a "factor other than sex," it treated that defense, as well as the three other numbered exceptions, as affirmative defenses on which the employer bears a significant burden of persuasion.

Why would plaintiffs resort to the Equal Pay Act, with its narrow proscription of sex-based wage discrimination, when Title VII prohibits other forms of sex-based wage discrimination (see Section 3 below) as well as sex discrimination affecting different terms and conditions of employment?

The answer lies in varying enforcement and remedial schemes.

Although the Equal Employment Opportunity Commission has enforcement responsibility and may file civil actions under EPA, a private plaintiff need not exhaust state or federal administrative remedies before proceeding to court. Moreover, the EPA action need not be filed until two or, in the case of a willful violation, three years after the accrual of an EPA claim, far longer than the 180–day or 300–day administrative filing deadlines of Title VII.

Further, EPA remedies are governed by the generous provisions of the Fair Labor Standards Act (FLSA), 29 U.S.C.A. §§ 216 and 217. These sections authorize recovery not only of unlawfully withheld wages (the rough equivalent of Title VII "back pay") but also of an equal amount denominated "liquidated damages." EPA liquidated damages will be available, under the terms of the Portal-to-Portal Act of 1947, 29 U.S.C.A. § 251 et seq., when an employer knows that, or recklessly disregards whether, its conduct is in violation of the statute. See McLaughlin v. Richland Shoe Co. (1988).

In 1974, FLSA was amended to extend the reach of EPA to state and local government employers. The constitutional validity of this extension was assured when the Supreme Court, overruling National League of Cities v. Usery (1976), rejected a Tenth Amendment challenge to the power of the federal government to regulate wages and hours of state and local government entities under the FLSA. Garcia v. San Antonio Metropolitan Transit Authority (1985).

C. AGE DISCRIMINATION IN EMPLOYMENT ACT OF 1967

The ADEA prohibits age discrimination against employees or job applicants over the age of 40. ADEA was amended in 1986 to remove the then current upper age limitation, 70, for the vast majority of covered employees. The only exceptions still pertinent relate to tenured professors, law enforcement officers and firefighters, who are subject to involuntary retirement at age 70 (professors) or younger. See Act of October 31, 1986, Pub. L. No. 99–592.

ADEA covers employers who have 20 or more employees for 20 weeks in a year; labor unions having 25 members; and employment agencies. The Older American Act Amendments of 1984 specifically protect U.S. citizens "employed by an employer in a workplace in a foreign country." At a minimum this covers overseas employees of American corporations.

State and local governments were included in the term "employer" by amendments in 1974. Age discrimination claims against these entities are constitutional exercises of Congressional authority under the Commerce Clause. EEOC v. Wyoming (1983). See also the discussion of *Garcia,* overruling *National League of Cities*, in connection with the Equal Pay Act, supra. In fact, some lower courts have now held the ADEA to constitute the exclusive remedy for age discrimination in government employment. See Zombro v. Baltimore City Police Department (1989). The Act does not include the federal government as an "employer," but special provisions of the act protect federal employees other than members of the U.S. military.

Like the BFOQ defense, the prima facie theories of liability under ADEA parallel those of Title VII, from which its language was derived. Age discrimination in hiring, firing or classifying employees or job applicants is forbidden, as is bias in employment advertisements or referrals.

Section 623(d) of ADEA provides protection against retaliation in the same terms as § 704(a) of Title VII. The ADEA provision has likewise been construed to shield a wide range of on-the-job "opposition" in addition to formal participation in ADEA proceedings. See, e.g., Grant v. Hazelett Strip–Casting Corp. (1989).

The BFOQ defense declared by § 4(f)(1) was delimited stringently by the Supreme Court in *Criswell*. BFOQ is now the employer's only real defense to an age-based forced retirement, since § 4(f)(2), after its amendment in 1978, no longer countenances use of benefit plans to compel retirement at any age. Public Employees Retirement System of Ohio v. Betts (1989). But Section 4(f)(2) also provides that an employer does not violate the Act merely by observing the terms of an age-discriminatory "bona fide seniority system or any bona fide employee benefit plan such as a retirement, pension, or insurance plan, which is not a subterfuge to evade the purposes of this chapter. . . ." In *Betts,* the Supreme Court, rejecting the unanimous position of the courts of appeals and the EEOC, recently gave this exemption an expansive reading. First, the Court held that the exemption pertains to plans that regulate any fringe benefit (for example, disability plans) and not just to retirement, pension, or insurance plans. Second, as a matter of law, a plan provision adopted before an employer becomes subject to ADEA cannot be deemed a "subterfuge" to evade the Act's purposes. Third, even a plan provision adopted thereafter will not be considered a subterfuge except in the unlikely event that the plaintiff is able to prove that it was "intended to serve the purpose of discriminating in some nonfringe-benefit aspect of the employment relation," such as discrimination in hiring or compensation. Bills have been introduced in both the House and the Senate to reverse *Betts* and codify EEOC's long-standing test under which age-based distinctions in benefit programs are valid only if justified by a substantial business purpose, such as the greater expense of providing a benefit to an older worker.

EEOC is charged with enforcement of the Act, and ADEA provides criminal penalties for intentional or willful interference with its processes. It investigates claims of age discrimination, attempts conciliation, and has the power to file civil actions. Although an EEOC suit generally precludes private relief, individual actions are the major means of enforcement, and procedures and remedies are borrowed from the Fair Labor Standards Act. An individual may seek injunctive relief, back wages, statutory "liquidated" damages equal to the amount of back wages, and attorney's fees. A 1978 amendment clarifies that jury trials are available on liquidated damages claims as well as on claims for lost wages. Liquidated damages are available, however, only if the employer knows that its conduct violates ADEA or acts with reckless disregard to its obligations thereunder, not merely when it knows that the Act is potentially applicable. See Part B, above, treating damages under the EPA.

The standards for administrative charge filing under ADEA are even more relaxed than those under Title VII. The major superficial similarities are the twin requirements that a complainant file a charge of discrimination (1) with EEOC, within 180 days of an alleged violation, or within 300 days in a deferral state; and (2) with an appropriately empowered state agency, if one exists, which then must be deferred to for a maximum of 60 days or until it dismisses or surrenders jurisdiction. But EEOC itself is given only 60 days of deferral, in contrast to the 180 days specified by Title VII, and plaintiffs may proceed to federal court without having received a "right to sue" letter from that agency.

In addition, the Supreme Court has liberally construed the ADEA's requirement that a state filing precede the filing of an ADEA action in federal court. A complainant's failure to file a state agency charge before commencing a federal action is not fatal; the federal court will simply stay its proceedings until a state charge is filed and the state deferral period elapses. Oscar Mayer & Co. v. Evans (1979). Similarly, a complainant need not comply with state limitations rules in order to maintain the ADEA judicial action. Id. The plaintiff need only file an ADEA complaint within the 2– or 3–year limitations period applicable under the Portal-to-Portal Act. See discussion of limitations periods under the EPA in Part 2, above.

In only one respect is ADEA more stringent. No class action may be maintained under Federal Rule 23, which in appropriate circumstances permits class members to be bound without their specific consent. Rather, under 29 U.S.C.A. § 216 of ADEA, a would-be "class member" who has not filed a charge must affirmatively "opt in" by giving a written consent to joinder as a party plaintiff.

D. TITLE VI OF THE CIVIL RIGHTS ACT OF 1964

Title VI of the Civil Rights Act of 1964, 42 U.S. C.A. § 2000d et seq., prohibits discrimination based on race, color or national origin (but not sex or religion) in all federally assisted programs and activities, i.e., those that receive financial support by way of grants, loans, or contracts. Discrimination is actionable under Title VI only where the primary objective of the federal assistance is to provide employment. 42 U.S.C.A. § 2000d–3. Federal agencies are required to engage in coordinated enforcement efforts with the U.S. Attorney General. They must, for example, refuse to grant or continue assistance after notice to the offending party and failure of attempts to secure voluntary compliance.

The Supreme Court, in a case under a companion statute that prohibits sex discrimination in federally-assisted education programs, limited sanctions to the particular discriminating program or activity within the recipient institution. *Grove City College* (interpreting Education Amendments of 1972, Title IX, 20 U.S.C.A. §§ 1681–1688). The Civil Rights Restoration Act of 1987, Pub.L. No. 100–259 (1988), overturns this holding by defining the "program or activity" sanctionable under Titles VI and IX to include "all" of a recipient's operations. A second holding of *Grove City College,* that federal assistance funnelled directly to students constitutes assistance to the educational institution itself, appears undisturbed either by subsequent decisions, cf. United States Department of Transportation v. Paralyzed Veterans (1986), or by the Restoration Act.

A private right of action that supplements administrative enforcement has been judicially implied for violations of Title VI, and direct proof of discriminatory intent is not essential. Guardians Association v. Civil Service Commission (1983). There remains some question, however, whether damages are available for unintentional violations, or if the plaintiff is limited to back pay. See Consolidated Rail Corp. v. Darrone (1984).

E. TITLE IX, EDUCATION AMENDMENTS OF 1972

The Education Amendments of 1972, Title IX, 20 U.S.C.A. §§ 1681–1688, prohibit sex discrimination in federally financed or assisted educational programs and activities. Noncompliance can result in the cessation of federal funding. The Supreme Court has implied a private right of action under Title IX, Cannon v. University of Chicago (1979), and its prohibitions extend to employees as well as students. North Haven Board of Education v. Bell (1982). The 1987 Civil Rights Restoration Act, overruling *Grove City College* in this respect, clarified that Title IX's sex discrimination prohibition pertains to all of a recipient's operations, not merely to the particular program or activity receiving federal assistance. But the Restoration Act also exempts from Title IX entities controlled by religious organizations if application of Title IX would conflict with the organization's religious tenets.

F.   CIVIL RIGHTS ATTORNEY'S FEES AWARDS ACT

The Civil Rights Attorney's Fees Awards Act, a 1976 amendment to 42 U.S.C.A. § 1988, permits a discretionary award of attorney's fees as a part of the costs recoverable by prevailing parties, other than the United States, in actions pursuant to 42 U.S.C.A. §§ 1981, 1982, 1983, 1985, and 1986, as well as Titles VI and IX. The Act parallels separate statutory authority to award attorneys' fees to prevailing parties in actions under EPA and ADEA, see FLSA § 16(b), and under Title VII, see § 706(k). The principles governing eligibility for and computation of awards are largely interchangeable among these statutes.

Although a plaintiff must receive at least some relief on the merits in order to become a "prevailing party" eligible for fees, success on a "significant issue," even if it is not a "central" one, will suffice. Texas State Teachers Ass'n v. Garland Independent School District (1989). A plaintiff adjudged to be a prevailing party should ordinarily receive a fee award absent "special circumstances," such as the plaintiff's egregious misconduct. See Christiansburg Garment Co. v. EEOC (1978); these circumstances are scarcely ever found. Zimmer, Sullivan & Richards, *Cases and Materials on Employment Discrimination,* 663–664 (2d ed. 1988).

To achieve success on a "significant issue" and thus be eligible for fees, the plaintiff need only obtain some relief, by settlement or otherwise, which changes his legal relationship with the defendant and is more than merely technical or *de minimis*. Fees may be awarded for relief obtained in state proceedings, Sullivan v. Hudson (1989); New York Gaslight Club, Inc. v. Carey (1980); and awards may be made *pendente lite* when a plaintiff has achieved some interim relief on the merits, for example an injunction. See Hanrahan v. Hampton (1980).

Degree of success is critically important in calculating the amount of a "reasonable" award of attorney's fees. A "lodestar" figure is calculated by multiplying the numbers of hours reasonably expended, on matters on which a plaintiff has prevailed, by a reasonable hourly rate. The lodestar is based on market rates in the relevant community, and therefore fees awardable to nonprofit legal services organizations may not be limited to actual costs. Blum v. Stenson (1984). Similarly, fee awards may compensate for the work of law clerks and paralegals, again at market rates. Missouri v. Jenkins (1989).

There is a strong presumption that the lodestar represents a reasonable fee, and upward or downward adjustments may take into account only factors not used in arriving at the lodestar. See Hensley v. Eckerhart (1983); Pennsylvania v. Delaware Valley Citizens' Council for Clean Air (1986). The lodestar may not be adjusted upward to compensate for an attorney's "risk of loss," unless perhaps evidence is produced to show that the possibility of an enhanced fee was required in order to attract counsel. Pennsylvania v. Delaware Valley Citizens' Council for Clean Air (1987) (O'Connor, J., concurring). Fees may be augmented to compensate for delay in payment (but not for risk of nonpayment), and that adjustment is not barred by the Eleventh Amendment in an action against a state. *Missouri v. Jenkins,* supra.

Additional adjustment factors include the novelty and difficulty of the questions presented, the extent to which the demands of the case preclude other legal employment, the undesirability of the case, awards in similar cases, and the experience, reputation and ability of the attorneys. No single adjustment factor can substitute for the basic multiplication of a reasonable billing rate by the number of hours reasonably expended on successful claims. For this reason, the attorney's fee award may not be limited by a contingent-fee arrangement that yields a lesser sum than the lodestar. Blanchard v. Bergeron (1989).

While a prevailing plaintiff is ordinarily to be awarded attorney's fees in all but special circumstances, the Supreme Court has interpreted § 706(k) to preclude attorney's fees to a prevailing defendant unless the plaintiff's action was "frivolous, unreasonable, or without foundation. . . ." *Christiansburg Garment Co.,* supra. Of course if a plaintiff is found to have asserted a claim in subjective bad faith, the case for awarding the defendant attorney's fees is even stronger. The plaintiff's failure to establish a prima facie case, the unprecedented nature of a claim, the defendant's offer of a settlement, or the dismissal of an action before trial all figure in determining whether a claim is sufficiently frivolous, unreasonable, or groundless to justify taxing attorney's fees against a plaintiff.

The *Christiansburg* test has recently been applied to govern the award of attorneys' fees against unsuccessful intervenors. The Supreme Court characterized as "particularly welcome" a union's intervention challenging a proposed settlement of a sex discrimination action in order to protect "the legitimate expectations of . . . [male] employees innocent of any wrongdoing." It encouraged intervention by holding that intervenors would be liable for plaintiffs' cost of defending a settlement only when the intervention is "frivolous, unreasonable, or without foundation. . . ." *Independent Federation of Flight Attendants v. Zipes,* supra. In effect, then, intervention becomes per se a "special circumstance" that warrants denial of a fee award to a prevailing plaintiff.

G. HANDICAP DISCRIMINATION AND THE REHABILITATION ACT OF 1973

There is no national comprehensive prohibition against handicap discrimination by private employers, although pending legislation, if enacted, would ultimately extend the ban to most employers covered by Title VII. The current provision with the broadest reach, § 504 of the Rehabilitation Act of 1973, 29 U.S.C.A. § 701 et seq., enjoins federal funds recipients from excluding or discriminating against any "otherwise qualified handicapped individual" in "any program or activity receiving federal financial assistance." The Civil Rights Restoration Act of 1987 overruled *Grove City College* with respect to Section 504, thereby effectively banning handicap discrimination in all the recipient institution's operations, not merely in programs or activities for which federal assistance is granted.

Section 504 is enforced by the administrative procedures of Title VI, which may lead to termination of funding or refusal to extend future assistance. In addition, the Supreme Court, without expressly deciding whether Section 504 gives rise to a private right of action, has approved the award of relief in such a case and held that employers may violate the statute even if the federal aid they receive is not for the primary purpose of promoting employment. See Consolidated Rail Corp. v. Darrone (1984). By contrast, lower courts have held that there is no private right of action right under Section 503 of the Act, which requires federal government contractors to "take affirmative action to employ and advance in employment qualified handicapped individuals."

In 1974, Congress amended the definition of "handicapped individual" for Section 504 purposes to include not just those with actual physical impairments, "but also those who are regarded as impaired and who, as a result, are substantially limited in a major life activity. . . ." School Board of Nassau County v. Arline (1987). Moreover, a person suffering impairment of major life activities from tuberculosis is considered handicapped even though his disease is contagious. Id. But to be eligible for relief, a plaintiff must generally also be "otherwise qualified," or able to perform the "essential functions" of the particular job. And while inability to function may not be inferred simply from the fact of a handicap, a tuberculosis sufferer may not be "otherwise qualified" if his contagion poses "a serious health threat to others." Id.

Lower courts after *Arline* have found that AIDS victims may qualify as handicapped individuals, at least where they experience a related physical impairment. Congress has somewhat awkwardly codified the *Arline* approach by excluding from the definition of "individual with handicaps" a person with "a currently contagious disease or infection" who, as a result, "would constitute a direct threat to the health or safety of other individuals or . . . is unable to perform the duties of the job." Section 9, Civil Rights Restoration Act of 1987, Pub.L. No. 100–259, 102 Stat. 28 (1988). This approach is seemingly more restrictive than the Court's, because an employer must ordinarily make "reasonable accommodation" to individuals with handicaps, even those who are not "otherwise qualified." Although accommodation does not require an employer to fundamentally alter its program or incur "undue financial or administrative burdens," Southeastern Community College v. Davis (1979), it provides an applicant or employee an opportunity to demonstrate that a handicap, while apparently preventing routine performance of an essential job duty, is surmountable. By classifying certain victims of contagious diseases as non-handicapped in the first instance, Congress may have foreclosed this opportunity.

H. ALIENAGE DISCRIMINATION AND THE IMMIGRATION REFORM AND CONTROL ACT OF 1986

Discrimination on the basis of alien status, not prohibited by Title VII or the Reconstruction Civil Rights Acts, receives special treatment in the Immigration Reform and Control Act of 1986 (IRCA), 8 U.S.C.A. § 1324b. Discriminating on the basis of "citizenship status" against an "authorized" alien—one admitted for permanent residence or eligible for U.S. employment under the terms of the Act—is an "unfair immigration-related employment practice" that may subject an employer to civil or criminal penalties. Another section prohibits employers from hiring, recruiting, or referring "unauthorized aliens." The IRCA creates an employment verification system under which an employer must verify a worker's identity and employment authorization. 8 U.S.C.A. § 1324a.

Complaints of discrimination on the basis of citizenship status or national origin are heard by administrative law judges within the Department of Justice, with judicial review in the courts of appeals.

I. CIVIL RIGHTS ACT OF 1968, TITLE I

The Civil Rights Act of 1968, Title I, 18 U.S.C.A. § 245, establishes criminal penalties for intentional violations of the civil rights of individuals. The list of possible violations includes: conduct which injures, attempts to injure, intimidates or interferes with a person's employment rights because of race, color, religion, or national origin. No prosecutions under the Act are permitted without certification by the Attorney General, the Associate Deputy Attorney General, or designated Assistant Attorneys General that a federal prosecution is in the public interest and necessary to secure substantial justice; this certification procedure cannot be delegated.

J. INTERGOVERNMENTAL PERSONNEL ACT OF 1970

State and local governments which receive monies or financial assistance under federal programs and grants through the Intergovernmental Personnel Act of 1970, 42 U.S.C.A. § 4723, must refrain from discriminating in employment on the grounds of race, color, national origin, sex, religious creed and political affiliation. Elected officials and their personal staffs are exempt. The Office of Personnel Management supervises, administers, and enforces the Act, and no private right of action is provided.

K. VIETNAM ERA VETERANS READJUSTMENT ACT OF 1974

The Vietnam Era Veterans Readjustment Act of 1974, 38 U.S.C.A. § 2011 et seq., requires federal contractors with contracts of $10,000 or more, their subcontractors, and federal agencies to engage in affirmative action to employ certain disabled veterans and veterans of the Vietnam Era. The EEOC supervises compliance by federal agencies, while the Department of Labor handles veterans' claims of handicap discrimination under government contracts. There is no private right of action.

L. AGE DISCRIMINATION ACT OF 1975

The Age Discrimination Act of 1975, as amended, 42 U.S.C.A. § 6101 et seq., prohibits discrimination at any age in programs or activities receiving federal financial assistance. The Civil Rights Restoration Act of 1987 extends the age discrimination ban from particular federally-assisted programs or activities to recipients' entire operations. Any administering federal agency or interested person is authorized to file suit against fund recipients. Interested persons may also seek administrative relief.

M. FOREIGN BOYCOTT LAWS

The Export Administration Act of 1969, as amended, popularly known as the Foreign Boycott Laws, 50 U.S.C.A.App. § 2407, authorizes the President to prohibit the facilitating of discrimination by foreign governments against "any United States person" on the basis of race, religion, sex or national origin. It also expressly prohibits furnishing racial, religious, gender, or national origin information about any "United States person," or any owner, officer, director, or employee of such person. Violations of the Act or regulations promulgated under it can result in criminal penalties.

N. LABOR MANAGEMENT RELATIONS ACT

The National Labor Relations Board ("NLRB"), in administering the Labor Management Relations Act ("LMRA"), may encounter unlawful discrimination during union representation campaigns, certifications, fair representation disputes, duty to bargain situations, or other unfair labor practice proceedings. A certified union's duty of fair representation may be enforced by aggrieved black union members or applicants for union membership in private federal damages actions, Steele v. Louisville & Nashville Railroad (1944), and probably in NLRB unfair labor practice proceedings.

See DelCostello v. International Brotherhood of Teamsters (1983). But minority employees are not protected from union discipline when, bypassing their union, they raise employment discrimination grievances directly with an employer. Emporium Capwell Co. v. The Western Addition Community Organization (1975). An employer probably has a duty to bargain over employment discrimination issues, but employer discrimination standing alone will not constitute an unfair labor practice absent a link between the employer's alleged discriminatory conduct and interference with rights conferred by the LMRA. See Jubilee Mfg. Co. (1973), enf'd sub nom. United Steelworkers of America v. NLRB (1974).

Although election results may be overturned if either a union or an employer has appealed directly to race hatred during a campaign, a union is not foreclosed from invoking the election procedures of LMRA because it has a history of racial discrimination. Compare Sewell Mfg. Co. (1962) with Handy Andy, Inc. (1977). Some courts of appeals, however, have found that the NLRB is constitutionally compelled to withhold certification from an illegally discriminating union. See NLRB v. Heavy Lift Serv., Inc. (1979); NLRB v. Mansion House Center Management Corp. (1973). In any event, the Board may revoke a union's certification if it breaches the duty of fair representation by engaging in discriminatory practices.

O. EXECUTIVE ORDERS

A number of Executive Orders issued under the authority of the President prohibit employment discrimination. These orders usually establish federal policy in a particular area, require affirmative action programs, and specify responsibility for enforcement. No private rights of action are created, and enforcement and implementation are usually left to the executive agency or department involved.

By far the most important for present purposes is Executive Order 11246. As amended, it prohibits employment discrimination by government contractors on grounds of race, religion, sex, or national origin. It also demands that contractors take "affirmative action" by means of "goals" and "timetables" to boost the representation of protected group members in major job categories to levels that reflect the availability of qualified members of the protected group. There is no specific legislative basis for the Order, but lower courts have followed the lead of the Third Circuit in holding that Congress should be "deemed to have granted" the President the "general authority" to so protect federal interests. Contractors Ass'n v. Secretary of Labor (1971).

Executive Order 11141 prohibits age discrimination by government contractors and subcontractors; Executive Order 11478 prohibits race, color, religion, sex, national origin, handicap, and age discrimination by the federal government. Other executive orders establish coordinated enforcement efforts and special programs for minority and women's enterprises.

P. U.S. CONSTITUTION

In limited circumstances the Constitution provides direct protection against certain forms of employment discrimination. There are two principal sources of protection. First, the Fifth Amendment provides that federal action may not work deprivations of life, liberty, or property without due process; the Fourteenth Amendment prohibits the same deprivations and denials by state and local governments. Second, the Fourteenth Amendment prohibits states from denying to persons within their jurisdiction the equal protection of the laws; to some degree this prohibition has been judicially extended to federal action as part of the Fifth Amendment right of due process. See Bolling v. Sharpe (1954).

The Supreme Court has recognized implied damages actions by federal employees to enforce constitutional guarantees against discrimination when no other remedy is available. Davis v. Passman (1979). But if a statute silent on preserving a judicial damages remedy for a constitutional violation creates an administrative remedy, an implied constitutional claim is precluded if the administrative system is comprehensive and provides "meaningful" remedies, even if no statutory remedy is afforded the particular putative plaintiff. Schweiker v. Chilicky (1988) (no implied damages remedy for alleged unconstitutional termination of social security benefits given elaborate benefit-restoration procedures of Disability Benefits Reform Act); compare Bush v. Lucas (1983) *with* Spagnola v. Mathis (1988) (en banc) (no implied damages remedy for, respectively, major or minor federal civil service personnel actions that allegedly violated First Amendment rights in the face of, respectively, elaborate and sparse administrative procedures and judicial review provided under the Civil Service Reform Act). Even more clearly, constitutional claims will not be implied so as to circumvent limitations in a statute that does specifically authorize a judicial damages remedy. For example, the courts of appeals, with the Supreme Court's apparent approval, see *Jett*, have unanimously rejected attempts to circumvent the *Monell* "official policy" requirement for municipal liability under § 1983 by implying a more permissive right of action directly from the Fourteenth Amendment.

The Supreme Court has also recognized that a state cause of action for employment discrimination gives rise to a property interest that may not be impaired without Fourteenth Amendment due process. Logan v. Zimmerman Brush Co. (1982). Finally, judicial scrutiny may be had of government actions that create "suspect classifications" potentially violative of the equal protection standards of the Fifth and Fourteenth Amendments. See National Education Association v. South Carolina (1978); Califano v. Goldfarb (1977).

CHAPTER 20

MISCELLANEOUS EMPLOYEE PROTECTION LAWS

A. EMPLOYEE RETIREMENT INCOME SECURITY ACT OF 1974 (ERISA)

Congress enacted the Employee Retirement Income Security Act, 29 U.S.C.A. § 1001 et seq., for the purpose of safeguarding employee retirement and pension benefits. The act established minimum standards for employee participation, vesting standards which create nonforfeitable rights, and funding guidelines. Generally speaking, federal laws preempt all state laws and causes of action which relate to ERISA pension or welfare plans, directly or indirectly. Ellenburg v. Brockway, Inc. (1985). For example, ERISA preempts state tort and contract actions involving ERISA covered plans. See e.g., Jackson v. Martin Marietta Corp. (1986) (contract); Dependahl v. Falstaff Brewing Corp. (1981) (tort). As a result of preemption, damages in an ERISA proceeding are limited, but attorney's fees are recoverable. Punitives are not allowed. Massachusetts Mut. Life Ins. Co. v. Russell (1985). Investments are regulated, and minimum standards of fiduciary conduct for trustees and administrators are established, with civil and criminal enforcement measures provided. ERISA

278

plan administrators have a special fiduciary relationship toward plan participants and beneficiaries. Most federal courts of appeal had applied an arbitrary and capricious standard of review to decisions of plan administration denying benefits. However, the Supreme Court in Firestone Tire & Rubber Co. v. Bruch (1989), placed limits on the utilization of this standard of review, and provided for de novo review, unless a plan expressly grants the necessary discretion to an administrator to construe terms and determine benefits. Payment of pensions has been assured through the Pension Benefit Guaranty Corporation, which administers the termination insurance provisions. The Retiree Benefits Bankruptcy Protection Act of 1988 also affords workers health, disability, and life insurance protection from insolvent businesses.

B. NATIONAL LABOR RELATIONS ACT

The National Labor Relations Act, as amended, primarily governs employer-union relations. The act grants employees important rights to create or become members of unions, to choose representatives and to bargain collectively, and to engage in or refrain from "concerted activities" for mutual aid and protection. This concerted activity protection is afforded non-union employees, and the National Labor Relations Board (NLRB) frequently intervenes to protect non-union employees so long as their activities are related to wage or working conditions. For example, NLRB involvement based upon "concerted activity" could arise in an employment situation if an employee solicited additional employee support for a group health insurance plan. See Edward Blankstein, Inc. v. NLRB (1980). For a more complete summary of the various federal legislation regulating unions, management, strikes, boycotts, etc., see D. Leslie, Labor Law in a Nutshell (2d Ed. 1986).

C. FEDERAL CONSTRUCTION PROJECTS

Two important federal acts protect workers employed on federal construction projects. The Miller Act contains a performance bond requirement, and the act permits persons supplying labor and materials to sue in federal district court to collect monies owed for unpaid wages or supplies. The Copeland or "Kickback" Act prohibits by criminal penalty any attempt to force or induce workers to pay kickbacks from wages under federal construction contracts.

D. FEDERAL CREDIT LAWS

The Consumer Credit Protection Act, Title III, prohibits the discharge of an employee because of a garnishment for any one indebtedness. The Consumer Credit Protection Act; Title VI (called the Fair Credit Reporting Act) regulates the use of credit reports for employment purposes. It should be noted that state laws frequently regulate garnishments. Additionally, blacklisting, employer statements and "service letters" relating to former employees are often areas of state regulation. Some states also regulate or prohibit wage assignments.

E. JURY SERVICE

The Jury System Improvement Act of 1968, as amended, protects any employee's job security in the event the employee is called to serve on a federal jury. See Shea v. County of Rockland (1987) (damages are limited to economic losses). A number of states have enacted similar employee protection laws for state jury service.

F. UNJUST DISCHARGES

Traditionally, the employment at-will concept freely allowed the employer or the employee to terminate the employment relationship at any time and for any reason without further obligation. See Adair v. United States (1908). However, recent litigation and legislation concerning wrongful terminations or unjust discharges have dramatically changed this entire area of the law. See generally, Smith v. Atlas Off–Shore Boat Service, Inc. (1981).

The common-law doctrine of employment-at-will has been the subject of rapid revision by state and federal legislation and judicial decision. Federal and state laws concerning unions, civil service employees, and fair employment give certain classes of employees fairly comprehensive protection from certain types of discharges.

The following theories or laws may provide an employee with a remedy for an unjust discharge or wrongful termination: (1) violation of public policy; see Sheets v. Teddy's Frosted Foods, Inc. (1980) (discussion of illegal act and whistleblowing); (2) breach of an implied contract of employment, usually based upon employment handbooks or oral representations; see Toussaint v. Blue Cross & Blue Shield (1980) (handbook); Schipani v. Ford Motor Co. (1981) (oral representations can override written disclaimers); (3) breach of implied covenant of good faith and fair dealing; see Wagenseller v. Scottsdale Memorial Hospital (1985); (4) breach of express employment contract; (5) promissory estoppel; see Grouse v. Group Health Plan, Inc. (1981) (job change in reliance on employment offer that was later revoked); (6) common law tort actions growing out of the discharge, including but not limited to prima facie tort, intentional infliction of emotional distress, fraud, defamation, tortious interference with contract, invasion of privacy; some jurisdictions recognize a separate tort action for the discharge itself, under the headings of wrongful discharge, retaliatory discharge, abusive discharge, or unjust discharge, etc.; and (7) state and federal statutory protections.

A non-exclusive list of federal statutory protections against discharge includes: the Labor Management Relations Act, 29 U.S.C.A. § 141 et seq.;

Age Discrimination in Employment Act, 29 U.S. C.A. § 621 et seq.; Rehabilitation Act of 1973, 29 U.S.C.A. §§ 701, 796i; Equal Pay Act, 29 U.S.C.A. § 206(d); Civil Rights Act of 1964, 42 U.S.C.A. § 2000e–17; Civil Rights Act of 1866, 42 U.S.C.A. § 1981; Civil Rights Act of 1871, 42 U.S.C.A. § 1983; Alcohol Abuse and Alcoholism Prevention Treatment and Rehabilitation Program for Government and Other Employees Act, 42 U.S.C.A. § 290 dd; Vietnam Era Veterans' Readjustment Assistance Act of 1974, 38 U.S.C.A. § 2011 et seq.; Occupational Safety and Health Act, 29 U.S.C.A. § 660; Mine Safety and Health Act, 30 U.S.C.A. § 815; Railroad Safety Act, 45 U.S.C.A. § 441; Longshore and Harbor Workers' Compensation Act, 33 U.S.C.A. § 948; Selective Service Act, 38 U.S.C.A. § 2021; Vocational Rehabilitation Act, 29 U.S.C.A. § 793; Energy Reorganization Act, 45 U.S.C.A. § 5851; Consumer Protection Act, 15 U.S. C.A. § 1674; Employee Polygraph Protection Act, 29 U.S.C.A. § 2001 et seq.; Whistleblower Protection Act of 1989, 5 U.S.C.A. §§ 1213–1222, 2302; Bankruptcy Act, 11 U.S.C.A. § 525(b); Clean Air Act, 42 U.S.C.A. § 7622; Toxic Substances Control Act, 15 U.S.C.A. § 2622; Federal Water Pollution Control Act, 33 U.S.C.A. § 1367; Solid Waste Disposal Act, 42 U.S.C.A. § 6971; Comprehensive Environmental Response, Compensation and Liability Act, 42 U.S.C.A. § 9610; Civil Service Reform Act, 5 U.S.C.A. § 2303; Fair Labor Standards Act, 29 U.S.C.A. § 215(a)(3); Migrant and Seasonal Agricultural Worker Protection Act, 29 U.S.C.A.

H. POLYGRAPHS

For the most part, the Employee Polygraph Protection Act of 1988, 29 U.S.C.A. § 2001, prohibits the use of polygraphs by employers with regard to job applicants or employees. Limited exceptions are made for some government contractors, some providers of security services, some drug industries, and some instances involving employee crime. The act is administered by the Secretary of Labor, and employees are given a private right of action.

I. NOTICE OF PLANT CLOSINGS

Most lay-offs or plant closings by employers with 100 or more employees are subject to the notice requirements of the Worker Adjustment and Retraining Notification Act of 1988, 29 U.S.C.A. § 2101. Employers must give 60 days notice to the employees' union or to the employees in the absence of a union, prior to such actions. Failure to comply with the act can result in employer liability for backpay and benefits to employees, and the imposition of fines. Enforcement actions are to be brought in federal district court.

J. MIGRANT FARM WORKERS

The Migrant and Seasonal Agricultural Worker Protection Act, 29 U.S.C.A. § 1801 et seq., attempts to regulate migrant and seasonal farm labor by requiring farm labor contractor registration; by regulating workers safety, housing, and transportation; and by requiring employers to keep certain records. Enforcement provisions include a private right of action for act violations. See Barrett v. Adams Fruit Co. (1989) (act preempts exclusive remedy provision of Florida's workers' compensation law).

K. CONTAGIOUS DISEASES IN THE WORK PLACE

Contagious disease in the workplace, and the increasing number of employees with AIDS (Acquired Immune Deficiency Syndrome), have focused attention on new employer-employee legal issues in recent years.

Employees covered by the Vocational Rehabilitation Act of 1973, 29 U.S.C.A. § 701 et seq., may have a private right of action for discrimination due to disease. See Consolidated Rail Corp. v. Darrone (1984). In addition, workers with contagious diseases may qualify as "handicapped" or "injured" for purposes of the Vocational Rehabilitation Act. School Board of Nassau County v. Arline (1987).

Of great importance to workers with diseases are medical benefits that are usually protected by the Employee Retirement Income Security Act of 1974, (ERISA) 29 U.S.C.A. § 1140. ERISA protected benefits plans may afford relief from acts of discrimination in connection with discontinuation of health insurance, denial of disability payments or pensions, or forced retirements.

It should also be noted that the Occupational Safety and Health Act, (OSHA) 29 U.S.C.A. § 651 et seq., imposes duties upon employers to provide safe workplaces free from recognized hazards, which can include contagious and other diseases.

An employer who discloses that a worker has a contagious disease may face common law claims for invasion of privacy. Also, states that have adopted fair employment practices laws in the handicap area may offer workers an additional remedy for discrimination. Finally, an employer could face state tort liability for any intentional exposure of workers to contagious diseases. See Chapters 3, 8, supra. Furthermore, the employer could be liable for third-party harm by way of negligent hiring and retention of workers with contagious diseases.

APPENDIX

PROPOSED NATIONAL WORKERS' COMPENSATION STANDARDS ACT

96th CONGRESS   S.420

1st SESSION

To strengthen State workers' compensation programs, and for other purposes.

IN THE SENATE OF THE UNITED STATES

FEBRUARY 9 (legislative day, JANUARY 15), 1979

Mr. WILLIAMS (for himself and Mr. JAVITS) introduced the following bill; which was read twice and referred to the Committee on Human Resources.

288

A BILL

To strengthen State workers' compensation programs, and for other purposes.

Be it enacted by the Senate and House of Representatives of the United States of America in Congress assembled, That this Act may be cited as the "National Workers' Compensation Standards Act of 1979".

FINDINGS AND DECLARATION OF PURPOSE

SEC. 2. (a) The Congress finds and declares that—

(1) many thousands of American workers are killed or permanently disabled and millions more are incapacitated from injuries and disease arising out of and in the course of their employment;

(2) injuries, disease, and deaths arising out of and in the course of employment, constitute a burden upon interstate commerce and have a substantial adverse effect upon the general welfare;

(3) work-related injuries and diseases frequently occur during the workers' most productive years which often results in hardship for dependents and families;

(4) the vast majority of these injured and ill workers, and their families, are dependent on

State workers' compensation systems for economic security, medical treatment, rehabilitation, and reemployment assistance when they suffer an injury, disease, or death arising out of and in the course of their employment;

(5) American workers and the national interest are best served by an adequate, prompt, and equitable workers' compensation system;

(6) many existing State workers' compensation laws do not provide an adequate prompt and equitable system of compensation for injuries, diseases, or deaths arising out of and in the course of employment;

(7) the basic national objectives for a comprehensive workers' compensation system include (A) broad coverage of employees and work-related injuries and diseases; (B) substantial protection against interruption of income; (C) provision of prompt and adequate medical care and rehabilitation services in order to correct work-related injuries and to restore such injured workers to gainful employment; (D) encouragement of safety and health protection; and (E) an effective system for delivery of benefits and services;

(8) the National Commission on State Workmen's Compensation Laws, in its 1972 report, found that existing State workers' compensation laws did not meet minimum standards of adequacy and fairness;

(9) although in recent years there have been improvements in many State workers' compensa-

tion laws, to a great extent existing State workers' compensation laws still fail to meet the minimum standards recommended by the National Commission on State Workmen's Compensation Laws; and

(10) the improvements that are necessary to insure that a prompt, adequate, and equitable system of workers' compensation is available to all American workers can and should be achieved without delay, and there is a need for the Federal Government to encourage and assist the States in meeting this responsibility and to establish Federal minimum standards for State workers' compensation programs which assure adequacy, promptness, and fairness, while at the same time maintaining the primary responsibility and authority for workers' compensation in the States.

(b) It is the purpose of this Act through the exercise of the power of Congress to regulate commerce among the several States and with foreign nations, and to provide for the general welfare, to—

(1) establish minimum standards for workers' compensation programs for employees throughout the Nation;

(2) establish appropriate procedures for providing employees with workers' compensation benefits in accordance with such standards in a State which does not meet such standards;

(3) encourage and provide technical and financial assistance to the States to make improvements in existing workers' compensation systems—

(A) to provide all workers and their families an adequate, prompt, and equitable system of workers' compensation;

(B) to restore disabled workers through medical and vocational rehabilitation services to the fullest possible physical, mental, and economic usefulness; and

(4) accomplish the foregoing objectives in such a way as to maintain the primary authority and responsibility for workers' compensation in the States.

DEFINITIONS

SEC. 3. For the purposes of this Act—

(1) the term "Secretary" means the Secretary of Labor;

(2) the term "Advisory Commission" means the National Workers' Compensation Advisory Commission established under this Act;

(3) the term "employer" means any person engaged in commerce or an industry affecting commerce, but shall not include the United States, or any State or political subdivision thereof;

(4) the term "person" includes one or more individuals, labor unions, partnerships, associa-

tions, firms, insurance funds, mutual companies, corporations, companies, joint-stock companies, trusts, unincorporated organizations, societies, trustees, trustees in bankruptcy, or receivers;

(5) the term "employee" means any individual employed by his or her employer or any individual who is treated as an employee for purposes of the workers' compensation law of any State, except that such term does not include—

(a) any individual who does not receive wages as defined in section 3121(a) of the Internal Revenue Code (26 U.S.C. 3121);

(b) any individual employed in domestic service in or around a private home by any employer who did not during any calendar quarter in the same or previous calendar year, employ one or more household domestic workers for compensation of $1,000 or more; or

(c) any individual employed as an agricultural laborer by any employer who did not during any calendar quarter during the preceding calendar year employ more than thirty workdays of agricultural labor. For the purposes of this subsection, "workday" means any day during which an employee performs any agricultural labor for not less than one hour. The person who operates a farm shall be deemed to be the "employer" of agricultural workers employed on that farm for the purposes of this Act, except where another person within the definition of "employer" in subsection (3) of this section has agreed in writing with the operator to accept workers' compensation responsibility and has informed the Secretary of his intention to accept such responsibility when applying for a registration certificate under the Farm Labor Contractor Registration Act of 2963, as amended; or

(d) any individual whose employment is covered by (i) subchapters I and II of chapter 81 of title 5, United States Code, (ii) the Act entitled "An Act relating to the liability of common carriers by railroad to their employees in certain cases", approved April 22, 1908 (35 Stat. 65, 45 U.S.C. 51–60), (iii) the Longshoremen's and Harbor Workers' Compensation Act (33 U.S.C. 901–950) and extensions thereof, or (iv) section 20 of the Act entitled "An Act to remove certain burdens on the American merchant marine and encourage the American foreign carrying trade, and for other purposes", approved June 26, 1884 (46 U.S.C. 688);

(6) the term "physician" means a person licensed to provide health care services, and includes but is not limited to surgeons, podiatrists, dentists, clinical psychologists, optometrists, chiropractors to the extent specified in the Federal Employees' Compensation Act (5 U.S.C. 8101(2)), and osteopathic practitioners within the scope of their practice as defined by State law, and any other individual licensed to provide health care services reimbursable without referral from a

physician under the workers' compensation law of any State;

(7) the term "compensation" means benefits made available under the applicable State workers' compensation law or pursuant to entitlements created by this Act, to the disabled employee or to the survivors of a deceased employee, and shall include, but not be limited to—

(a) "monetary benefits" paid to disabled employees or their survivors;

(b) "medical benefits" including payments for or provision of services of physicians, hospital care, nursing care, ambulance, prosthetic devices, and other related services, drugs, medicines;

(c) "rehabilitation benefits" including payment for or provision of medical and vocational services to reduce disability and to restore the physical, mental, and vocational functioning of a disabled worker;

(8) the term "statewide average weekly wage" means the average weekly earnings of workers on private payrolls within the State, as determined under the Federal Unemployment Tax Act (26 U.S.C. 3304);

(9) the term "State workers' compensation agency" means that agency, court, or official designated in each State as responsible for the

administration or enforcement of the workers' compensation program within such State;

(10) the term "State workers' compensation law" means the law or laws of a State which provide compensation for death or disability resulting from injuries (including diseases) arising out of and in the course of employment or other similar test of work relatedness applicable under such law.

STANDARDS FOR WORKERS' COMPENSATION BENEFITS

SEC. 4. The minimum standards for State workers' compensation laws shall be as follows:

(a) All employers and employees as defined in this Act shall be covered, and coverage shall be compulsory, rather than elective.

(b)(1) Monetary benefits payable for total disability or for death shall be not less than 66⅔ per centum of the employee's average weekly wage subject to the following limitations:

(A) During the one-year period commencing January 1, 1982, with respect to disability or death occurring during such year, the maximum weekly benefits payable shall not be less than 100 per centum of the statewide average weekly wage during the first four of the last eight calendar quarters preceding January 1, 1982.

(B) During the one-year period commencing January 1, 1984, and for every year thereafter, the maximum weekly benefits payable with respect to disability or death shall be not less than 150 per centum of the statewide average weekly wage during the first four of the last eight calendar quarters preceding January 1, of the year in which the death or disability occurs.

(C) Minimum weekly monetary benefits for permanent total disability and death during any one-year period shall be at a rate not less than 50 per centum of the statewide average weekly wage during the first four of the last eight calendar quarters preceding January 1 of such year or the employee's actual weekly wage, whichever is less.

(D) The maximum and minimum weekly benefits provided herein which are in effect on the date of the occurrence of the disability or death shall be applicable for the full period for which benefits are payable with respect to such disability or death.

(2) For the purpose of paragraph (1) of this subsection, payment of benefits at the rate of 80 per centum of the spendable earnings of a totally disabled or deceased employee shall be deemed to be not less than $66\frac{2}{3}$ per centum of such employee's average weekly wage if spendable earnings are not less than the employee's gross average weekly wage reduced by an amount de-

termined to reflect amounts which would be withheld from such wage under Federal and State income tax laws and under subchapter A of chapter 21 of the Internal Revenue Code of 1954 (relating to social security taxes) if the amount withheld were determined on the basis of the reasonably anticipated liability of such employee for tax for the taxable year in which such payments are made without regard to any itemized deductions but taking into account the maximum number of personal exemption deductions allowable.

(c)(1) Monetary benefits in the case of death at not less than the rate specified in subsection (b) of this section (including the maximum limits specified therein) shall be payable to the deceased employee's surviving spouse for life or until remarriage, with at least two years' benefits payable upon remarriage, except that if there is one or more surviving child, at least 50 per centum of the benefits payable under this paragraph shall be payable to such surviving children (share and share alike), such benefits to be payable to each child until at least age eighteen (or age twenty-five if the surviving child is a full-time student in an accredited educational institution), or for life if any such surviving child is physically or mentally incapable of self-support at the time of death of the employee provided the compensation need not continue if such child becomes capable of self-support. If there is no surviving spouse, the amount of benefits payable to any surviving children shall include the amount which would otherwise have been payable to such surviving spouse.

(2) State law may provide an offset of death benefits against the survivor's insurance benefit payable under the Social Security Act, but only to the extent that such death benefits are reduced by no more than 5 per centum of the surviving spouse's share of the survivor's insurance benefits under the Social Security Act for each $10 of the deceased employee's average weekly wage in excess of $100, and further provided that in no case shall the reduction exceed 50 per centum of the surviving spouse's share of the survivor's insurance benefits under the Social Security Act.

(d) There shall be no time or dollar maximum limitation on the total amount of compensation payable in case of death or total disability.

(e) There shall be no time or dollar maximum limitation on the type or extent of medical benefits determined to be necessary by the State workers' compensation agency in any case.

(f) There shall be no exclusion of any disease and compensation due to disease shall not be denied on the basis that a disease (1) is not peculiar to or characteristic of a particular occupation or employment; (2) is not the result of an accident, or the onset of such disease was unrelated to any accident or accidental occurrence;

(3) does not appear on a list of compensable diseases where exclusion from the list renders a disease conclusively noncompensable, or appears on a list of diseases which are conclusively noncompensable if such disease might, under some circumstances, arise out of and in the course of employment; or (4) is an ordinary disease of life or is a communicable disease, if the risk of contracting such a disease is increased by the nature of the employment. Nothing in this section shall preclude any State from including in its law, rebuttable presumptions concerning the circumstances under which particular diseases may be found to have arisen or not to have arisen out of and in the course of employment.

(g) A disabled employee shall be entitled to prompt rehabilitation services subject to the supervision and approval of the State workers' compensation agency. The State workers' compensation agency shall determine the appropriate rehabilitation services in each case to accomplish to the extent possible the objectives of restoring the physical, mental, and vocational functioning of the disabled employee, and his or her return to employment, consistent with the nature of the disability incurred. The State law may permit a maximum time limit on rehabilitation of not less than two years. Expenses incident to rehabilitation shall be considered a part of the rehabilitation benefits and shall not be borne by the disabled employee. Rehabilitation benefits are additional benefits and shall not reduce or replace any other available compensation.

(h) At such time as a disabled employee is able to resume work, the employer shall take reasonable steps to reemploy such employee in the same position or occupation such employee held prior to the disability, or if the employee is unable to perform the duties of his or her former position or occupation, to any other available position for which such employee is qualified, unless taking into consideration all the relevant circumstances, requiring such reemployment would constitute an undue hardship on the employer.

(i) Subject to the approval, direction, control, and supervision of the State workers' compensation agency, a disabled employee shall be entitled to select a physician for diagnosis and treatment from among all physicians licensed by the State, or from a group or panel of physicians designated previously by the State workers' compensation agency.

(j) Compensation may be denied by reason of an injured worker's refusal to accept medical or rehabilitation service ordered by the State workers' compensation agency, except where such refusal is based on a choice, made in good faith, treatment through prayer or spiritual means.

(k) Whenever employment requires travel between States or between the United States and any other country, an injured or ill employee or the eligible survivors of such employee may claim benefits under the workers' compensation law of a State if the employment was principally localized in that State; or the employee was hired or appointed in that State; or the injury, disease, or death for which benefits are claimed occurred in that State. This section shall not be construed as authorizing recovery of compensation under more than one State's law.

(*l*) The waiting period for monetary benefits shall be not longer than three days and the period for qualifying for retroactive benefits during such period shall be not longer than fourteen days.

(m) An original claim for compensation for disability or death may be filed within two years after the onset of disability or death. The time for filing a claim or notifying the employer of the injury (or disease) shall not begin to run until the employee has a compensable disability and is aware, or by the exercise of reasonable diligence should have been aware, of the causal relationship of the compensable disability to the employment. There shall be no time limitation on the filing of a claim based on recency of employment, unless the Secretary promulgates a standard under section 5 which includes such a time limit.

(n)(1) No compromise or release of any compensation shall be effective unless approved by the State workers' compensation agency, based on a determination by such agency that such compromise or release is in the best interest of the claimant, and will not adversely affect any program of rehabilitation.

(2) No compromise or release of medical or rehabilitation benefits shall be effective unless approved by the State workers' compensation agency, based on the evaluation of a physician designated by that agency that the compromise and release will sufficiently provide for future medical and rehabilitation care necessitated by the employee's injury or disease, and a determination by the agency that such compromise and release is otherwise in the best interest of the employee.

(3) No waiver, release, or similar instrument relating to future coverage or compensation under any State workers' compensation law that is executed prior to the occurrence of any injury or death shall be effective under any circumstances. Any waiver, release or similar instrument which does not comply with the provisions of this paragraph shall be void.

PROPOSALS FOR THE COMPENSATION OF OCCUPATIONAL DISEASE

SEC. 5. (a) The Secretary of Health, Education, and Welfare is authorized and directed to undertake studies of employment-related disease for the purpose of developing and recommending proposals for appropriate standards for (i) determining whether particular diseases arise out of and in the course of employment; (ii) establishing criteria for diagnosing diseases; and (iii) establishing criteria for determining whether death or disability is due to such diseases. In determining subjects for and design of studies pursuant to this section, the Secretary of Health, Education, and Welfare shall give priority to the recommendations of the Secretary of Labor and the National Workers' Compensation Advisory Commission established under section 17 of this Act (hereinafter called the "Advisory Commission"). In carrying out the studies required by this section, the Secretary of Health, Education, and Welfare shall consult with the Director of the National Institute of Occupational Safety and Health and such other public and private organizations as are appropriate with respect to employment-related diseases. The results of such studies shall be published and distributed to the States, and shall be furnished to the Secretary of Labor.

(b) The Secretary may develop recommended standards for (i) determining whether diseases arise out of and in the course of employment; (ii) establishing the criteria for diagnosing such diseases; and (iii) establishing criteria for determining whether death or disability is due to such diseases or for modifying or revoking such standards. Such recommendations may include reasonable rebuttable presumptions wherever appropriate.

(c)(1) Such recommended standards shall be developed in accordance with the following paragraphs:

(2)(A)(i) When the Secretary receives a recommended standard from the Secretary of Health, Education, and Welfare pursuant to subsection (a), and determines not to propose a recommended standard based on that recommendation, the Secretary shall within sixty days after receipt thereof, publish in the Federal Register his determination not to do so and his reasons therefore.

(ii) Whenever the Secretary, upon the basis of studies or recommended standards published under subsection (a) or other information or studies submitted to him by an interested person or by a State or on the basis of information developed by the Secretary, determines that a standard should be proposed to establish minimum standards relating to occupational disease compensation, the Secretary shall prepare a recommended standard and shall appoint an advisory committee composed of not less than three medical, scientific, or other experts of suitable experience, training, or education related to the subject matter of the proposal.

(B) When the Secretary has determined to propose a recommendation for consideration by an advisory committee, the Secretary shall forward it to the advisory committee established to consider such proposal, and shall provide the committee all pertinent information developed by the Secretary or the Secretary of Health, Education, and Welfare, or otherwise available to the Secretary, including the results of research, demonstrations, and experiments. The advisory committee shall consider such proposal and shall determine (i) whether in the advisory committee's opinion the standard is consistent with available scientific and medical knowledge concerning the subject matter of the proposal and (ii) the advisory committee's recommendations for modifications of such proposal to make it consistent with available scientific and medical knowledge concerning the subject matter of the proposal or otherwise to improve the proposal. The advisory committee shall submit a report of its consideration of such proposal to the Secretary within one hundred and eighty days of the date of its appointment or within such shorter period as may be prescribed by the Secretary, but in no event may such period be less than ninety days.

(3) Within sixty days of the receipt of the report of the advisory committee, the Secretary shall determine whether to solicit public comment on the recommended standard. If the Secretary determines to do so, he shall publish that determination and the recommended standard in the Federal Register. If he determines not to recommend said standard, he shall publish that determination in the Federal Register, and his reasons therefore. In either event, the Secretary shall at the same time forward a copy of the advisory committee's report to the Advisory Commission.

After publication of a recommended standard in the Federal Register, the Secretary shall afford interested persons a period of thirty days after such publication in the Federal Register to submit written date or comments on the proposal. Such comment period may be extended by the Secretary upon findings of good cause, which the Secretary shall publish in the Federal Register.

(4) On or before the last day of the period provided for the submission of written date or comments under subparagraph (4)(A), any interested person may file with the Secretary written objections to the recommended standard, stating the grounds therefore and requesting a public hearing on such objections. If the Secretary determines that a public hearing on such proposal would assist in developing pertinent information about such proposal and its subject, the Secretary shall, within sixty days after the last day for filing such objections, publish in the Federal Register a notice specifying the proposal to which objections have been filed and a hearing requested, and specifying a time and place for such hearing. Any hearing under this subsection for the purpose of hearing relevant information shall commence within sixty days after the date of publication of the notice of hearing. Hearings shall be conducted by the Secretary, who may prescribe rules and make rulings concerning procedures in such hearings to avoid unnecessary costs or delay. A verbatim transcript shall be taken of any such hearing and shall be available to the public.

(5) Within one hundred and eighty days after the closing of the record of any such hearing, or, in the case of a recommended standard concerning which a public hearing was not held, within one hundred and eighty days after the period for filing such objections has expired, the Secretary shall publish such proposed standard in its original or modified form in the Federal Register as an advisory standard for compensation of death or disability due to disease arising out of and in the course of employment, or shall publish in the Federal Register the determination not to do so and the reasons therefore.

(6) Any advisory standard published pursuant to this section shall be based on and shall be consistent with available scientific and medical knowledge.

(7) The Secretary may require by subpoena the attendance of witnesses and the production of evidence in connection with any proceeding initiated under this section. If a person refuses to obey a subpoena under this subsection, a United States district court within the jurisdiction of which a proceeding under this subsection is conducted may, upon petition by the Secretary, issue an order requiring compliance with such subpoena.

(d)(1) Any such advisory standard published in the Federal Register pursuant to this section shall immediately upon publication become applicable as an advisory standard which may be considered by each State workers' compensation agency with respect to determining the compensation of death or disability due to disease arising out of and in the course of employment. In any subsequent review of the workers' compensation law of a State made by the Secretary of Labor pursuant to section 7 of this Act, the Secretary shall evaluate and note the extent to which the law of such State complies with the advisory standard; however, the Secretary shall not make any certification of State compliance or noncompliance with any such advisory standard by a State. In determining the extent of compliance with any such advisory standard by the State, the Secretary shall evaluate the statutory law of the States, and the administrative and judicial interpretation of the law by the State workers' compensation agency and the courts of such State.

(2) The Secretary's annual report filed pursuant to section 16 of this Act shall note the extent of State compliance with any advisory standard published pursuant to this section.

(3) Three years after the publication of the first such advisory standard, and at least every three years thereafter, the Secretary shall evaluate the compliance by the States with all published advisory standards, and shall forward to the Congress a report of the degree of such compliance and the Secretary's recommendation with respect to any of the published advisory standards which should be considered by the Congress as mandatory Federal standards for the compensation of death or disability due to diseases arising out of and in the course

of employment. The Secretary shall at that time forward to the Congress the report of the advisory committees which considered any such standards and the record of any public hearings which may have been held in connection with the Secretary's consideration of any such advisory standard, and any medical, scientific, or other data relevant to such standards. The Secretary may, in addition, recommend to the Congress alternative means of establishing mandatory occupational disease standards, including the delegation of comprehensive standard-setting authority.

(e) In developing and considering any recommended standard for compensation of death or disability due to disease, the Secretary shall determine the estimated number of individuals who are employed or formerly employed and who may be affected by the disease or diseases which are the subject of the recommended standard, and the estimated cost of providing compensation pursuant to such recommended standard. The Secretary shall also consider the adequacy and effectiveness of the workers' compensation system to compensate the victims of such disease or diseases, and shall consider alternative methods of providing such compensation which may be more effective in providing fair and adequate compensation. The Secretary shall include such information in the report to the Congress made pursuant to paragraph (d)(3) and may propose alternative methods of providing such compensation in lieu of or in addition to any proposal to provide such compensation through the workers' compensation system of the States.

STUDY OF COMPENSATION OF PARTIAL DISABILITIES AND OF BENEFIT ADEQUACY

SEC. 6. (a) The Secretary shall conduct a study of the compensation of partial disabilities arising out of and in the course of employment. In conducting such study, the Secretary shall compare the efficiency, effectiveness, and adequacy of the means by which the several States compensate partial disabilities arising out of and in the course of employment. In connection with such studies, the Secretary may enter into contractual arrangements with one or more States or political subdivisions thereof, other Federal agencies, or private agencies; and may establish experimental programs to test the efficiency, effectiveness, and adequacy of various means of compensating partial disability arising out of and in the course of employment. Not later than three years following the date of enactment of this Act, the Secretary shall make a written report to the Congress on his study of the compensation of partial disability. Such report shall contain recommendations for legislation to amend this Act to provide minimum Federal standards for State workers' compensation laws relating to the compensation of partial disabilities due to injury or disease arising out of and in the course of employment.

(b) The Secretary shall conduct a study of the desirability and feasibility of a Federal minimum standard requiring periodic adjustment of benefits for death or total disability to reflect changes in the statewide average weekly wage. In considering this matter, the Secretary shall evaluate the adequacy of workers' compensation benefits, the availability of other sources of compensation for those receiving death or total disability benefits as a result of work-related causes, and shall consider the effect of inadequate workers' compensation benefits on other compensation programs. Such study shall also include an estimate of the cost of providing periodic benefits adjustment for those receiving death or total disability benefits, and shall evaluate the feasibility of alternative procedures for providing such adjustment of benefits. Not later than three years following the enactment of this Act, the Secretary shall make a written report to the Congress on the results of this study, including recommendations for legislation to amend this Act to provide such adjustments. The Secretary's annual report filed pursuant to section 16 shall include a report on the economic effect of the failure to require adjusting benefits to reflect changes in the statewide average weekly wage.

(c) The Secretary shall consult with the Advisory Commission concerning the studies and reports required by this section.

CERTIFICATION AND SUPPLEMENTAL COMPENSATION

SEC. 7. (a) On or before the effective date of section 4 of the Act, the Secretary of Labor shall review the workers' compensation law of each State to determine whether such law meets the applicable standards for State workers' compensation programs contained in section 4 of this Act. If the Secretary determines that State law meets all of the requirements of section 4, the Secretary shall so certify and the State law shall be deemed fully certified during the period covered by such certification.

(b) If the Secretary finds that the law of any State fails to meet one or more of the standards of section 4 of this Act, the Secretary shall certify the State law only to the extent that it meets such standards, and the Secretary shall specify those standards which the State law fails to meet. During any period in which the State law has not been fully certified, any employee shall be entitled to receive from his or her employer, with regard to any injury or disease arising out of and in the course of employment with such employer, compensation in accordance with the provisions of this Act with which the State is not in compliance (hereinafter referred to as "supplemental compensation").

(c) After initial review provided by subsection (a), the Secretary shall annually review the workers' compensation law of each State, including the judicial and administrative interpretations of the law, to determine whether it meets the requirements of section 4 of this Act. Pursuant to such reviews, the Secretary shall modify the certifications previously issued under subsection (a) as appropriate.

(d) Except with respect to section 4(f), in certifying a law of a State as meeting the requirements of section 4, the status of any individual as an employee or independent contractor, whether death or injury has been suffered, whether an injury or death arose out of and in the course of employment, and the degree of disability, if any, shall be determined solely by State law.

ENFORCEMENT OF SUPPLEMENTAL COMPENSATION

Sec. 8. (a)(1) Any claimant who is aggrieved by an order or award of a State workers' compensation agency, insofar as it fails to award compensation at least equivalent to supplemental compensation may within ninety days after such order or award becomes final file a petition for review of the State workers' compensation agency's order or award, insofar as it fails to award such compensation, with the Benefits Review Board (hereinafter referred to in this section as the "Board") established in section 21 of the Longshoremen's and Harbor Workers' Compensation Act, as amended or as it may be amended from time to time (Act of

March 4, 1927) (hereinafter referred to as the "Longshore Act").

(2) For the purpose of this section, the order or award of a State workers' compensation agency shall become final for the purpose of paragraph (1) on the date on which no appeal or review of such order or award shall be available to any party subject to such order or award or any further appeal or review would be futile.

(b) State law shall govern the determination of the status of any individual as an employee or an independent contractor, and the determination of whether death or injury (including disease) has been suffered, whether an injury (including disease) or death arose out of and in the course of employment, and the degree of disability, if any.

(c)(1) In review proceedings under this section, the decision of the Board shall be based upon the evidence in the record before the State workers' compensation agency except that the Board, in its discretion, may (i) in any case in which the State workers' compensation agency has refused to assert jurisdiction over the claim, refer the case to the Office of Workers Compensation Programs of the Department of Labor for processing in accordance with the provisions of the Longshore Act, or (ii) in any case where the State agency has refused to assert jurisdiction over the claim or has otherwise precluded the introduction of such evidence permit the parties to submit additional relevant evidence in a hearing before an administrative law judge in accordance with sections 19 and 21 of the Longshore Act.

(2) Where new evidence is not submitted, the findings of fact by the State workers' compensation agency, insofar as they involve eligibility for supplemental compensation shall be conclusive if supported by substantial evidence on the record as a whole. Findings of fact and conclusions of law in the determination of the State workers' compensation agency on issues covered solely by State law shall be conclusive, and not subject to review in any proceedings under this section.

(3) Where the Board finds that the employer has failed to provide supplemental compensation to which the petitioner is entitled, the petitioner shall be awarded such compensation together with the reasonable costs and expenses of litigation, including reasonable attorney's fees.

(4) Any order issued by the Board shall be enforceable and reviewable in accordance with section 21 of the Longshore Act.

(5) Any award of the Board shall be automatically modified to take into account subsequent orders or awards of the State workers' compensation agencies with respect to issues solely covered by State law. With respect to issues not solely covered by State law, procedures for the modification of Board awards or orders shall be in accordance with section 22 of the Longshore Act, except that references in that section to "the deputy commissioner" shall mean "the Board" and the word "his"

in the first sentence of that section shall be read "its" and shall refer to the Board.

(6) Sections 14, 17, 18, 19, 21, 21a, 23, 24, 25, 26, 27, 31, 34, 35, 38, and 39(a) and (c) of the Longshore Act shall be applicable with respect to claims for supplemental compensation payable under this Act during any period in which the workers' compensation law of that State is not fully certified. The Secretary shall by regulation modify the provisions of section 14 of the Longshore Act to conform the payment of supplemental compensation to the payment schedule of the applicable State's law, and may by regulation modify the applicability of any other of the foregoing provisions as appropriate to carry out the purposes of this Act.

EMPLOYMENT DISCRIMINATION

SEC. 9. No person shall discharge or in any manner discriminate against any employee because such employee has filed any complaint or instituted or caused to be instituted any proceeding under or related to this Act or has testified or is about to testify in any such proceeding or because of the exercise by any employee on behalf of himself or others of any right afforded by this Act. Any employer who violates this section shall be liable to a penalty of not less than $100 or more than $1,000, as may be determined by the Secretary. All such penalties shall be paid to the Secretary for deposit in the special fund as described in section 44 of the Longshore Act, and if not paid may be recovered in a civil action brought in the appropriate United States district court. Any employee so discriminated against shall be restored to his employment and shall be compensated by his employer for any loss of wages (including fringe benefits) arising out of such discrimination: *Provided*, That if such employee shall cease to be qualified to perform the duties of his employment, he shall not be entitled to such restoration and compensation. The employer alone and not his carrier shall be liable for such penalties and payments. Any provision in an insurance policy undertaking to relieve the employer from liability for such penalties and payments shall be void.

EXCLUSIVITY AND THIRD PARTY LIABILITY

SEC. 10. (a) The compensation to which an employee is entitled under the applicable State Worker's Compensation laws and the supplemental compensation, if any, to which he or she may be entitled under this Act, shall constitute the employee's exclusive remedy against the employer, the employer's insurer or any collective-bargaining agent of the employer's employees and any employee, officer, director, or agent of such employer, insurer, or collective-bargaining agent (while acting within the scope of his or her employment) for any illness, injury, or death arising out of and in the course of his or her employment.

(b)(1) Notwithstanding any other provision of this law, or any other law, in any liability action against a third party brought as a result of illness, injury or death arising out of and in the course of employment, this section shall govern the rights of the employee (or his or her representative or survivors) and the employer or insurance carrier, the collective bargaining agent, and the third party.

(2) For the purpose of this section, liability actions against third parties shall include but not be limited to all actions brought for or on account of personal injury, disease, physical or mental impairment, disability, or death caused by or resulting from the manufacture, construction, design, formula, preparation, assembly, testing, warning, instruction, marketing, packaging, or labeling of any product. It shall include, but not be limited to, all actions for damages based upon the following theories: strict products liability; negligence; breach of warranty, express or implied; breach of or failure to discharge a duty to warn or instruct, whether deliberate, negligent, or innocent; misrepresentative, concealment, or nondisclosure, whether fraudulent, negligent, or innocent.

(3) Any judgment against a third party in a liability action described in this section shall be reduced by an amount equal to the amount paid to the injured employee or his or her survivors as compensation pursuant to any State workers' compensation law and any supplemental compensation paid pursuant to this Act and the present value of

all future compensation and supplemental compensation payable.

(4) No employer, or insurer of such employer shall have any lien upon any judgment rendered in any such third party liability action brought as a result of any illness, injury or death arising out of or in the course of employment with such employer, nor any right of subrogation in connection with any such third party liability action.

(5) No third party may maintain any action for indemnity, contribution or other monetary damages against any party immune from suit by the employee by subsection (a) based on the liability of such third party to any employee of such employer as a result of any action described in this Section.

EMPLOYER RESPONSIBILITY FOR ELECTIONS AND INSURANCE

SEC. 11. (a) Every employer shall be responsible for payment of all supplemental compensation which may be payable to its employees under Section 8 of this Act.

(b) Every employer shall secure the payment of supplemental compensation payable under Section 8 of this Act—

(1) by insuring and keeping insured the payment of such supplemental compensation with any stock company or mutual company or association, or with any other person or fund, while such person or fund is authorized to insure work-

ers' compensation or supplemental compensation under the laws of the United States or of any State, or by the Secretary, to insure payment of supplemental compensation under this Act; or

(2) by qualifying as a self-insurer under the law of each State with respect to which the employer has not satisfied the requirements of paragraph (1) of this subsection, except that the Secretary may, by regulation, impose additional or alternative conditions on qualification for self-insurance in the event that the Secretary finds that the qualification requirements in a State are insufficient to assure the payment of supplemental compensation provided by this Act.

(c)(1) Any employer not subject to a State workers' compensation law because such law fails to comply with Section 4(a) of this Act shall, where permitted, elect coverage under such law so as to provide coverage under the State law to each individual who is an employee of such employer.

(2) If the Secretary has not certified under section 7 that a State law is in compliance with Section 4(a), employers in the State who are permitted to elect such coverage under the State law but who have not done so, shall be subject to a civil penalty not to exceed $25 per employee for each day of noncompliance in a suit brought by the Secretary.

(d) Each contract of insurance under which workers' compensation benefits are provided to or for the employee any employer shall be deemed to provide benefits in accordance with the minimum standards contained in section 4 of this Act. The Secretary may by regulation provide for exceptions to or exemptions from this subsection consistent with the purposes of this Act.

(e) Each contract of insurance which provides coverage for comprehensive personal liability, either alone or as part of a homeowner's or tenant's policy, shall be deemed to provide benefits in accordance with the minimum standards contained in section 4 of this Act with respect to domestic employees to the extent that such employees are entitled to workers' compensation under this Act, unless the employer has otherwise secured payment of such compensation pursuant to this section.

GRANTS TO STATES

SEC. 12. (a) The Secretary is authorized during the fiscal year of enactment of this Act, and the two succeeding fiscal years, to make grants to any State to assist such State—

(1) in identifying needs and responsibilities in the area of workers' compensation,

(2) in developing programs for meeting the requirements of section 4,

(3) developing and publishing a guide to the evaluation of disability,

(4) establishing one or more disability evaluation units to assist in the determination of the degree of disability,

(5) utilizing the services of impartial physicians in the evaluation of impairment and the degree of impaired workers,

(6) establishing systems for the collection of information concerning workers' compensation as provided in section 13 of this Act,

(7) increasing the expertise and enforcement capabilities of personnel engaged in workers' compensation programs, or

(8) otherwise improving the administration and enforcement of State workers' compensation laws consistent with the objectives of this Act.

(b) The Governor of the State shall designate the appropriate State agency for receipt of any grant made by the Secretary under this section.

(c) Any State agency designated by the Governor of the State desiring a grant under this section shall submit an application therefor to the Secretary.

(d) The Secretary shall review the application, and shall approve or reject such application, and, if the application is rejected, shall promptly inform the Governor and the applicant of the reason for the rejection.

(e) The Federal grant shall not exceed 66⅔ per centum of the total cost of the projects described in the application. In the event the Federal share for all States under such subsection is not the same, the difference among the States shall be established on the basis of objective criteria.

(f) There is hereby authorized to be appropriated for the fiscal year of enactment, the sum of seventy-five million dollars, to be available without fiscal year limitation; and for each of the following four fiscal years such sums as are necessary for the purpose of carrying out the provisions of this section.

STATISTICS

SEC. 13. (a) The Secretary shall develop and maintain a program of collection, compilation, and analysis of workers' compensation data in order to carry out the purposes of this Act.

(b)(1) The Secretary shall, by regulation, require that the following reports be submitted to the State workers' compensation agencies with respect to claims for injuries or illnesses arising out of and in the course of employment except with respect to claims for medical benefits only in each State—

(A) A report by the employer within a reasonable time of the injury or illness which identifies the employer and the employee; states the date, time, and place of the accident or the exposure; gives a brief explanation of the occurrence of the injury or exposure; describes the injury or illness dates of diagnosis and initial treatment, dates of lost time and return to work; identifies physicians and hospitals involved in treatment and the insurance carrier, if any; and provides such additional information required by the Secretary's regulations.

(B) A prompt report by the employer or the employer's insurance carrier, after the first compensation payment or denial of the claim, which identifies the employee, the employer, the carrier, if any; the dates of injury or illness and diagnosis; the amount of the compensation paid, specifying the date and amount of the first compensation payment; the employee's average weekly wage if less than the applicable maximum; the nature and extent of the disability; the medical payments to date; and, if the case has been closed or the claim denied, the total compensation, and the reason for closing the case or denying the claim.

(C) A prompt report by the employer or the employer's insurance carrier, after the last compensation payment, which identifies the employer, the employee, the carrier, if any; provides pertinent data concerning the compensation specifying monetary, medical, and rehabilitation benefits paid; provides information concerning the nature and duration of the impairment and disability; and states the reason for the termination of benefits and closing of the case. The Secretary may by regulation require the filing of periodic reports with respect to claims continuing two years after the first compensation payment.

(2) In promulgating regulations with respect to reports required under this section, the Secretary shall consider and evaluate the reporting requirements of the several States with the objective of developing and encouraging the adoption of a uniform data collection and reporting system under this Act.

(3)(A) The Secretary's regulations shall require that all reports required by paragraph (1) of this subsection be filed with the State workers' compensation agencies. The Secretary shall further require, as a condition of any grant made for the purpose of assisting the State to improve their data collection processing, that such agencies shall periodically, but no less frequently than annually, submit to the Secretary a report analyzing workers' compensation cases in such States, based on the data contained in the reports required by the Secretary's regulations issued pursuant to paragraph (1) of this subsection. The analyses of the State workers' compensation agencies shall contain such information as the Secretary shall prescribe by regulation.

(B) With respect to any State which does not agree to collect data and provide analyses of workers' compensation cases as provided in this section, the Secretary's regulations shall require that all reports required by paragraph (1) of this subsection be filed directly with the Secretary.

(c) The Secretary shall annually file with the Congress and make available to the public, a report and evaluation of workers' compensation information compiled pursuant to this section.

(d) The Secretary may make grants to States as provided in section 12 to assist them in developing programs for the collection and evaluation of data and reports required by regulations of the Secretary issued pursuant to this section.

RESEARCH

SEC. 14. (A) The Secretary is authorized to engage in research and to engage in such pilot projects and demonstration programs as the Secretary shall deem warranted, for the purpose of—

(1) developing recommendations for improving the workers' compensation programs of the several States and the compensation program under this Act;

(2) developing recommendations for means of more economically assuring that workers will have the benefits described in section 4; and

(3) monitoring and promoting academic study of workers' compensation and the development of improvements to the workers' compensation program of the several States and the workers' compensation program under this Act.

(b) The Secretary shall conduct a study of the adequacy of the workers' compensation system for compensating individuals for disability or death due to occupational diseases, including the availability and cost of providing such coverage through traditional insurance or self-insurance. Such study shall also include particular attention to work-related diseases characterized by long latency periods between exposure to toxic substances or other harmful physical agents and the onset of disability or death, including the feasibility and desirability of providing such coverage through re-insurance pools, trust funds, or other means of apportioning liability. The Secretary shall submit his report, together with his recommendations to the Congress no later than two years after enactment of this Act.

(c) In carrying out his functions under this Act, the Secretary, with the consent of any State or political subdivision thereof, accept and use the services, facilities, and employees of the agencies of such State or political subdivision thereof, with or without reimbursement.

AUDITS

SEC. 15. (a) Each recipient of a grant under this Act shall keep such records as the Secretary shall prescribe, including records which fully disclose the amount and disposition by such recipient of the proceeds of such grant, the total cost of the project or undertaking in connection with which such grant is made or used, and the amount of that portion of the cost of the project or undertaking supplied by other sources, and such other records as will facilitate the administration of such grants.

(b) The Secretary and the Comptroller General of the United States, or any of their duly authorized representatives shall have access for the purpose of audit and examination to any books, documents, papers, and records of the recipients of any grant under this Act which are pertinent to such grant.

ANNUAL REPORT

SEC. 16. Within one hundred and twenty days following the convening of each regular session of each congress, the Secretary shall prepare and submit to the President for transmittal to the Congress a report upon the subject matter of this Act, the progress toward achievement of the purpose of this Act, and the needs and requirements in the field of workers' compensation.

ADVISORY COMMISSION

SEC. 17. (a) There is hereby established a National Workers' Compensation Advisory Commission (hereafter in this section referred to as the "Advisory Commission") to be composed of nine members appointed by the Secretary from among persons who by reason of training, education or experience are qualified to carry out the functions of the Advisory Commission. Three members shall be appointed from among representatives of employees'; three members shall be appointed from among representatives of employers, one of whom shall be a representative of insurers; and three members shall be representatives of the general public, one of whom shall be a representative of State governments. The Secretary shall designate one of the public members to serve as Chairman or Chairwoman. Five members of the Commission shall constitute a quorum. The terms of office of the members of the Commission shall be three years, except that of the members first appointed, three members shall be appointed for a term of one year, three members shall be appointed for a term of two years, three members shall be appointed for a term of three years.

(b) The Commission shall—

(1) monitor the progress of the State in making improvements in their workers' compensation laws and in meeting the standards provided in section 4;

(2) monitor the administration of the workers' compensation programs in the States;

(3) provide technical and other assistance to the Secretary in improving the implementation of this law and the administration of the workers' compensation program, including recommendations to the Secretary of administrative or legislative action necessary to improve workers' compensation programs.

(c)(1) The Commission or any authorized subcommittee or members thereof, may, for the purpose of carrying out the provisions of this Act, hold such hearings, take such testimony, and sit and act at such times and places as the Commission deems advisable. Any members authorized by the Commission may administer oaths or affirmations to witnesses appearing before the Commission or any subcommittee or members thereof.

(2) Each department, agency, and instrumentality of the executive branch of the Government, including any independent agency, is authorized to furnish to the Commission, upon request made by the Chairman or Chairwoman, such information and assistance as the Commission deems necessary to carry out its function under this section.

(d) Subject to such rules and regulations as may be adopted by the Commission, the Chairman or Chairwoman shall have the power to appoint and fix the compensation of an executive director, and such additional staff personnel as is deemed necessary, without regard to the provisions of title 5, United States Code, governing appointments in the competitive service, and without regard to the provisions of chapter 51 and subchapter III of chapter 53 of such title relating to classification and General Schedule pay rates, but at rates not in excess of the maximum rate of GS–18 of the General Schedule under section 5332 of such title, and procure temporary and intermittent services to the same extent as is authorized by section 3109 of title 5, United States Code. The Commission is authorized to enter into contracts with Federal or State agencies, private firms, institutions, and individuals for the conduct of surveys, the preparation of reports, and other activities necessary to the discharge of its duties.

(e) Members of the Commission shall receive compensation for each day they are engaged in the performance of their duties as members of the Commission at the daily rate prescribed for GS–18 under section 5332 of title 5, United States Code, and shall be entitled to reimbursement for travel, subsistence, and other necessary expenses incurred by them in the performance of their duties as members of the Commission.

SEPARABILITY

SEC. 18. If any provisions of this Act, or the application of such provision to any person or circumstance, shall be held invalid, the remainder of this Act, or the application of such provision to persons or circumstances other than those as to which it is held invalid, shall not be affected thereby.

EFFECTIVE DATE

SEC. 19. (a) The provisions of section 4 of this Act shall take effect two years after the date of enactment of this Act, and shall apply to deaths or disabilities occurring thereafter.

(b) Except as otherwise provided, all other provisions of this Act shall take effect immediately upon enactment.

INDEX

333

ASSUMPTION OF RISK
See also Federal Employers' Liability Act; Tort Liability of
Employer
Origin of doctrine, 4

ATTORNEYS
Attorney as employee, 52

ATTORNEY'S FEES
Fair Labor Standards Act, 160
Job anti-discrimination, 263

BACK INJURY
As accident, 79
Unusual strain, 81

BASIS FOR COMPUTING COMPENSATION
See Death Benefits; Wage Loss

BENEFITS
Black Lung program, 171
Fair Labor Standards Act, 154
Social Security Insurance programs, 179, 181, 184
Unemployment compensation, 144
Claims procedures, 146
Eligibility, 144

BOILER INSPECTION ACTS
Coverage, 15

BONA FIDE OCCUPATION QUALIFICATION
Age Discrimination in Employment Act, 257
Title VII, Civil Rights Act of 1964, 198

BORROWED EMPLOYEE
Control test, 46
Liability of lending and borrowing employer, 53

BROTHERS AND SISTERS
As dependents, 92

FEDERAL EMPLOYERS' LIABILITY ACT
Generally, 14
Assumption of risk abolished, 15
Coverage, 14
Negligence, 15

FEDERAL INSURANCE CONTRIBUTIONS ACT
See Social Security Insurance Programs

FEDERAL UNEMPLOYMENT TAX ACT
Federal Unemployment Tax Act, 141
Tax on employers, 143

FELLOW SERVANT RULE
See Tort Liability of Employer

FIFTH AMENDMENT
See Job Anti-discrimination Legislation

FINANCING
Social security insurance programs, 175
Unemployment compensation, 143

FOURTEENTH AMENDMENT
See Job Anti-discrimination Legislation

FULL FAITH AND CREDIT
See Conflict of Laws

GOOD CAUSE
Unemployment compensation disqualification, 145

GRANDPARENT
As dependent, 92

HANDICAP
See "Odd Lot" Doctrine; "Second Injury" Problem

HAZARDOUS BUSINESSES
Compensation limited to, 11

HEALTH INSURANCE
See Social Security Insurance Programs

PROHIBITED ACTIVITY
Accidents on premises while employee engaged in prohibited actvity, 65, 66, 67, 76

PROXIMATE CAUSE
Violation of statute as, under FELA, 15

PSYCHOSIS
Held compensible, 80

PUBLIC EMPLOYMENT
Coverage, 148, 153, 162, 174
    Equal Pay Act, 253
    Fair Labor Standards Act, 153
    Job Anti-discrimination Legislation, 194
Covered by compensation, 13, 46, 47

PUBLIC OFFICIALS
Covered as employees, 46, 47

RADIATION INJURY
Special statute, 83

RAILROAD EMPLOYEES
See Federal Employers' Liability Act

RECORD KEEPING
OSHA inspections, 167

RECREATION
Accident during recreation period, 74

REGULAR RATE OF PAY
Fair Labor Standards Act, 154

RELATIVES
See Death Benefits

RELATIVES BY MARRIAGE
As dependents, 92

REMEDIES
Fair Labor Standards Act, 160

STANDARDS
Occupational Safety and Health Act, 162, 164
    Basis for, 162, 164
    Enforcement, 166
    Procedure and review, 167

STATUTE OF LIMITATIONS
Death, statute of limitations for, 113
Fair Labor Standards Act, 160
From date injury becomes or should have become apparent to
    claimant, 113
From date of injury, 113
Occupational disease, 86
Survivor's right, when statute had run against decedent, 113

STEPCHILD
See Child

STRAIN
See Exertion; Heart and Blood Vessels; Hernia

STRANGER
Accident while assisting stranger, 75

STREET RISKS
Injuries in street as arising out of employment, 65

SUICIDE
Post accident, 78

SUPPLEMENTAL SECURITY INCOME
Benefits, 186
Federal Benefit Rates, 187

SURVIVAL OF ACCRUED COMPENSATION
Generally, 108

SURVIVORS
See Child; Widow

TAXES
Federal Unemployment Tax Act, 141, 142

UNEXPLAINED ACCIDENTS AND DEATHS
During course of employment, 69

UNJUST DISCHARGES
Employees-at-will, 281

UNLAWFUL EMPLOYMENT PRACTICES
See Job Anti-discrimination Legislation; Title VII, Civil Rights
    Act of 1964

VICE–PRINCIPAL
See Tort Liability of Employer

VIOLATION OF ORDERS
Employee injured while violating orders, 76

VIOLATION OF RULES
Violation as affecting course of employment, 76

WAGE LOSS
Generally, 97

WAGES
Social security insurance programs, 178
Unemployment compensation, definition, 144

WAITING PERIOD
Effect of, 114, 144
Purpose of, 114

WEATHER
Act of God, 64

WHOLLY DEPENDENT
See Death Benefits

WIDOW
Generally, 89

WIFE
See Widow

WILLFUL AND WANTON MISCONDUCT
See Tort Liability of Employer

WILLFUL VIOLATIONS
Fair Labor Standards Act, 160
OSHA, 168

WORKERS' COMPENSATION INSURANCE
Constitutionality, 24
History, 8

WORKERS' COMPENSATION PRINCIPLE
Compromise aspects of, 28
Economic basis, 29, 31
Fault abolished, 27
Implications for other areas of tort, 30
Interrelationship with Social Security, 127
Interrelationship with Unemployment Compensation, 128
Nature of, 28
Social insurance, 30

†